ALEJANDRO TSAKIMP

Fourth World Rising series editors:

Gerald M. Sider *The College of Staten Island*, CUNY

Kirk Dombrowski *John Jay College of Criminal Justice*, CUNY

STEVEN RUBENSTEIN

Alejandro Tsakimp

A Shuar Healer in the
Margins of History

University of Nebraska Press

Lincoln and London

Photographs are courtesy of the
author.
© 2002 by the Board
of Regents of the University
of Nebraska Press. All rights
reserved. Manufactured in the
United States of America ⊗

Library of Congress Cataloging-
in-Publication Data
Rubenstein, Steven, 1962–
Alejandro Tsakimp: a Shuar healer
in the margins of history / Steven Rubenstein.
p.   cm.—(Fourth world rising)
Includes bibliographical references and index.
ISBN 0-8032-3929-7 (cloth: alk. paper)—
ISBN 0-8032-8988-x (pbk.: alk. paper)
1. Tsakimp, Alejandro.   2. Shuar Indians—
Biography.   3. Shamans—Ecuador—
Biography.   I. Title.   II. Series.
F3722.1.J5 T777   2002
299′.88372—dc21
2002018014

Contents

CONTENTS

I dedicate this work to Alejandro Tsakimp,
my Shuar father, my teacher, my friend.

ILLUSTRATIONS

Photographs

Maps

Charts

Series Editors' Introduction

Alejandro Tsakimp is the third volume in Fourth World Rising, a series of contemporary ethnographies from the University of Nebraska Press. The series focuses on contemporary issues, including class, gender, religion, and politics: in sum, it addresses social and cultural differentiation among and between native peoples as they confront those around them and each other in struggles for better lives, better futures, and better visions of their own pasts. This focus thus represents a departure from many of the monographs produced by anthropologists about native peoples, which often have sought to reproduce either visions of ways of life now long past or else pasts refracted through current idealization. In the process, traditional anthropology has helped enshrine a backward-looking focus to native culture that has, at times, been influential in the way laws are framed and even in how native peoples come to see their own identity.

Ideas, especially when enshrined in law and lent the authority of governments, have power. And the idea that native cultures and societies are historical artifacts rather than ongoing projects has served to narrow the politics of native identity or indigenism worldwide. One purpose of this series is to change this focus and broaden the conception of native struggle to match its current complexity.

This is especially important now, for the last two decades have provided prominent examples of native peoples seeking to recast the public—ultimately political—basis of their native identity in ways other than the reproduction of often fanciful, even fictional, pasts. Our hope is that by offering a variety of texts focused on these and other contemporary issues, structured for classroom use and a general audience, we can help change the public perception of native struggle—allowing people to see that native cultures and societies are very much ongoing (and to a surprising extent on their own terms) and that the issues they confront carry important practical and theoretical implications for a more general understanding of cultural and political processes.

The primary geographical and topical emphasis of the Fourth World Rising series is the native peoples of the Americas, but the series will also include comparative cases from Australia, Africa, Asia, the circumpolar Arctic and sub-Arctic, and the Pacific Islands. Yet beyond its unique topical and contemporary focus, four critical theoretical and political features distinguish the series as well:

1. A focus on the struggles native peoples must fight, with the dominant society and with each other, whether they wish to or not, in order to survive as peoples, as communities, and as individuals, as well as the struggles they choose to fight.

2. A consideration of how the intensifying inequalities within and between native communities—emerging from social, cultural, and economic differences among native peoples—create unavoidable antagonisms, so that there cannot be any simple lines of cleavage between a dominant, oppressive, and exploitative state on the one side and its long-suffering victims on the other. Thus the series pays particular attention to gender, identity, religion, age, and class divisions among native peoples, along with differences in the goals and strategies that emerge from these struggles.

An emphasis on internal differences and tensions among native peoples is not at all intended to let the dominant states and societies off the hook for their policies and practices. Rather, this perspective calls to the foreground how internal complexities and divisions among native peoples and communities shape their struggles within and against the larger societies in which they find themselves. Indeed, it is precisely these internal differences among and between native peoples (and how these differences unfold over time and through native peoples' complex relations to one another) that give native people their own history and their own social processes that are, ultimately, partly separate from the history imposed upon them by the dominant society.

3. An emphasis on the praxis of native struggles: what works, and why, and with what intended and unintended effects; who benefits within native communities and who loses what, and why. The series monographs are thus not advocacy tracts in the conventional sense of that term, though they are undeniably political constructs. Rather, the emphasis on contemporary social processes and the political praxis of participants, advocates, and anthropologists serves as a stimulus for dialogue and debate about the changing pressures and possibilities for

particular native societies and the political situations confronting native peoples more generally.

4. An attempt to clarify the situation facing those whose concerns and fundamentally decent impulses lead them to want to help the victims of domination and exploitation. Such honorable commitments need to be developed in the midst of realizing that the radiant innocence of an earlier applied anthropology, and of many aid programs, along with the social world that sustained this innocence, has crumbled. It is no longer possible to say or to think "*we* will help *them*." Now we must ask who is helped and who is hurt both by the success and by the frequent failure of aid programs, and why, and how.

The primary audience for this series is students in college courses in anthropology, political science, native and ethnic studies, economics, and sociology. Yet the series achieves its importance among a college and popular audience by being developed for a second audience as well. One of the major purposes of this series is to present case studies of native peoples' current struggles that have broader strategic relevance to those engaged in similar or complementary struggles and to advocates whose concerns lie more directly along the lines of what has worked in the past or in other areas, what has not, and with what consequences.

Hence this volume becomes part of a new way of both doing and teaching anthropology and native studies. On one level, the case studies seek to bring together activists, native peoples, and academics, not simply by dramatizing the immediacy of native struggles, but also by dispelling the notion that native societies derive their nativeness from being internally homogeneous and externally timeless. On a second level, the series as a whole helps those currently teaching native studies to pursue an engaged, contemporary perspective and a broad geographic approach—allowing for and in fact encouraging a global, contemporary native studies that is deeply rooted both in a fundamental caring for native peoples' well-being and in the realities of internal differentiation among native peoples.

Gerald Sider
Kirk Dombrowski

Acknowledgments

This book is based on research conducted between 1988 and 1992, which was supported by grants from the Foundation for Shamanic Studies, the Fulbright Foundation, and the MacArthur Foundation; and on research conducted during the summer of 1998, which was made possible by a grant from the Ohio University Research Council; I am grateful for their support. I would also like to thank the Ohio University College of Arts and Sciences and Department of Sociology and Anthropology for a one-quarter release time from teaching that made the writing of this book possible.

The thanks I owe people for their support, encouragement, and assistance during my initial fieldwork is for far greater things than the words on the following pages.

Above all else I must thank my parents, Kenneth and Francine Rubenstein; they would have supported me in any vocation, and I cherish their pride in the choices I have made. Other members of my family have provided emotional comfort and relief, and often cheer, when most needed: Laurie Rubenstein, Leslie Rubenstein, Jeff Gratz, and Cathy Berkman. I must also acknowledge, with gratitude and affection, William Dial, Joel Buchband, Elissa Heil, Sean Goldstein, Bruce Rosenberg, Chris Rosenberg, Sara Mahler de Dominguez, Daniel Ornstein, Marian Alexander, Ray Goldberg, Elana Daniels, Lorraine Newman, Aaron Mackler, Jessica Elfenbein, Robert Feinstein, Haim Lapin, Joyce Burton, Janice Gitterman, Debbie Gitterman, Maria Mendoza, Amanda Thorpe, Cris San Miguel, Shelly Masur, Josh Masur, Denise Holzka, Sue Buchsbaum, Andrew Stromberg, Lillian Solis, Gabrielle Marzani, Rebecca Tolen, Fulvia Heubler, Maria Angeles Ronda, and Suzanne Fitzgerald.

Whenever I was on the verge of losing my mind or soul while in Ecuador, I knew I could turn to a number of people for love and comfort, and frequently for free food: Ernesto Salazar, Myriam Ochoa, Leon Doyon, Meg Criley, Laurie Laird, Sheila Webb Nordland, Ramiro Penaherrera, Fernando Davila, Lorena Mora, Maria Ornes, Kevin Barnard, Stephen Robinet, Tom Doyle, Doug Speicher, Greg York, Brian King, David Smith, Robert Caldwell, Anita Tapia, Lauro Lopez, Ruth Molina, Pepe and Jenny Pozo, Ester Arcos, Maria Arcos, Patricia Arcos, Helmut Gantner, Miguel Puwáinchir, Amalda Nekta, Silverio Jíntiach', Felipe Tsenkush, Pepe Sardi, Sonia Sardi, Vicente and Maria Zuniga, Estela Zuniga, Otto Campana, Cristina Zuniga, Elke Mader, Olga Garcon, Juan Bosco Mashu, Patricia Tankámash, and Maria Tsamaraint (rest in peace).

A number of people played a key role in my working with Shuar: Jane Bennett-Ross (rest in peace), Michael Harner, Peta Kelekna, Janet Hendricks, Norman Whitten, and Michael Brown; their encouragement and guidance were invaluable. I also owe a debt of gratitude to the members of my dissertation committee, who planted the seeds out of which much of this project grew: Robert F. Murphy (rest in peace), Libbet Crandon-Malamud (rest in peace), Joan Vincent, William Fisher, Michael Brown, Angela Zita, and Michael Taussig. I would also like to thank others who have helped me continue my education after graduating and who have helped me reach new insights about my research, especially Davydd Greenwood and Joan Scott.

Some of my informants are also my friends, and I have already acknowledged them. To the names of Juan Mashu, Pepe Sardi, and Miguel Puwáinchir, I must also add Pedro Kunkumas, José Chau, Dr. Juan Chau, Enrique Chiriap, Congressional Deputy Augusto Abad, and Dr. German Mancheno. My debt to them is immeasurable. They were always happy to take time out of their busy schedules to talk to me, and they bent over backward to give me some insight into their lives and times. I cannot name every person I spoke to, but nearly everyone I interviewed offered me humor, pathos, passion, and kindness, as well as abundant information. They took their role as teachers as seriously as I take mine as student. I apologize to those I may have left out, but I offer this work as a monument to their assistance nevertheless.

Darissa Phipps served as my research assistant during the summer of 1998, and I thank her for her help. Several students at Ohio University assisted me in the preparation of the manuscript: Rex Jackman, Jerry Marcus, Adriana Jaramillo, and Israel Lagos. Several students read and commented on various drafts of the manuscript and offered valuable suggestions: Lisa Brooten, Sara DeAloia, Eric Cruciotti, Amy Jones, Darissa Phipps, Derek Collins, Meghan Moran, and Kristen Stroup. I would also like to thank the following colleagues for their comments: Michel Alexiades, Diane Ciekawy, Diccon Conant, Glenn Goodwin, Walter Hawthorne, Didier Lacaze, Elke Mader, David Lazar, Daniela Peluso, Marie Perruchon, Tim Simpson, David Smith, and Christopher Zurn. I also appreciate the insightful comments and constructive suggestions of two anonymous reviewers. I also want to thank my copyeditor, Jane Curran, for her invaluable help in finding inconsistencies and errors in the text, and the editors and staff at the University of Nebraska Press. Most of all I must thank the editors of this series, Kirk Dombrowski and Gerald Sider, for their encouragement and their careful, critical, and constructive readings of the manuscript.

A Note on Transcription
and Shuar Orthography

As with any language, there is a fair amount of variation in the way Shuar pronounce many words. Some sounds do not easily transcribe into English. For example, many Shuar words end with an unvoiced vowel. Such words thus have variant spellings: Shuar or Shuara; Tserem or Tserembo; Tsakimp or Tsakimpio. Many place an apostrophe following the final consonant to indicate the unvoiced vowel ending: Chiriap or Chiriap'. These variations reflect the inevitable inconsistencies of a previously oral language only recently adapted to writing.

As the Shuar Federation has published a considerable number of Shuar texts, it is playing a role in establishing conventional spellings of such words. Following the Salesian missionaries, the Federation has adapted Spanish orthography to its language (thus, j is a velar fricative and is pronounced as a spirant h). The only exceptions are the k following an n, which is pronounced as a hard g; the p following an m, which is pronounced as a b; and the t following an n, which is pronounced as a d. Thus, my Shuar name Nanki is pronounced Nangi; the name Chúmpi is pronounced Chúmbi; and the name Nantu is pronounced Nandu.

In general, I have tried to follow Federation orthography in the spelling of Shuar words. I follow Mundo Shuar 1977 for the spelling of names of plants, Abya-Yala 1986 for the spelling of names of animals, SERBISH (1988a) for the spelling of place-names, and SERBISH (1988b) for the spelling of personal names.

Nevertheless, Federation orthography often differs from that used by ethnographers and often suggests a pronunciation different from Alejandro's. In the case of Shuar kinship terminology I have transcribed Alejandro's pronunciation. I have thus transcribed his word for brother as yatsuru, his word for male affine, or in-laws, as saich, and his word for son as uchiru. Readers who consult SERBISH 1988b, Harner 1984, and

Hendricks 1993, however, will find alternate spellings. The Federation transcribes the word for brother as yatsu, the word for male affine as sai, and the word for son as uchirí. Harner and Hendricks transcribe the word for brother as yachi, the word for male affine as sái, and the word for son as uchi.

A Note on Shuar Names

Attentive readers will notice inconsistencies in the composition of Shuar names: some have one name, others two or three or four. Such inconsistencies do not necessarily reflect personal choices but rather historical processes.

Prior to colonization, Shuar generally had one name and did not distinguish between private and public, or informal or formal, uses. For example, Alejandro's grandfather's name was Pítiur, and Pítiur's son's name was Tsakimp. Missionaries, however, encouraged Shuar to take on Spanish names as well. Thus, Pítiur's son Tsakimp took on the additional name Andrés. Similarly, Tsakimp's son Yurank' was given the Spanish name Alejandro.

Government representatives soon insisted that for official purposes Shuar assume surnames as well. Shuar followed the Spanish custom of following their names with those of their fathers and mothers. Thus, although Tsakimp and Suanúa named their second son Yurank' Alejandro, the child's legal name is Yurank' Alejandro Tsakimp Suanúa. (The fact that Alejandro's grandfather had but one name might reflect a precolonial practice or the fact that Alejandro does not remember the name of his great-grandparents.)

If this practice had been institutionalized, Alejandro's first-born son would have been named Etsa Lorenzo Yurank' Kintanúa. Instead, it was the names themselves that have been institutionalized; patronyms have become surnames. Thus, Etsa Lorenzo's last name was Tsakimp. What was once the name of a person has become the name of a family.

Ecuador

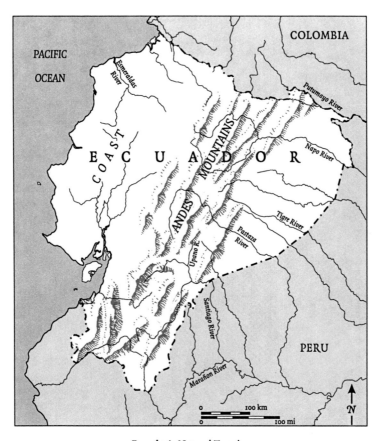

Ecuador's Natural Terrain

xxiii

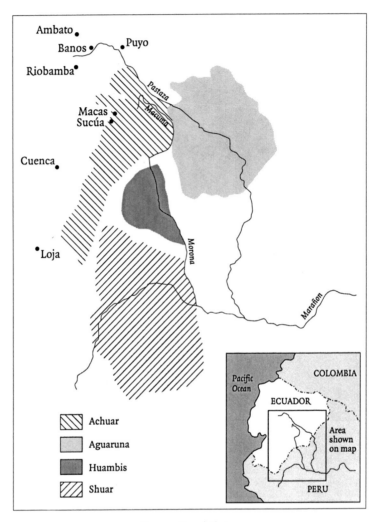

Jivaroan Populations

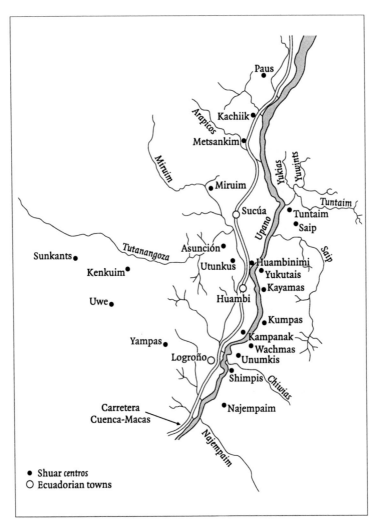

The Shuar Federation

ALEJANDRO TSAKIMP

Part 1: Introductions

I

Meeting Alejandro

Perhaps forty thousand Shuar live in the Ecuadorian province of Morona Santiago. They were formerly, and today are vulgarly, known as Jívaro.[1] The Shuar achieved fame in the latter half of the nineteenth century for their practice of shrinking the severed heads of slain enemies. Like many other sub-Andean hunter-gardeners, they lived in small clusters of semi-nomadic households, connected by the loosest of kin and political ties. In response to Ecuadorian colonization of the region in the twentieth century, they coalesced into nucleated settlements called *centros*: eight to thirty homesteads located around a central plaza. These *centros* are organized into a federation with an elected leadership and an increasingly professionalized bureaucracy. One can safely say that today *Shuar* is the name of a tribe. In the language of the same name, however, the word *shuar* simply means "person," and this is the story of one person, Alejandro Tsakimp.

The first time I heard about Alejandro Tsakimp was in November 1988. That was the day my colleague Janet Hendricks saw me sitting under the umbrellas on Avenida Rio Amazonas in Quito, Ecuador.

Amazonas Avenue is a far cry from the Amazon rain forest, where I intended to conduct my doctoral dissertation research. Quito is the capital of Ecuador, a densely populated city high in the Andes. During the day the sun is often strong enough for people to walk about in shirt-sleeves, but in the mornings and evenings they wear sweaters and coats to warm themselves against the mountain chill. Amazonas is one of the main thoroughfares in the northern half of the city, running from the airport in the north, past the upper-middle-class neighborhoods along the Carolina Park, through the more commercial neighborhood of Mariscal, until it ends at the El Ejido Park.

Mariscal is home to a number of government offices but is dominated by a plethora of folk-art and souvenir shops, trendy bars, and bistros. Tourists and exchange students mingle with homeless Indians and young boys from the slums in the southern part of the city who come to Mariscal to shine shoes and beg. I often sat at one of the many sidewalk tables at one of the three conveniently adjacent restaurants that served as a hub for this activity. Huge umbrellas sheltered the tables from the strong midday sun and the occasional afternoon rain and served as a useful landmark for tourists and a meeting place for friends.

Such settings, where men and women of different races, classes, and nationalities variously engage with and avoid one another, are gold mines for anthropologists fascinated by the culture of modernity. My thoughts, however, were wandering eastward, over the Andes and down into the rain forests of the Upper Amazon—to a site for what I thought would be a different kind of anthropological research. What first drew me to anthropology was its claim that to understand human nature, one must understand humanity in all its diversity. I grew up in a middle-class suburb of New York and wanted to experience life in a society as different from my own as possible. Having grown up Jewish in a Christian society, I already felt like I lived in two different cultures, but I wanted to know what it was like to live in a society without cities, without "the state," without capitalism. In his memoire *Tristes Tropiques*, Claude Lévi-Strauss argued that the most basic human truths can most easily be recognized in the simplest societies. Since I had spent a couple of months after college studying Spanish in Guatemala, I, like Lévi-Strauss, looked to the Amazon to escape modernity.

During my second year of graduate school, however, I began reading ethnographies of lowland South America and learned two important facts. First, no Amazonian society is "pristine"; European conquest and colonization of the Americas in the sixteenth century set off waves of epidemics and migrations that destroyed old societies and created new ones. Second, every Amazonian people today lives under the legal jurisdiction of some state. Moreover, states not only regulate people's lives; they also regulate people and places in different ways, in effect, legislating social and spatial differences. I thus learned that isolation and cultural difference are not absolute but relative, and are the effects of colonialism rather than signs of its absence.[2]

Then I read Michael Harner's *Jívaro: People of the Sacred Waterfalls*, and learned how the Shuar rebelled against colonial authorities in 1599, and how they formed a federation in 1964 to defend themselves against neocolonialism and the Ecuadorian state. Ernesto Salazar's "The Federación Shuar and the Colonization Frontier" describes the democratic, hierarchical organization of the Federation, but Harner remarked that shamanism and accusations of witchcraft are still prevalent among Shuar. The Shuar had seemed to develop a formal political apparatus to manage their relations with the modern state, while maintaining informal traditional beliefs and practices. I proposed to study the possible coexistence or antagonism between leaders of the Federation and shamans and was awarded grants from Columbia University (underwritten by the MacArthur Foundation) and Fulbright/International Institute of Education. I arrived in Ecuador in October 1988. This was my second time in the country. The first time I had stayed two weeks; this time I hoped to stay for more than a year — and I ended up staying until January 1992.

The first time I went to Ecuador was in August 1987. I wanted to see the place I hoped would become my home for a year or two, and I wanted to meet with officials of the Shuar Federation. The seat of the Shuar Federation is in Sucúa, a town of over four thousand people in the province Morona Santiago. Although some Shuar live in Sucúa, most of its inhabitants are *colonos*, settlers. The first *colonos* were poor peasants who came down from the highlands beginning around the late 1890s and increasingly in the early 1900s, traveling for days over muddy foot trails. Some came in search of gold, but most came hoping to acquire land (usually by trading some machetes, shotguns, or clothing with Shuar) in order to raise a few head of cattle. After the road connecting the province to the highland city of Cuenca was completed in the mid-1970s, more people came down to take advantage of new commercial opportunities. Today most *colonos* live along the road in the Upano River valley. Many Shuar also live in the valley, but most live east of the Upano, on the other side of the Cutucú — the last foothills of the Andes.

Sucúa is an hour bus ride south of Macas, the largest city (eleven thousand people in 1987) in, and capital of, the province. At that time planes flew to and from Quito on Mondays and Fridays, and I spent Monday night in Macas. Today when I think of Macas I think of the Chinese restaurant, playing cards with some Peace Corps volunteers I befriended, and the huge depiction of "Our Lady of Macas" on the church overlooking the Upano. Of my first night in Macas, however, I remember only my encounter with a North American tourist staying at the same small hotel as I. He wanted to spend a few days hunting in the forest and had gone to Sucúa to ask for permission from the Federation. "All I want to do is go hunting and fishing!" he shouted, as he paced on the balcony. "But they accused me of being a spy for the CIA!"

I remember more of Sucúa, but only details—it is hard for me now to recapture how I felt. On the one hand Sucúa has become for me a second home; it is as familiar to me as any place I have lived, and I can barely remember that time when all was new and strange. On the other hand, Sucúa has grown and changed a lot over the past twelve years, as more and more of its youth have moved to the United States and elsewhere to work and have returned with dollars to finance the construction of new houses and stores. When I first arrived the main street was unpaved and almost all of the buildings were made of wood. There was one theater that usually showed kung fu and porn movies, but I had the strange luck to be there to watch an incredibly decrepit print of *Raiders of the Lost Ark*. In the evenings men congregated in one of the three or four restaurants to drink cheap Ecuadorian beer or cheap Ecuadorian rum. By the time I left in 1992 the theater had closed down because too many people owned VCRs. Today many homes have cable television as well. There are now a number of discotheques where people can drink Bacardi, Don Q, or Havana Club.

I do remember my first sight of the Federation headquarters—a two-story building notable for a beautiful depiction, shaped out of steel rods, of a traditional Shuar homestead (a woman carrying a basket of manioc, a man with a blowgun, and a shrunken head hanging by the doorway) and the group of Shuar hanging out in front. I met with the vice president of the Federation and a couple of the directors, and expressed my interest in learning more about the Shuar and the accomplishments of the Federation. They seemed sympathetic—at least they did not accuse me of working for the CIA—but regretted to inform me that they had declared a moratorium on anthropological research.[3] I could try again next year, but for the moment they could not help me.

I had two more days to spend in Sucúa and did not want to see *Raiders of the Lost Ark* again. As I ate some fried meat in one of the small restaurants, I asked the proprietor what I could do. "You could go for a walk to the Upano," he suggested, and then he gave me directions: just before the old airstrip, turn left and walk for about an hour. As I walked I thought about the Shuar I had watched in front of the Federation, variously

6

arguing passionately or laughing, and about the dignity projected by the vice president. As the road began to slope down I could see the vast expanse of the valley; forest punctuated by pasture and gardens. Of course, I had hiked in forests in New York, but here the glaring equatorial sun revealed shades of green with a luminosity I had never before seen.

As I walked farther, I ran into several cows in the middle of the road. Years ago, in Guatemala, I had an encounter with a bull that does not bear repeating, but that left me with a paralyzing anxiety in the face of cattle. Perhaps five minutes passed as I waited for the unobliging cows to move off the road. Then, I heard a voice from behind: "Are you walking to the river?" I replied, with questionable honesty, "Yes," and found myself walking around the cattle in order to hear what the man was saying to me. His name was Juan Bosco Mashu, he was Shuar, a teacher, and he was going to visit his first wife in Saip on the other side of the river. When we reached the river he showed me a garden that someone was maintaining. "Here," he pulled something out of the ground and gave me half. I bit into it, pungent and spicy—it was ginger. We talked a little more, and I asked him to have a beer with me when he returned to town.

I went to Ecuador for the second time fourteen months later. I had enough money to support myself for one year and hoped to stretch it out for two. I wanted to proceed with my work slowly and cautiously and decided to stay in Quito for a month or two to work on my Spanish (almost all Shuar are bilingual) and make periodic trips to Sucúa to explore the possibilities of fieldwork—I was afraid that the Federation moratorium on research would still be in effect, and I had no idea what I would do if this were the case. I decided that the first step would be to find Juan.

I had learned that machetes are among the most prized tools used by people in the Amazon, owing to their versatility and practicality. Indeed, I would soon discover, everyone in Morona Santiago owned at least one. Ironically, though, the best machetes were imported from the United States and sold only in the highlands. Moreover, even the cheapest machete constitutes a considerable expense for most Shuar. While in Quito I bought an imported machete as a present for Juan and then bought a ticket for Macas.

This time I had no intention of spending a night in Macas. From the airport I walked straight to the bus terminal. I paid for the ticket and turned around to face . . . Juan! He had come on business with the Education Ministry and was on his way back to Sucúa. We sat next to each other in the bus, and each time we drove past a ravine he recounted for me a different accident in which a bus ran off the road. He was now living with his second wife in a Shuar settlement called Utunkus; he invited me to have lunch at his home the next day, and we agreed to meet in Sucúa in the morning to walk out together.

Back in Quito, sitting under an umbrella and sipping coffee, I considered my options. Juan had introduced me to a number of people working in the Shuar Federation, and I wondered if he had any leverage with them. Also, I met an English woman who was planning to move to Sucúa in the hopes of teaching English at the Shuar Federation. She had befriended Miguel Puwáinchir, the new president, and said she would introduce us.

It was at this moment that I heard someone shout my name.

It was Janet Hendricks, who had conducted fieldwork among the Shuar in 1982 and had written *To Drink of Death*, a masterful life history of a Shuar warrior named Tukup'. I had first written to her when I began considering working among the Shuar, and she read and commented on various drafts of my research proposal. I knew that she had been planning a brief trip to Ecuador, but I was uncertain when and where our paths would cross. She sat down, and I told her about my initial trips to Sucúa and my fears about not receiving permission. Although she encouraged me not to worry about the Federation, she did question the next step in my research. I was planning to ask permission to live in a Shuar community east of the Cutucú range, but she thought I should stay in the Upano valley. It was in the valley, where population density is highest, game is least available, and land is a more precious resource, that Shuar are struggling most directly against the effects of colonialism. If I wanted to study changes in shamanism and new accusations of witchcraft, she told me, I should work in a Shuar community as close to the road as possible. And suddenly I realized that, despite all I had learned about the relationship between indigenous culture and colonialism, I still harbored fantasies of living in as simple and isolated a community as possible. "Here is the name of a shaman you should meet," she told me. "He is a great guy, fascinating, and perfect for your project." I looked at what she had written: "Alejandro Tsakimp, in San José."

A couple of weeks later I made another trip to Sucúa and set off to find Juan. I more or less remembered the way we walked to San José, and I assumed that once I was in the community, people could direct me to his house. I bought a bag of candy to give to his children and set off on the road out of Sucúa around 10:00 A.M. Shortly after the airstrip I turned right and cut through someone's farm, until the path descended to the Utunkus (in Spanish, Tutanangoza) River, the *de facto* boundary between settler territory and Shuar territory. Rivers such as the Utunkus have been carrying water from the Andes down into the Amazon for millennia. They are neither very wide nor deep, but they are very swift and even treacherous when it rains, and they have cut deep ravines and gorges through the land. In lieu of a bridge, the municipality had constructed a *tarabita*, a gondola suspended over the river, and a rope and pulley system, with which one could cross from one side to the other.

When I reached the top of the riverbank, I saw a house and called out. A woman appeared; I offered her some candy (desperately hoping for something to drink) and reminded her that I was a friend of Juan's and had passed through a few weeks earlier. She remarked that she thought Juan was gone, but pointed me toward his house. I set out and promptly got lost in the tall grass. I turned around and called to her, and she sent her daughter to show me the way. The young girl ran past me, practically skipping down an incredibly steep and rocky path, over a stream, up another hill, and then pointed to a path leading into the forest. I was tired but remembered this path and thanked the girl. Twenty minutes later I reached a familiar pasture and stopped to rest a bit. Then I looked up. All around me were high grasses; I could see the trail back into the forest, but not forward.

Stupidly, I decided to climb a nearby hill in the hope of getting a better view, but when I reached the top I found myself back in forest. No trail, no vista, just tall grass, trees, rotting logs, and vines that seem to want to drag me down. It was now one P.M. and hot. For half an hour I sweated and stumbled around looking for anything like a path. Yet in every direction I looked the forest either got thicker or dropped precipitously. On the verge of panic, I decided to close my eyes for a few minutes. Standing at the edge of a small ledge, I realized that the only way down was down, and I jumped. Somehow, I managed to slide not only back to the same pasture but to the correct trail. I brushed myself off and continued my search for Juan.

When I reached the next house, I collapsed and explained who I was and who I was looking for. The woman took my bag of candy, gave me water to drink, and explained that Juan had moved to Santiago, where he had taken a new job teaching.

Recalling Janet's note, I asked the woman where I could find Alejandro Tsakimp. She pointed me back to the trail, and I managed to keep to it without getting lost. When I ran into some young men and explained who I was now looking for, one of them said, "He's my uncle—I'll take you there!"

It was around 4:00 P.M. when we finally reached Alejandro's house, a simple wooden structure with a zinc roof, set in a small clearing surrounded by forest. The nephew called out, and a man with long black hair and shining dark eyes came out smiling at me. I told him I was a friend of Janet's. "Oh, yes!" he said, as he held out his arms to embrace me. He had been expecting me, he said, and was happy to meet me. As we hugged I wondered to myself how he could possibly have known I was coming—I didn't think Janet had gone back to Sucúa since I saw her in Quito. In time I learned how much delight he took in meeting new people; often during the course of my fieldwork he would introduce me to tourists he had met and to whom he had given Shuar names. Well, much of fieldwork relies on circumstance and luck. At the moment I put my confusion aside; relieved to have made contact, all I wanted now was something to drink.

Alejandro escorted me into the cool darkness of the house, and his wife Maria brought me grapefruit juice. I explained that I had first come looking for Juan—"Oh, he isn't here anymore," Alejandro told me—and how I had left Sucúa at 10:00 A.M. and had gotten lost. Everyone was laughing, and Alejandro asked me why I came from the northern entrance to the community. "There is another entrance?" I asked. "There is a bridge over the Utunkus just south of here," he explained, "you can be back on the road in half an hour!"

Alejandro invited me to have supper with him, and Maria brought us chicken noodle soup. I explained to him that I was interested in learning more about shamanism and the Federation, but that I was worried that the Federation might not give me permission.

"So what?" he responded. "I am a Shuar. The Federation has no right to tell me what to do. I am a man and do what I please. If the Federation won't give you permission, you can still work with me."

Alejandro addressing the community at Nayumpim

I should have known that an attempt to study conflict among and between shamans and Federation leaders would inevitably place me in moral and political dilemmas. Before colonization and incorporation into the Ecuadorian state, Shuar maintained an egalitarian society (meaning that people of the same age and gender have equal access to resources, prestige, and power) without coercive leadership. They continue to value liberty to an extent inconceivable in the United States, where almost every aspect of our lives is governed by law or some bureaucratic regulation. Indeed, Federation officials do not claim the right to tell Shuar what to do. But they do claim that the right to represent Shuar collectively, however recent in Shuar history, is a legitimate and necessary function. After all, Alejandro's individualism not only recalls a past Shuar egalitarianism; it echoes the discourses of colonialism: individual citizenship, private property, private contract, and alienated labor. These are discourses through which native communities have been destroyed and their lands taken from them. Today Shuar such as Alejandro are caught between these two, at times deceptively similar, discourses.

The Shuar Federation is also caught between these discourses. On the one hand, it gives individual Shuar a voice, not only through its democratic organization but also through its radio service, which allows any member of the Federation to broadcast messages. Moreover, it gives Shuar a powerful collective voice in both local and national politics and has been instrumental in securing "global," or collective, title to land for its members and thus protecting Shuar against colonization. On the other hand, it has effectively transformed Shuar into agents of colonialism by channeling access to capital and promoting cattle ranching. Since officials and employees of the Federation receive salaries from the state, the organization is also facilitating the division of Shuar into two classes, professional and agrarian. Leaders of the Federation are thus caught within a set of practices that simultaneously unite and divide Shuar.

It did not take long for me to realize that my original proposal to study the conflicts between shamans and the Federation in terms of the clash between tradition and modernity was ill-conceived. For both shamans and leaders of the Federation, the conditions of possibility for being either "traditional" or "modern" take confusingly similar forms. It is thus very difficult to appeal to one way of life in order to resist the other. Put another way, Shuar find themselves in a situation where their attempts to be either subversive or conservative (in their stance toward their culture, political organization, or the state) unintentionally, but unavoidably, get tangled up.

Coincidentally, anthropologists such as myself also often find themselves to be both subversive and conservative. This paradox has its roots in the history of the discipline. Anthropology was first made possible by the waves of European colonial and neocolonial expansion in the eighteenth and nineteenth centuries, but many of the first anthropologists saw in knowledge of other societies leverage to question and criticize elements of their own culture. Traditionally, we untangle the contradictions between these two stances by separating them. Lévi-Strauss once observed that "while often inclined to subversion among his own people and in revolt against traditional behavior, the anthropologist appears respectful to the point of conservatism as soon as he is dealing with a society different from his own" (1973: 383).

Conservatism in the field is usually both methodologically sound and politically expedient. Respecting a different culture is a means of escaping the blinders of our own and a precondition for understanding. Moreover, anthropologists need the cooperation and assistance of those whose culture they study. (I had not come to study "the Shuar" as such; I had come to study their culture, and in this project Shuar were my teachers, not my subjects).

Such conservatism is also morally charged, for as much as it reflects an attitude of detachment and acceptance, it also involves taking a particular side in what is often a highly partisan confrontation. After all, even today most anthropological research occurs in colonial situations, where government officials, missionaries, corporations, and settlers vie for control over indigenous land and labor. In such contexts what appears to be conservative abroad, or in a local context, is necessarily subversive at home, or in a global context.

Ever since Franz Boas, the founder of American academic anthropology, was censured by the American Anthropological Association for criticizing the government's use of anthropologists as spies during the Great War, anthropologists have struggled over their relationship to the state. This issue resurfaced in the 1960s, when the CIA and the Department of Defense sponsored anthropological research in Southeast Asia and Latin America. In the postcolonial and post-Vietnam era anthropologists reached a consensus that their first loyalty was to the people with whom they worked, rather than their government or sponsors.[4]

As Lévi-Strauss's formulation manifests, this stance resolves the conflict between subversive and conservative by locating one at home and the other in the field. This distribution of loyalties works only if the anthropologist's home is a complex society in turmoil and if the field site is relatively simple and stable. That is, anthropologists have assumed that geographic distance marks cultural difference and can thus keep divided loyalties safely apart.

This distance (if it was ever as great as anthropologists and their Western readers imagined) has collapsed in Morona Santiago. As I walked back to Sucúa from Alejandro's house, I realized that the Upper Amazon was perhaps an even more complex space of modernity than the umbrellas on Avenida Río Amazonas in Quito. So what happens to professional ethics when the society in which one works is conflicted and the culture one studies is contested? To whom should I be loyal, when Shuar themselves differ over what it means to be Shuar and who has a right to represent the Shuar? How can I tell who represents the interests of the Shuar, and who represents the interests of capital or the state? What constitutes subversion or conservatism?

I never had to resolve this dilemma. I met Miguel Puwáinchir, the president of the Federation, and gave him a copy of my research proposal; he read it, we talked about it, and he gave me a letter authorizing my research. In order to live in Utunkus I had to meet with and explain my work to the community; they voted to allow me to live among them.[5] I worked closely with Alejandro, but also with other shamans who were his rivals. With the exception of one Federation official and one resident of Utunkus, everyone was willing to talk to me.

To this day I do not know what I would have done had Puwáinchir denied me permission and had Alejandro persisted in his offer to help me anyway. Nor do I hope to resolve through this book the practical issue of how to conduct fieldwork—complex questions such as these can only have contingent solutions that are found in practice, not in reflection. Nevertheless, this practical issue calls into question some basic theoretical assumptions about culture, fieldwork, and ethnography (a book describing and analyzing a particular society, based on participant-observation fieldwork). I confront such assumptions in the remainder of part 1. Before proceeding with Alejandro's story, we need to reflect on how such stories have been read in our culture, how they have been and how they might be used, and how they are produced. Consequently, the introductory chapters of this book are not meant to "introduce" Alejandro or the Shuar in the sense of naming and describing them. On the contrary, they are meant in part to introduce some of the dangers and difficulties involved in naming and describing them. Of course, it is inevitable that readers will form their own ideas about Alejandro and his society. Each introductory chapter, therefore, is also meant more constructively to provide different perspectives from which people may read his stories.

In chapter 2 I deconstruct Lévi-Strauss's separation of home and the field by critiquing the related opposition between history and culture.[6] I effect this deconstruction through a consideration of a series of texts describing Shuar and Shuar culture, written by ethnographers and adventurers, missionaries and administrators. These texts are not just discursive practices but symptoms of other practices through which land and labor have been exploited and people sometimes killed. Nevertheless, however subversive I may try to be through my reading and writing, deconstructing texts in the United States is both easier and safer than trying to make a living, or even just living, in the contradictory circumstances of the Ecuadorian Amazon.[7] In chapters 3 and 4 I discuss the value of life history in furthering this deconstruction.

That I never really had to live out the conflict between individual and collective Shuar interests attests only, I believe, to my relative insignificance in the Shuar political landscape. For people such as Miguel Puwáinchir and Alejandro Tsakimp, however, this struggle is a fundamental condition of their lives. It is the unavoidable consequence of their history and sets the terms through which they must respond to Euro-Americans and to one another. Shuar, especially shamans such as Alejandro, have to negotiate their own problems with power on a regular basis—and in the process, they deconstruct the contradictions in which they live. I am writing this book with the hope that a reflection on Alejandro's life will make possible a greater appreciation of this dilemma—and that an appreciation of its complexity will make possible a better understanding of Alejandro.

2

History and Culture

The complexity of Alejandro's situation has a paradoxical effect. Sometimes the importance and meaning of his stories are obscure, while other times they are so clear as to seem clichéd. When someone finds a story confusing or unimpressive, it is easy to conclude that there is some fault in either the writer or the reader. It is important, though, to consider the possibility that these effects may have more to do with what the story is about, or the circumstances under which it was recounted. If we are to take the complexity of Alejandro's situation seriously, we must also take seriously the difficulties and dangers in reading his stories.

When Alejandro first told me that he would work with me even if the Federation would not authorize my work, I asked myself why he was telling me this and what, exactly, he meant. At the time I was concerned only with the practical dimension of these questions: How, exactly, should I proceed in my work? Long after I began working with Alejandro and leaders of the Federation, however, these questions lingered. For they are theoretical questions as well: How do I make sense of another person? This is a matter of hermeneutics, a matter of interpretation and understanding. These are problems that many anthropologists and historians grapple with as they seek to understand people living in other places or at other times.

As I thought about these questions, however, I began to suspect that my own culture might limit for me the possible answers. Hermeneutic problems are not just the result of cultural distance; they are the result of political and economic engagement. Writers and readers of ethnography exist in a relationship with Ecuador and Shuar—a relationship that further complicates our attempts to write and read about them. Centuries of colonialism have produced not only particular ways that Euro-Americans and Native Americans act toward one another; they have also produced particular ways in which we talk about one another. These discourses are inherently political because they were produced in and reflect a colonial context. More significantly, though, they have been used to justify not only genocide or ethnocide; in the guise of defending traditional cultures they have also been used to justify, and in some cases to facilitate, the exploitation of indigenous land and labor (see Torgovnick 1990 and Trouillot 1991 for analyses of the construction of these discourses, and Asad 1973, Escobar 1995, Ferguson 1994, Ferguson and Whitehead 1992, Friedlander 1975, Gordon 1992, James Scott 1998, Stocking 1991, Taussig 1987, Todorov 1984, and Wilmsen 1989 for illustrations of their application in colonial practice).[1] I grew up surrounded by images of Indians and the Amazon, and as a graduate student supplemented these popular images by reading scholarly treatises before I left for Ecuador. I was afraid that some of these ways of talking about, and depicting, Indians were actually distorting, rather than furthering, my understanding of Alejandro.

Nevertheless, I realized, I could not escape them, even by leaving New York and moving to Ecuador. The fact is, there is no possibility for a pure encounter between a Euro-American and a Native American; Alejandro and I each brought to our first meeting desires and expectations shaped by hundreds of years of Euro-American/Native American encounters. So our relationship involves not only how we understand each other but also how we understand this history. Ultimately, it involves how we understand ourselves.

More importantly, our relationship involves how we struggle within and against colonialism to find new ways of understanding each other and ourselves. This struggle moved me far beyond the hermeneutic question "What does the person I am studying mean?" It led me to questions like "What does it mean that I am studying another person?" and "What is at stake in the different ways other Euro-Americans have talked about Indians?" These are matters of "critical theory," which asks under what conditions different kinds of knowledge are possible or impossible and questions the uses to which different kinds of knowledge are put.[2] At stake in these questions is not only the relationship between knowledge and power but the possibility that these two words really refer to the same thing.

The critical approach leads me to reconsider the ethnographies and histories I read before meeting Alejandro.[3] Now, reconsidering previous research is also a hallmark of science. This may surprise some, for many Westerners have invested in "science" a religious-like authority. The history of science, however, is not just about the progressive accumulation of knowledge; it is also characterized by periodic revolutions in how we think about the world (see Kuhn 1962). From one perspective, science is profoundly anti-authoritarian: all science rests on the admission that the scientist may be wrong; that another person, using scientific methods, can confirm or disprove previous research; and that no scientific proposition can therefore be posited as "true," as having been "proven," in any absolute sense. Indeed, any scientific proposition must be posited in a form that makes it possible to prove the proposition false (see Popper 1959).[4]

Thus, when Michael Harner went to the field he brought with him the earlier ethnographies of the Shuar by Rafael Karsten (1935) and M. W. Stirling (1938), and he reviewed them with his Shuar informants. I had brought Harner's monograph with me and at one point decided to do the same. This book, *Jívaro: People of the Sacred Waterfalls*, is a classic example of traditional ethnography, presenting an abstracted portrait of Shuar culture written in the present tense—the "ethnographic present."[5] The result of my experiment was tedious. I would read a sentence, and Alejandro (who, as a young boy, knew Harner) would say, "That's right." I would read a paragraph and he would say "Yes." Occasionally, he would remark "Not anymore, but yes, when I was younger." I consider these responses in part to testify to the accuracy of Harner's depiction of Shuar culture.

But accuracy is not an end in itself; in the positivist project it is a precondition for using knowledge, not a use itself. So what, exactly, is the use of an account of the past, in the present? (Of course, one might argue that the primary use of "accuracy" is to establish authority. This only begs the question of the uses of authority, which I address below when I revisit the issue of the ethnographic present.) I soon realized that Alejandro's responses also reveal the difference between Harner's scientific concerns and my own critical concerns. I was not interested in correcting a study that did not seem to need correction; I was interested in exploring issues that it did not address. I learned that a story that perfectly illustrated one of Harner's general points could just as well lead in very different directions. I began my research by trying to document the history of local conflicts, but as I listened to such accounts as the following, I could not help wondering about the relationship between Western notions of "history" and "culture" and how we talk about violence. I ended up learning that there is far more at stake in the ethnographic enterprise than accuracy; how we talk about violence may itself be a form of violence, and how we talk about power is itself a form of power.

The following extended account comes from my interview with Alejandro and from an interview with his sister Teresa. As in the chapters that constitute Alejandro's life history, I have edited the remarks to provide a coherent narrative in Alejandro's (or Teresa's) own words. I have occasionally inserted my own comments or explanations into the narrative. In such cases, my words are in italics in order to distinguish them from Alejandro's or Teresa's.

I once asked Alejandro if he knew of any shamans who had been killed. He thought back to when he was four or five years old, and told me a story that echoed all that I had read and heard about the Shuar.

It was sometime around 1950, give or take two years, he told me, when Chúmpi killed Tséremp. Both men were in-laws of Alejandro's father, Andrés.[6] *Chúmpi and Alejandro's mother were parallel cousins and therefore, following Shuar kinship terminology, brother and sister. Tséremp was the brother of Andrés's second wife.*

But Tséremp was also an uwíshin, a person who had special powers to harm or heal others. According to Alejandro, Tséremp boasted of his power to kill. And so when Chúmpi's son Augustin became sick, Chúmpi suspected Tséremp.

First, according to Alejandro, Chúmpi sought Tséremp's help. He took the sick lad to the uwíshin and begged Tséremp to examine and cure the boy.

"He is cold and suffers from spasms," Chúmpi said, but Tséremp just said, "It's nothing."

But the boy remained seriously ill, and Chúmpi went to Andrés.

"I don't know what will happen," Andrés said. "I too am sick. And I know that it is my own in-law, Tséremp, who is doing this. I don't know what to tell you."

So Chúmpi said "Come, now with me; they have screwed with you, but they aren't going to screw me. You have to help me."

Alejandro's older sister Teresa remembered more of what happened that day:

The afternoon sky grew dark, *she recalled*; there was thunder, and then it rained. *Teresa was at the home of her older brother, Valentín, and his wife Tsapik'. Valentín had gone out hunting and returned with a guatuza, an agouti, when Chúmpi arrived.*

So Chúmpi and Valentín walked about ten meters away from the house and talked.

"Your father Andrés Tsakimp is really sick, because you cannot act. I am going to give you a spear so you too can kill Tséremp. I will shoot him, and if he doesn't die, you finish him off with the spear."

But Valentín said, "No, I am Christian. I cannot kill a person."

"No," Chúmpi says, "no, no, what are you, a woman? Don't you feel sorrow for your father? If your papa dies . . . Nephew, you, why don't you want to accompany me? Suppose your father dies today, is it good that Tsarimbo continues ensorcelling, continues doing evil to us? We have to kill this evil witch—a deed for a deed!"

But my brother Valentín kept saying, "No, I am a Christian, I cannot kill."

But Uncle Chúmpi convinced him. "Just the same, let's go," Uncle Chúmpi says, "let's go."

After Tsapik' and Teresa had cooked the guatuza and prepared to eat, Valentín said, "I am going to go to Chúmpi's. He says his son is dying, and I am going to go find out."

It was as if he got lost! "When is he going to come home?" we asked ourselves, "When is he going to come?" How it rained! There was thunder and lightning, and when I went out to fetch water, I heard a noise like a tiger. Later, people said that it was the cry of the soul of the late Tséremp. When they killed him his soul went out of his body and made this sound. But we were young women—we were afraid to go out to see what had happened.

Then, after they killed Tséremp, the rain and thunder stopped. There was nothing but the moon, really shining, and my brother came back. He entered the house in silence and lay down in bed.

I was there and couldn't contain myself, and I told my sister-in-law, "Sister-in-law, why did my brother return so early in the morning, what was he doing? Ask him!"

So Tsapik' asked her husband, "Where did you go? Where did you go?"

But what could my brother say? He was silent.

"Where were you, Valentín? Where did you go?"

What could my brother say?

Then we heard a scream, and we ran out. I said to my sister-in-law, "Who is it, crying in these hours, in the middle of the night, so close to dawn, who cries?"

She replied, "I don't know." Then she said, "There was a fight."

"Why is that woman crying? Who is it?"

"It is Suanúa, the wife of Tséremp. They must have killed Tséremp."

Then my sister-in-law says, "Let's go see." I was afraid they would kill us, but we left the little ones secure in the bed, and we ran off.

When we saw Suanúa she was naked, and in her hand was a cloth, a piece of clothing she had grabbed as she ran out of her house. We met her in the middle of the forest, in the path. How she was screaming! There were so many screams that we went back to get the babies.

There in the middle of the forest we met my father and stepmother. "What happened?"

My stepmother said, "Daughter, they killed my brother."

"Who killed him?"

"I don't know. They were Shuar from Asunción," she said, knowing full well that they were from right here in San José.

We met Suanúa and said, "Grandmother, grandmother, put on your clothes."

"Aaaaaahh" she cried, "aaaahh, they killed my Tséremp, they killed him. Why did they kill him?"

"Who killed him?" I asked.

"I don't know. It was Shuar from Asunción, to avenge the death of Wampíu."

Wampíu was a Shuar who lived in Asunción, and people say he too died of witchcraft.

Then we went to see where they killed him — they killed him in his own bed! Everything was shot up! And my uncle, my father's own brother, Pedro, had cut Tséremp in the chest with a machete. The shotgun hadn't killed Tséremp, so Pedro cut until the machete penetrated the heart.

"Tséremp was a powerful *uwíshin*," Alejandro concluded, "but he fell because of the many bad things that he had done."

Is this history? If history is a record of causes and effects, then this looks like history — it tells the story of what caused Chúmpi to kill Tséremp. Nevertheless, while I have no doubt that something violent occurred between Chúmpi and Tséremp decades ago, I have no way of knowing whether it happened this way or not. I heard the story from two people, but one was a little boy at the time, and both are partisan — related to the parties in the fight. Then again, everyone in Utunkus is related in one way or another; the only people who could ever tell such a story would have to be partisan.

But I do not think that such a story can be ignored on this account. For me, it is sufficient that the story exists. Rather than get bogged down in the futile task of questioning whether these events actually happened, it would be more productive to ask what the story of these events means and to what uses may such a story be put. Indeed, given all that I had read about the Shuar, the significance of this account of witchcraft and feuding seemed obvious the first time I heard it. As an anthropologist, however, I have been trained to question the obvious. The meaning of an account is never obvious, for it changes as the story is put to different uses. The pressing questions are, What are the different ways people may read this story? To what uses might these different readings be put?

In the case of this story, as I discuss below, Alejandro put the story to different uses. One time, as we have seen, was to answer a direct question I posed. But he brought up the story himself in the context of other discussions. He used the story to make a moral point to me when I asked him what his father taught him about shamanism, and he used the story to make a historical point when I asked him how he came to live in Sucúa.

In this chapter, however, I explore three prevalent ways that Euro-Americans have read stories like this. First, I examine the way the word history has been applied to the Shuar. In fact, what histories there are of the Shuar seem to ignore such stories, viewing them as examples of Shuar culture rather than accounts of historical events. Second, therefore, I turn to ethnography, and how anthropologists have used notions of culture to tell stories about Indians. (I limit myself to a discussion of Karsten, Stirling, and Harner for two reasons: they serve to illustrate a particular point I would like to make about a tension in the ethnographic endeavor, and these are the books I relied on most heavily before I began my initial fieldwork.) Finally, I examine a popular treatment of the Shuar, a book representative of the growing Euro-American interest in Native Spirituality.

Many of these works provide much useful information about the Shuar, their physical environment, and their history. But they also reveal something about their authors, and in this chapter I am less interested in what these books say than in how they say it. This approach reveals that studies that seem quite different—historical versus ethnographic, academic versus popular—are nevertheless bound by certain common assumptions concerning history, culture, and Native Americans. These assumptions reflect our own culture—my own culture—and I have no illusions about my own ability to escape them. Given the real power that my society has had over indigenous people, directly in the United States and indirectly in Ecuador, I do, however, believe it is important to question these assumptions. Moreover, I hope that by confronting these assumptions I may make possible a fourth way to read this story.

"The Jívaros," noted M. W. Stirling, of the Smithsonian Institution's Bureau of American Ethnology, "first appear in history when the Inca, Tupac-Yupanqui, undertook the conquest of the realm of Quito about the middle of the 15th century." Stirling went on to explain that although Tupac-Yupanqui conquered the Cañari of the highlands, neither he nor his son, Huayna-Capac, were able to conquer the Shuar in the lowlands. The Shuar were thus "left in peace to continue their customary fighting among themselves. The conquest of the Incas by the Spaniards simply meant a new adversary for the Jívaros" (Stirling 1938: 3–4).

These remarks are especially interesting because they reveal as much about our own culture as they do about that of the Shuar. I am most interested in what they suggest about how we talk about "history." For although Stirling's remarks seem clear and straightforward, and his vocabulary unexceptional, it is worth pausing for a moment to puzzle over how one might "first appear in history." What, exactly, does "history" mean in this sense? Certainly it cannot mean "time," for the Shuar lived and acted in the world long before their encounter with the Inca.

The Shuar "appear" in history—so history is a place where one may be seen. But not everyone, it seems, is in this place: one's appearance in history is an event. How one gets to appear in this place may tell us something about what it is like. Perhaps this place is some sort of written record. The most literal gloss for "history," then, might be "a history book," or "a historical document." If this were the case, however, the date of their appearance would be the date that the book or document was written. In fact, Stirling cites two history books, one written in 1878 and the other in 1882. Yet Stirling dates their first appearance in the fifteenth century.

The appearance in history, for Stirling, is occasioned not by the act of writing but by another act—in the case of the Shuar, a war. The Shuar appear in history when the Inca go to war against them. Moreover, in this story all hinges on the actions of the Inca, the emperor. When the emperor sends his army into new territories, the people living there (whether they win or lose the war) suddenly find themselves "in history." "History," then, is the place where the emperor rules or seeks to rule.[7] It does not really matter who the emperor is, or even that he or she be called "emperor." When Stirling goes on to detail the "later history" of the Shuar, it is in fact a history of European and Euro-American adventures in, and attempts to colonize, the territory in which Shuar live. "History," then, is the space of the state, whether Inca, Spanish, or Ecuadorian.

Within the space of the state, Shuar appear cunning and fiercely independent. After the Spaniards defeated the Inca in the sixteenth century, they began to explore the foothills of the Andes and the tropical forests to the east, in search of gold. By 1552 they had established two settlements, Logroño and Sevilla del Oro. In 1582, the Spaniard Juan Aldrete wrote that the Shuar "are a very warlike people, and have killed a great number of Spaniards, and are killing them every day. It is a very rough land, having many rivers and canyons, all of which in general have gold in such quantity that the Spaniards are obliged to forget the danger and try to subject them for the profits which they can obtain and which the land promises" (cited in Harner 1984: 18).

According to other colonial accounts, however, the two groups lived and traded with each other in peace. Settlers offered the natives iron tools in return for labor in the mines, but the Shuar demand for tools did not match the European demand for gold. Thus, colonial officials further demanded tribute from the Shuar in the form of gold dust. The consequence was what Stirling called "the Jívaro Revolt."[8]

The seat of the Spanish empire was in Madrid; the king appointed viceroys to govern in the New World. The Viceroyalty of Peru (seated in Lima) was established in 1544 and was divided into three *audencias* (courts): La Paz, Bogota, and Quito. When Philip III was crowned Hapsburg emperor in September 1598, the Real Audencia de Quito (Royal Court of Quito) ordered the customary ceremonial oath of allegiance to the new king. The governor imposed a large tax on both Indians and settlers to pay for the expenses of the ceremony. When the colonists protested, he informed them that the tax was really a voluntary gift; when Shuar complained, though, the governor was silent and steadfast.

Since the forest is vast, the easiest way to avoid conflict in one place is simply to move to another. This is what many Shuar wanted to do, until one of them, named Quirruba, said that he had a better idea, but it would require all Shuar to submit to his leadership. After swearing all his followers to secrecy, Quirruba instructed them to seek as much gold as they possibly could. Upon learning the date of the arrival of the governor in Logroño, Quirruba sent emissaries to other Shuar who were subject to the tax to help raise an army. One part of this army would go to Huamboya, another to Sevilla del Oro, and Quirruba himself would lead the third part to Logroño. According to one account,

> The fatal day came with the arrival of the Governor at Logroño, without any aspect of the conspiracy having leaked out up to then. The Spaniards slept quite without worry in the unfortunate city when it was taken cautiously, at midnight, by the enemy army. This exceeded 20,000 Indians, according to recorded report, outside of the troops who had already marched to Sevilla and to Huamboya. Surrounding the city, they invaded and occupied all of its sections simultaneously, so that the Spaniards would not be able to unite, and they were forced to die in their own homes.
>
> The principal chief, Quirruba, who had carried out all of the preparations with great cunning, took possession of the house in which the Governor was staying. Surrounding the house, Quirruba entered it with sufficient troops, carrying all the gold that his nation had amassed for the celebrations; and at the same time the implements for melting it. They killed all the people who were inside, except for the Governor, who was in a state of undress because of the surprise. They told him that it was now time for him to receive the tax which he had ordered prepared.
>
> They stripped him completely naked, tied his hands and feet; and while some amused themselves with him, delivering a thousand castigations and jests, the others set up a large forge in the courtyard, where they melted the gold. When it was ready in the crucibles, they opened his mouth with a bone, saying that they wanted to see if for once he had enough gold. They poured it little by little, and then forced it down with another bone; and bursting his bowels with the torture, they all raised a clamor and laughter. (Quoted in Harner 1984: 21)

Quirruba's army proceeded to sack Logroño and Sevilla de Oro, killing almost all the men, old women, and young girls; the surviving colonists fled north to found Macas, which is today the capital of Morona

Santiago. Shuar and Euro-Americans for the most part avoided each other for the next 250 years.

Outside of the space of the state dwell "the people without history."[9] In this space, people act according to "custom." They act out of habit, often without calculation. And the custom of the Shuar, Stirling tells us, is to fight among themselves, as Chúmpi, Tséremp, Valentín, and Andrés fought. This nonhistory of the Shuar—we could call it myth, to use a word popular among anthropologists[10]—has been the dominant view of Shuar on the part of people who have and write history.

The myth of the savage Shuar was perhaps best expressed by the anthropologist Paul Rivet in 1907:

> The Jívaro does not have the submissive, humble, cringing appearance, I might almost say servile, of the civilized Indian; much to the contrary, everything in him reveals the free man, passionately loving liberty, incapable of putting up with the slightest subjection. The eye is quick, the look steady, the physiognomy mobile and expressive, their movements rapid and animated, their speech easy and assured . . . so one finds him in the forests in the midst of virgin nature whose pure splendor forms a magnificent frame for the indomitable savage. (quoted in Stirling 1938: 3)

How like my first impression of Alejandro, when he told me he did not care what the Federation would or would not allow. Yet the forest in which Alejandro lives is not virgin, and it was not virgin when Rivet wrote either. In Rivet's discourse, however, civilization and nature are opposed: civilization (the space of the state) is submissive, nature is free, and Shuar can belong only to one and not the other. But this discourse belongs not to Rivet—it is far older than anthropology and has its antecedents in the discourse of colonialism.

I would now like to review some examples from this discourse. What strikes me about these examples, despite the fact that they were written by different people over the course of more than three hundred years, is how similar they are. For scientists, such consistency usually suggests that the individual reports are accurate. For the critical theorist, however, it suggests the persistence in our own culture of unquestioned, and perhaps even unrecognized, biases. I do not believe that these biases reflect a conscious prejudice concerning Shuar. Rather, they reveal unquestioned assumptions about the very possibilities for being human.

For example, in 1582 Joan Pizarro prepared a report for the *encomendero* (grantee; someone to whom the Crown gave rights to Indian labor, in return for converting the Indians to Christianity) of the Shuar. He wrote that they "are a people living free from the subjection of any ruler, although each is a partial subject of the chief under whom they join together to make war and to rob and take the heads of their enemies. . . . Their chief is not chosen by inheritance but is the most cruel among them, he who formerly commanded them having died" (quoted in Stirling 1938: 43).

In 1815 a Dominican friar named José Prieto led an expedition to find the ruins of Logroño, during which time he sought to convert Shuar to Catholicism. He wrote, in an article that Stirling characterized as "the best ethnological account of the Jívaros prepared up to this time" (1938: 25), that "their inclination to make cruel and ferocious war on their fellow creatures distorts and obscures all their good qualities to such a degree that the Jívaros are reputed to be the most cruel enemies in all the world. Traveling from mountain to mountain, from forest to forest, from river to river, looking for other infidels like themselves in order to take their lives and dance with the heads of the dead is what most amuses, delights, and enraptures them" (quoted in Stirling 1938: 47).

In 1852 the bishop of Cuenca, Frey José Manuel Plaza, spent five months among the Shuar. His report to the Ecuadorian minister of state provides a consistent, though more detailed, account:

> The Jívaros live in that complete natural liberty which is so lamentable to the body as well as to the soul, since from it arises polygamy without the vigilance and toil of the priests being able to restrain it, resulting from this a repugnance towards embracing the Christian religion and consequently a state of slavery and abjection for the women, victims of pleasure, incontinence and libidinousness of the men; one can well affirm that these three passions form the distinct character of these infidels.
>
> Their dwelling, which they change every six years at the most, is exactly elliptical in shape, it holds several families and each one occupies a kind of berth made from Gadua bamboo-cane, in which one sees a blowgun, a lance, a shield, some feather ornaments, black seeds, and four to six leashed dogs. Round about this house there is

a plantation of yucca, bananas, cotton, toquilla, and guayuza. . . . As descendants of the old rebels of Logroño they preserve the maxim of not fighting as a unit but scatter throughout the woods and reduce their tactics to treachery. (quoted in Stirling 1938: 26)

F. W. Up de Graff, a North American adventurer who traveled around Ecuador from 1894 to 1901, declared:

> Contrary to what is generally supposed, these untamed sons of the forest are a compendium of all that is cunning, knavish, and diabolical; they have the courage of wild animals in battle, but unlike the latter, their guiding principle is "every man for himself." The truth is not in them. Their attempts at understanding the psychology of the white man are even more puerile than were those of the Germans in the Great War. A totally unenlightened race, they must be controlled by fear and superstition. (1923: 224–25)

After Up de Graff joined a party of Aguaruna in an attack on Huambiza (two other Jívaroan groups), he commented further on "Jívaro methods of warfare": "They are utterly distasteful to the white man—the true white man who is brought up to a code of fair play. The attackers display no bravery, the attacked have no chance to defend themselves. As a cat creeps up behind a bird which is digging up worms, so the Jívaro attacks his enemy. A square hand-to-hand fight he will not entertain. With all his paint and feathers he is, unlike the North American Indian, a coward at heart" (270).

In 1935 the ethnographer Rafael Karsten remarked:

> The Jibaros are no doubt at present the most warlike of all Indian tribes in South America. The blood-feuds within the tribes and the wars of extermination between the different tribes are continuous, being nourished by their superstitious belief in witchcraft. These wars are the greatest curse of the Jibaros and are felt to be so even by themselves, at least so far as the feuds within the tribes are concerned. On the other hand, the wars are to such a degree one with their whole life and essence that only powerful pressure from outside or a radical change of their whole character and moral views could make them abstain from them. (259)

And Stirling himself concluded that "at the present time the Jívaros are without doubt the most warlike group in all South America, and it is probable that this statement would hold true for the past century" (1938: 41).

It does not occur to Karsten and Stirling that every documented instance of Shuar violence is a response to state aggression, and that "the most warlike group in all South America" might in fact be the Europeans and their New World descendants. This is especially strange, because Stirling began his history by noting that "this same 'virgin nature,'" to which Rivet referred,

> friendly to those who have adapted themselves to her embrace, so hostile to those who have not, has enabled these children of the jungle to maintain the spirit of independence against the conquering might of the Inca, the greed of the gold-hungry conquistador, and the passionate zeal of the missionary. . . . The multi-faceted account of this prolonged struggle against military, theological, commercial, and territorial aggression constitutes one of the most colorful chapters in aboriginal American history. (1938: 3)

So Stirling explicitly framed his history as a struggle between the Shuar and the state.

Nevertheless, historians have characterized this struggle not as between equals but rather between essentially—and radically—different types of people. Civilized men are strong, hungry, and passionate; they are aggressive, they act. In this struggle, however, the uncivilized Shuar can only react. They live in the realm of nature and fight to stay in that realm. From the perspective of the state, of "civilization," they struggle from the outside and struggle only to stay the same.

Lévi-Strauss labeled societies that fight to stay the same "cold" societies (1966: 233–36). One way that they did this was through "myths" populated by *supernatural* beings. The supernatural creates a dimension outside of human action that props up the social order. Conversely, "hot" societies that embrace change—that is, state-level societies—write "history," stories that celebrate change. I would add, however, that people of the state have myths, too. The myths to which I am referring are not populated by supernatural beings, but by *natural* beings—that is, those beings who live "in the forests in the midst of virgin nature"—and thus likewise constitute a domain outside of human action. The result is an image of the Shuar that is frozen in—or rather, outside of—time (see Fabian 1983 for a more extensive and general discussion of these issues).

By presenting his narrative of Inca, Spanish, and Ecuadorian history as a history of the Shuar, Stirling removes violence from history, from the space of the state, and places it squarely in the mythic world of the Shuar. The "nature" of the Shuar is to be "warlike," and their life is one of ceaseless conflict. Now we can imagine their world as essentially unchanged from their first encounter with "history" in the fifteenth century up to the night Chúmpi and his confederates killed Tséremp, sometime around 1950.

For the conventional (and generally positivist) historian, effects have causes; the task of "description" is to provide an objective account of what has happened, and the task of "explanation" is to look to the past to identify the proper causes.[11] For the moralist, however, causes have effects, one's actions have consequences; the task of a myth is to instruct people how to act in the future. For a long time, the dominant Western myth was that of progress from a natural state to a civilized state (for Indians, more simply, from being creatures of nature to subjects of the state). In this context, accounts of Indian culture took the form of judgments; to be "natural" meant to be either childlike and innocent or wild and brutish. Westerners used events such as the death of Tséremp to portray Shuar as brutal savages free of the civilizing constraints of the state. The moral of such stories was that the state has an obligation to tame savages, and savages have an interest in submitting to civilization.

Of course, Alejandro and his father also used this story to pass judgment, but it was a judgment over an individual, not a society: "Tséremp was a powerful *uwíshin*, but he fell because of the many bad things that he had done." Anthropologists have argued that such men as Alejandro and Andrés did not look to the state or the state's myth of progress for a basis for their judgments, but rather they had one in their own culture. Such anthropologists have railed against ethnocentrism—the viewpoint that "one's own group is the center of everything," against which all other groups are judged (Sumner 1906: 13). Instead they promoted relativism—the theory that a culture can be understood only on its own terms.

Bronislaw Malinowski's first book, *Argonauts of the Western Pacific*, which was to become a veritable textbook on how to do ethnography, ends with this manifesto:

> What interests me really in the study of the native is his outlook on things, his *Weltanschauung*, the breath of life and reality which he breaths and by which he lives. Every human culture gives its members a definite vision of the world, a definite zest for life. In the roamings over human history, and over the surface of the earth, it is the possibility of seeing life and the world from the various angles, peculiar to each culture, that has always charmed me most, and inspired me with the real desire to penetrate other cultures, to understand other types of life.
>
> To pause for a moment before a quaint and singular fact; to be amused at it, and see its outward strangeness; to look at it as a curio and collect it into the museum of one's memory or into one's store of anecdotes—this attitude of mind has always been foreign and repugnant to me. Some people are unable to grasp this inner meaning and the psychological reality of all that is outwardly strange, at first sight incomprehensible, in a different culture. These people are not born to be ethnologists. It is in the love of the final synthesis, achieved by the assimilation and comprehension of all the items of a culture and still more in the love of the variety and independence of the various cultures that lies the test of the real worker in the Science of Man.[12] (1922: 517)

Unlike conquerors, explorers, missionaries, and earlier anthropologists, Malinowski tried not to see indigenous people as somehow more "natural." He asserted that they have as rich a culture as any society, which must be understood on its own terms.

Note, however, that the move from ethnocentrism to relativism involves not only shifting from one's own point of view to that of another; it also involves changing one's concern from judgment to understanding. If this leaves no room for ethnocentric judgments of Shuar by Westerners, it leaves little room for Shuar to pass their own judgments of the West. Like Rivet, Stirling, and others, Malinowski still thought of the people he was interested in as living outside the space of the state, outside the space of history. The moral of the new myth is that people such as the Shuar should stay the same.

This is evident in the classic ethnographies about the Shuar. Books by such anthropologists as Rafael Karsten and Michael Harner offer an account of Shuar culture that would be of use to anyone traveling among the Shuar and a vision of the world that would provide a moral basis for the kinds of violence Alejandro had told me about. Nevertheless, their style relies on three rhetorical techniques fundamental to Malinowskian ethnography (although they never claimed to be disciples of Malinowski). One is *abstraction*—a process that starts with particular, concrete events that occurred in different contexts (like Alejandro and Teresa's stories about Chúmpi and Tséremp); claims that the meaning of these events has little or nothing to do with the contexts in which they occurred, and that these events are really examples of particular *kinds* of events and patterns; and ends with generalizations (such as the composite account of Shuar culture I present in the following pages). The second technique is *reification*—the process by which these generalizations are given names and then treated as if they were particular, concrete things (for example, "the Shuar"). These two techniques are joined in the *ethnographic present*—the exclusive use of the present tense.

In the following several pages I provide a composite account of Shuar culture written in the classical style in order to call attention to some of the effects of Malinowski's model. Although this book (like other life histories) departs from this model, I include the classical account because so much ethnography available today is written in the same style. As you read this composite account, think about the effect these rhetorical techniques have on your impression of the Shuar. Imagine how it would have sounded in the past tense, and how it would have sounded had it provided different subjects in the sentences (for example, the names of individual people, or "*all* of the people in that part of the Ecuadorian Amazon," or "*some* people").

Population density in the Amazon is low, and Shuar social organization has responded to the relative abundance of land with atomized nuclei of extended households in dispersed settlements. Shuar houses contain on the average nine people and are "dispersed in loose-knit groupings of irregular size" (Harner 1984: 77). Sometimes two houses containing close relatives are found within three hundred yards of each other, but the nearest house is generally half a mile away. Households consist of a senior man, perhaps two wives, daughters, unmarried sons, and sons-in-law.

Vista of Upano valley

Men clear the forest using the slash and burn technique. Although the rain forest is lush, its soil is thin and poor in nutrients, and it is ill-suited for gardening or farming. Cutting down and burning patches of forest liberates the nutrients in the plants and trees, so that root crops can be planted for several years, until the nutrients have been exhausted. Women are responsible for the cultivation of manioc, the staple, and other tubers. Manioc is consumed boiled or, preferably, in the form of *nijiamanch'* (in Spanish, *chicha*), or beer. *Chicha* is made by women in a time-consuming process. The manioc is peeled, washed, and then boiled until soft. After it has cooled it is mashed by a wooden stick and stirred. As it is being stirred, the woman chews handfuls and spits them back into the pot. It is then left to ferment for a day or two. Average daily consumption by men has been estimated to be three to four gallons; by women one to two gallons; by children half a gallon (Harner 1984: 52).[13]

The cultivation of root crops exhausts the soil after a few years; men clear new gardens and allow the old ones to reforest. After repeating this process a few times, the family often abandons their house and gardens, now overrun with weeds, and moves to another location. Shuar recognize a family's rights to use a house and garden, but these use

Alejandro's grandson on a path in the forest at Nayumpim

rights do not translate into any notion of ownership or property. Anyone has the right to occupy land that has been abandoned.

Women tend gardens and make *chicha*. Through these practices Shuar consider women as valued workers. But men value women not only because of their role in subsistence production, but as links between men as well. Wives produce a surplus of *chicha* that is essential to a man's participation in or hosting of *tsantsa* feasts (to celebrate the return of a headhunting party) and entertaining guests. Preferential polygyny is in part a function of the disproportionate ratio of women to men owing to warfare (Harner estimated 2:1) and in part a function of the warrior's need to produce a surplus of food and drink (Harner 1984: 80–81).[14] Marriage, moreover, is seen as much as a way for a man to acquire a father-in-law as to acquire a wife. Marriage thus formalizes alliances between junior and senior warriors. Furthermore, Shuar practice uxorilocal residence: a married couple lives with the family of the bride until the birth of the first child; thereafter they live in

Esteban Tsakimp's traditional Shuar house

a house nearby. Young men serve their fathers-in-law as junior warriors as a form of bride-service in return for support in feuding and warfare.

Preferential cross-cousin marriage promotes conflict among brothers, who compete for wives.[15] Combined with uxorilocal residence, which isolates brothers from one another, this practice cements the bond between a young man and his father-in-law. This tendency suggests a relative weakening of the bond between the young man and his father (who establishes relations with his own sons-in-law)—which, in the absence of corporate descent groups (social groups based on descent that hold property in common for their members) inhibits the institutionalization of power.

Polygyny provides men with important choices: A young man can marry unrelated women and so forge alliances with various fathers-in-law, and a father can marry his daughters to different men to forge alliances with various younger warriors. Or a man can marry two sisters, cementing the relationship between the son-in-law and father-in-law. Uxorilocal residence promotes a preference for sororal polygyny (marriage to sisters) that further inhibits the institutionalization of power by limiting the number of sons-in-law a man would have. Departures from this practice can foster temporary and local concentrations of power. Nevertheless, the sexual division of labor, uxorilocal residence, bride-

Washing clothes in the river, at Nayumpim

service, bifurcate-merging kinship terminology and preferential cross-cousin marriage, and polygyny reproduce inequalities between males and females by constructing women as resources and between young and old men by structuring access to these resources.[16]

Although a man's role in the system of production is to clear gardens and to hunt, the ultimate expression of male power is the shrunken heads of casualties of war. Warfare consists of an organized raid against the homestead of a neighboring non-Shuar (generally an Achuar, who live to the east of the Shuar). During the return trip the warriors peel the victim's skin back from the upper chest and back, and cut the head off as close as possible to the collarbone. As soon as is convenient, the party stops by a river, and the headhunters slit the skin at the rear of the head, cut the skin away from the skull, and throw the skull in the river. The skin is boiled in water for about half an hour, during which time it shrinks by half. It is taken out to dry and turned inside out so that the remaining flesh can be scraped off. The skin is then turned right side out, and the slits and gaps are sewn together. The shrinking process is completed by rolling first hot rocks and then hot sand inside the skin. Finally, the skin is rubbed with balsa wood charcoal; the black soot is supposed to keep the *muisak*, or avenging soul, of the dead person from coming out and doing mischief. The result is a fist-sized shrunken head, or *tsantsa*.

The warriors then proceed to the homestead of the sponsor, one of the men who organized the raid, who hosts a two-day feast. After this feast the warriors return to their homes, where they personally host one or two additional feasts, which last five or six days. Up to 150 people attend these feasts, where they dance, eat, and drink huge quantities of *chicha*. Afraid that the *muisak* might take advantage of the inebriated state of the guests by fleeing the *tsantsa* and causing a possibly fatal fight, the sponsor and his supporters immediately stop any argument (Harner 1984: 183–93). This is important because the host uses the occasion of the feast as an opportunity to channel the power of the *muisak* into the bodies of close female relatives, commonly a wife or sister, which will enable them to work harder—of pressing importance because the preparations for a feast generally exhaust the household garden. The feast thus mystifies the power of women by ascribing it to men—the dead victim, the triumphant killer. The shrunken head is but a mask obscuring the subordination of women to men—the ultimate trophy. "It is not surprising, therefore, that the *tsantsa* feasts tend to be viewed by the Jívaro as the pinnacles of their social lives. It is also expectable, given the ethos of killing and counter-killing, that this, the greatest celebration, centers around the indisputable evidence of a triumph over a common enemy" (193). On the other hand, these feasts provide an excellent opportunity to surreptitiously poison an enemy, as more than a dozen women from different households circulate, serving *chicha* to all the men. Indeed, most poisoning is done at such feasts (173).

A Shuar could be harmed by other means, besides shotgun, spear, or poison. Many Shuar believe in the existence of what they call *tsentsak*, which they describe as little arrows or darts.[17] Most people are aware of *tsentsak* only through their effects: if one enters a person, that person will sicken and may die. *Tsentsak* are alive, but certain people learn how to master them and to store them within their own bodies. Thereafter, *tsentsak* will enter or leave a body only if a specialist puts them there or removes them. Shuar call such specialists *uwishin*, which they gloss in Spanish as *brujo* (witch), *curandero* (healer), or shaman. These men and women ingest an infusion called *natém* (from the vine *Banasteriopsis caapi*), which enable them to see and control *tsentsak*.[18]

Any Shuar can kill, but unlike warriors, shamans are not supposed to act solely to augment their own power. They exist to help others. Nevertheless, since the power to cure is the same as the power to kill, all shamans live under a cloud of suspicion and fear that one day they may be accused of murder. After all, one shaman can cure only a victim of some other shaman; in the very act of healing, shamans remind people of how dangerous a shaman can be. In fact, a diagnosis of witchcraft almost always involves an accusation, and such an accusation often leads to a revenge killing.

Although men claim that women gain power through the *muisak*, they claim that they acquire their own power by ingesting *maikiúa*. *Maikiúa* is the Shuar name for *Brugmansia* or *Datura*, which Ecuadorians call *floripondio* and North Americans call thorn apple; it is a flowering plant with high concentrations of scopolamine and other alkaloids. The use of *maikiúa* is organized primarily by the life cycle. Shuar take it on four occasions to gain power. First, newborn infants are given a little to make them stronger. Second, throughout their lives Shuar take *maikiúa* following an injury to the bones, for purely medicinal purposes. Third, children are also given *maikiúa* as a form of discipline (they see childish misbehavior as a sign of weakness; the *maikiúa* is less a form of punishment than a remedy that will make the children stronger and more mature).

Finally, Shuar men take *maikiúa* to acquire warrior power, or *arútam wakaní*. Such power allows them to kill without fear or regret. Boys of about eight years are taken by their fathers or uncles on a three- to five-day journey to a nearby waterfall. During the trip a boy drinks only tobacco water. At some point the child is given *maikiúa* and dreams. If the child is fortunate, he encounters his *arútam wakaní* and is taken by a desire to kill. As long as this force remains in his body, he is strong; if he acquires additional powers through repeated ingestion of *maikiúa*, he is invincible—immortal. But while the *arútam wakaní* is something that can be acquired, it can also be lost. Many adult Shuar repeat this experience throughout their lifetimes whenever they feel weak, especially since they believe that a Shuar could die in battle if he has lost his *arútam wakaní*. This practice, available to all men, provides a basis for the ideology of male egalitarianism and individualism, while transforming political inequalities between older and younger men into an artifact of the life cycle—men are powerful because they have ingested enough *maikiúa*, boys are weak because they have not.

Thus, just as social power is not institutionalized among Shuar, neither is personal power ever completely or securely possessed. Just as any man can gain an *arútam wakaní*, any man can lose it. Such power belongs neither to society nor to the individual. The warrior soul inhabits, but does not belong to, people. It walks about at night, as the warrior sleeps, and can be acquired by someone else. Shuar thus depend on a power that can be controlled neither absolutely nor permanently.

This subjective experience of power as detachable might seem fantastic to Westerners; whether a capacity or an achievement, power should be under the control of the individual. Nevertheless, this experience reflects the objective situation of the warrior, whose power is in fact contingent. Indeed, the very way individual power is constructed among Shuar determines its own limitations. While all adult men have an equal chance to achieve the status of warrior, the achievement itself increases the likelihood of their being assassinated. Although few might challenge a warrior who has killed dozens of people, he necessarily has many enemies. If Shuar power, being individual, is anti-social, then at the same time Shuar society is anti-power. The notion of the *arútam wakaní* begs the question of how easily the warrior can sleep. (adapted from Rubenstein 1995: 92–97, 100–102, 106–7)

According to Malinowski's model, this portrait of Shuar culture as a whole can help me understand the actions of Chúmpi and Tséremp. "Tséremp was a powerful *uwíshin*," Alejandro told me. He was supposed to cure people, but when Chúmpi asked him for help, he said "It's nothing." And so Chúmpi—perhaps with the help of Andrés and Valentín—killed Tséremp. Perhaps Tséremp had become too wealthy, too powerful, in his community. Or perhaps some simply feared that he could become too wealthy or powerful. Or perhaps he was a scapegoat. It does not always matter who is killed, because the persistence of violence among the Shuar, according to the ethnographic account of their culture, has the effect of inhibiting the development of the state and promoting egalitarianism among men. As soon as Chúmpi's son took sick, every shaman in the vicinity became vulnerable. But Tséremp betrayed himself, for, Alejandro told me, he did nothing. Alejandro was just a little boy when these events occurred; by the time he told me about these events, however, he had become a grandfather and a shaman himself and was acutely aware that he could share Tséremp's fate. For a shaman it is not enough even to be equal to others—the shaman must serve others, must care. A shaman must always do something. The story of Chúmpi and Tséremp thus seems to provide a Shuar perspective on persistent problems of the human condition—like sickness and death, grief and anger.

Ethnographies such as Harner's help us appreciate the poignancy of such stories. Indeed, Harner hoped that his ethnography would reveal to a general audience the complexity and dignity of Shuar culture. Moreover, he hoped that this portrait would be of use to Shuar: he felt that his ethnography should "serve . . . the grandchildren and great grandchildren of the people whose culture I was studying" (1984: xiv). Thus, he was gratified when the Shuar Federation commissioned a translation of his book into Spanish and was pleased by its intended uses:

> The translation was primarily intended for distribution to the general Ecuadorian population so it would learn that "Jibaros" had a complex cultural heritage which deserved respect as part of the national patrimony. . . . The secondary intended audience of the Federation translation was their own people, the Shuar themselves, especially in the regions of heavy missionization and colonization such as the Upano valley, so that the ethnography could "help us to rediscover our dignity and to regain the equilibrium that we need for an authentic development, based on our own values." (Aíjiu Juank, translated in Harner 1984: xv)

Although this passage is ostensibly about Harner's good intentions, it points to a danger in his work. While the use of the ethnographic present of his study renders time a non-issue, this revealing text signals that time is in fact a serious problem. Harner would like his book to be of use to future generations. The use of the past perfect in the first sentence of the extended quote, however, relegates Shuar culture to the past. The ethnographic present collapses the distance between the two times into one contradictory moment.

Harner resolves this paradox through abstraction and reification. He does not claim to be studying people, but rather their culture. Presumably he learned about this culture by talking to, watching, and living among a number of different individuals, over the course of a specific period of time. Although there has been considerable debate among anthropologists about what this word *culture* should mean and how it should be used (I review a portion of this debate in the following chapter), Harner seems to use this word to transcend differences between various Shuar, not only over space but over time as well. Although this is a standard practice in science, and necessary for any comparative analysis, it can be dangerous in other contexts.

Indeed, Eric Wolf warned that "by turning names into things we create false models of reality" and, more importantly, oppressive political relationships (1982: 6–7; see also Graham 1976, Ranger 1983). Of course, other anthropologists have claimed that truer knowledge of a people's culture will make possible better and more just governance (see Fortes and Evans-Pritchard 1940; Malinowski 1929). Peter Pels and Oscar Salemink, however, have argued that the issue is not the degree of *accuracy* of ethnographic knowledge, but rather the *form* that it takes. Through reification and the ethnographic present, traditional ethnography simultaneously binds a number of people both to one another and to a particular place, located geographically but outside of history. They are now capable and in need of being governed. In other words, how they are represented discursively is related to changing forms of political representation and control. It is no coincidence that this style of ethnography emerged during a time when states were seeking to control indigenous peoples, whether directly or indirectly, through the mediation of missionaries or indigenous leaders (Pels and Salemink 1994).

The quote from Aíjiu Juank's preface to the Spanish translation provides an example of this danger. Juank resolves this paradox through the seemingly benign (or beneficial) notion of authenticity. "Our own values" seems to be a reference to Shuar identity. In fact, it is about *identification*, the conflation of two different things. First, it identifies the past with the future; that is, the past has authority over the future. But there is another form of identification, not clear in Harner's text. Aíjiu Juank is not Shuar: he is a priest named Alfredo Germani, born in Italy, who has taken a Shuar name and claims (at least, in this text) the right to speak not only as a Shuar but on behalf of the Shuar. However sincere or noble Aíjiu Juank's intentions may be, his identification as Shuar signifies a claim of missionary authority over Shuar. His conception of "authenticity," far from being a signifier of validity or pride, is an instrument of authority.

The point is not that Harner's ethnography is, ironically, a tool of missionaries. Rather, the point is that despite anyone's best intentions, the questions of *who* will use this ethnography and *how* are open questions. For non-Shuar readers of this account, the present tense grants a sense of immediacy that is perhaps pleasurable. But it also gives them the power of the voyeur, the one who sees but is not seen. The safety of the voyeur relies not only on the lack of reciprocity but on distance: the ethnographic present, which distances Shuar from any possibility of a past or future, reassures the place of non-Shuar readers firmly in history.

For Shuar readers, however, this distance is a dangerous deception. As time passes and the conditions of Shuar life change, the present tense inevitably serves to present a portrait of the Shuar that is increasingly unreal. Were the text written in the past tense, readers could see it as a sign of their distance from their past, from their grandparents and great-grandparents; indeed, older Shuar such as Alejandro recognized this despite the use of the present tense. Many younger Shuar I met, however, were confused—some of them assumed Harner was describing the Achuar, who live further to the east (in effect transforming temporal distance into spatial distance, much as anthropologists used to transform spatial distance into temporal distance by characterizing indigenous peoples as "contemporary ancestors"); others simply concluded that Harner was wrong. Shuar who take all Harner's implicit claims at face value (i.e., that this is a portrait of how the Shuar are) can see it only as a sign of an identity crisis, that they somehow are not what they should be.

Shuar, in fact, are facing an identity crisis. As I learned when I met Alejandro, questions of identity and authority—who may speak for Shuar, what are Shuar values—can be neither ignored nor easily answered. Although Father Germani promoted the Shuar Federation, and through the Federation Shuar themselves have taken control over the Shuar reserve, the representation of the Shuar, both ethnographically and politically, is still an issue. Authoritative claims to Shuar authenticity that rely on the ethnographic present and reification do not resolve the crisis; they are, rather, one part of it (see Warren 1998 for an instructive example of this sort of identity crisis in Guatemala).

The ethnographic myth of the Shuar may be poignant, reasonable, and even fairly accurate. Nevertheless, this myth, frozen in time, denies

Shuar—both individually and collectively—a past or a future. It offers no account of how this moral order came to be,[19] or what keeps it going (although I do suggest that insofar as this portrait of Shuar society might be accurate, the political interests of adult men played a crucial role in promoting this sort of moral order). Consequently, it offers little room for people like Chúmpi and Tséremp to act differently. Indeed, as a depiction of a moral order, it suggests how Shuar are "supposed" to behave—risking the implication that if they behave differently, they are no longer Shuar. (Malinowski, aware that indigenous beliefs and practices were changing, thus mourned that "within a generation or two, they or their cultures will have practically disappeared" [1922: xvi].) Following a cultural script, Shuar are actors without agency. Rivet and others have written of this mythic space outside of the state as if it were a space of freedom. In fact, it is a prison.

This problem reveals itself in stark clarity when we turn to popular representations of indigenous people produced by non-academics who have been influenced by the Malinowskian project. Although Malinowski claimed that such myths are meaningful for people such as the Shuar, they were in fact produced for Western consumption, and he felt they should be meaningful for Westerners.

Indeed, there is much at stake in how Westerners use ethnographic knowledge. Malinowski wrote at a time when Europeans and Euro-Americans employed anthropologists to help govern conquered and colonized people. Even today governments and businesses appeal to anthropologists to help manipulate others. Although relativism is a useful attitude for anthropologists who are trying to understand different cultures, it is inadequate in colonial and imperialist contexts, when different cultures enter into unequal relationships. How could one apply a relativist attitude equally to Sioux and the United States, to the inhabitants of the Congo and Belgium, to the Trobrianders and the British?

These are questions that anthropologists in the early twentieth century seldom addressed directly. Nevertheless, they understood that their critique of ethnocentrism was itself a judgment, and that anthropology could not use relativism as an excuse for avoiding any responsibility to judge. Instead, they sought a basis for judgment that would not be culture-bound, but rather universal. For them, an understanding of the varied cultures of humankind could lead finally to a grasp of human nature[20]:

> There is, however, one point of view deeper yet and more important than the love of tasting of the varieties of human modes of life, and that is the desire to turn such knowledge into wisdom. Though it may be given to us for a moment to enter into the soul of a savage and through his eyes to look at the outer world and feel ourselves what it must feel to him to be himself—yet our final goal is to enrich and deepen our own world's vision, to understand our own nature and to make it finer, intellectually and artistically. In grasping the essential outlook of others, with the reverence and real understanding, due even to savages, we cannot but help widening our own. We cannot possibly reach the final Socratic wisdom of knowing ourselves if we never leave the narrow confinement of the customs, beliefs and prejudices into which every man is born. Nothing can teach us a better lesson in this matter of ultimate importance than the habit of mind which allows us to treat the beliefs and values of another man from his point of view. Nor has civilised humanity ever needed such tolerance more than now, when prejudice, ill will and vindictiveness are dividing each European nation from another, when all the ideals, cherished and proclaimed as the highest achievements of civilisation, science and religion, have been thrown to the winds. The Science of Man, in its most refined and deepest version should lead us to such knowledge and to tolerance and generosity, based on the understanding of other men's point of view. (1922: 517–18)

Writing while Europe was simultaneously recovering from the devastation of the Great War and inflicting devastation on its colonial subjects, Malinowski saw ethnocentrism as the greatest threat to peace and felt that relativism must lead to humanism—a loyalty to and love of humankind that transcends cultural difference. Even so, he undermined his own humanism by reiterating the distinction between savagery and civilization (which simultaneously erases differences between different kinds of "savages" while reifying the difference between "savage" and "civilized" societies).[21] He wanted to learn from others but could not learn from them as individuals—only as members of another culture.

Today many non-anthropologists share Malinowski's humanistic vision, and the travelogue in the style of Up de Graff's *Headhunters of the Amazon* has been replaced by reports of more spiritual adventures, such as John Perkins's *The World Is as You Dream It*.[22] Perkins's book is in many ways about the clash between the state and indigenous people, but his writing relies on the distinctions between civilization and savagery, between history and myth/culture. Really just an extreme example of Malinowskian anthropology, it reveals in sharp relief the ambiguous legacy of Malinowski's discourse and how fragile and perhaps illusory the humanistic project is.

Perkins takes issue with the traditional view of the Shuar: "The Shuar were considered fierce warriors; I heard many stories about their raids, head- hunting, and savage rituals, although from personal encounters I found them to be a compassionate people who were gravely concerned about the impact colonists were having on the fragile rainforest ecology" (1994: 13). In fact, he argues, it is we in the West who are savages. Capitalism is destroying the environment while ravaging the resources of the world for the benefit of a handful of people, he claims.

Traveling in the Amazon, Perkins is shocked by the devastation wrought by economic "development." He asks a Shuar shaman what he can do to help, and the shaman tells him to start by taking responsibility for the problems of his own culture. The Ecuadorian laws promoting colonization of the rain forest, he realizes, were modeled after the U.S. Homestead Act of the late 1800s. "And more colonists come because of the roads that are built by your oil, lumber, and mining companies," the shaman tells him. "He lay back and looked up at the roof. My eyes followed his to where the monkey sat on a rafter, chewing on what looked like a piece of sugar cane. 'If you want to help us,' he said slowly and deliberately, 'if you want to help these forests, then you should start with your own people. It is your people more than mine who need to change'" (1994: 31). This is a powerful rebuke, not only to Perkins (who explains that he has come to regret his role in promoting development as a Peace Corps volunteer and then as a consultant to the World Bank) but to Western claims to economic, scientific, and moral superiority.

I believe that Perkins's good intentions are hobbled by his own culture's centuries-old discourse of savagery and civilization. This is a discourse that, perhaps ironically, links Perkins to Rivet and Stirling in a number of ways. Fundamental to this discourse is a radical divide between civilization and savagery. Although his shaman friend is clear about the connections between the lives of the Shuar and the fortunes of the West, Perkins insists that the two "live in parallel worlds" (1994: 47). Thus, like Rivet—who distinguished between civilized (who are submissive and humble) and savage (who are free and passionate) Indians—Perkins describes two kinds of Shuar: "Some Shuar have given up their traditional ways and have tried to adopt Western customs. For the most part, they live impoverished lives in oil company ghettos. Others, determined to maintain their independence, have moved deeper into the forest to places east of the Cutucú Mountains, an ancient mist-enshrouded range that long ago split away from the Andes" (13). Perkins writes as if the first kind of Shuar, the Shuar who lives in history, is somehow no longer, not really, Shuar. Conversely, he consigns this second kind of Shuar, this "noble" savage, to a timeless realm that obliterates the distance between the present and the past. Their houses "might well have belonged to a North American Indian three hundred years ago" (15), and their eyes express "a timeless knowledge" (17).[23] And, like Rivet, Perkins identifies this timeless space with nature itself.

Thus, Perkins and writers such as Rivet and Stirling agree that there is a fundamental difference between *civilization* and *savagery*; they disagree only as to who is good and who is bad. For Perkins, savages are noble. Moreover, the distance between savagery and civilization is critical to their nobility in two ways: the greater the difference between them and us, the nobler they are; and because they are so noble, they can be our salvation. "In order for life to continue as we know it," Perkins concluded, "we must all change our dream from the one of materialism and domination that has ruled supreme for so long to a more spiritual, cooperative, and Earth-honoring one" (1994: xix). That is, we must become more like the Indians, insofar as they are radically unlike us. Their nobility, this salvation, cannot come from within our world, it can only come from the outside.

Of course, the notion that our salvation can only come from a source that is radically different from us has dominated Western thought since the rise of Christianity. (Before the apostle Paul, the word *messiah* meant a man, a descendant of David anointed king of Judea, but after Paul, it came to mean the son of God.) In Perkins's conception of the Shuar, the natural and the supernatural meet. In the process, I fear, the humanity of the Shuar—Perkins's friends and mine alike—is at risk. The Shuar to whom he introduces us are full of wisdom and compassion and even humor, but they are empty of individuality. Their virtues belong not to them, but to their culture; in Perkins's account, the shaman does not speak for himself but rather for "the Shuar." Although Perkins allows himself to belong to the West and to be critical of it, he denies this right to Shuar: they can criticize the West only from the outside and do not have any critical distance from their own culture.

Perkins's romanticization of the Shuar is most evident when he addresses the issue of *tsantsas*. When one of his companions asks an old shaman if Shuar still shrink heads, the man replies that the practice has declined and as a result, "the jungle has suffered" (1994: 61). At first members of Perkins's group can't believe that headhunting is virtuous, but the shaman explains that "We shrunk the head of our enemies . . . so their vengeful souls would stay inside and not come after us or our families" (61). After the shaman describes how shrunken heads are made, another of Perkins's companions stands next to him and admits, "Your view of life is beautiful" (62).

It does not seem to occur to this woman that the Achuar soul would not feel vengeful if his or her head had not been cut off in the first place. Nor does it occur to her that a practice that a man claims is a way of protecting his family may actually help him dominate and control his family. There is no room in this view of the Shuar for any real violence, in the sense of violation. In the end, it does not matter what the Shuar say or do as human beings and individuals, because it can only be beautiful.

Malinowski was offended that Westerners saw non-Western practices as quaint, amusing, or strange. But even he was "charmed" by, and felt a "desire to penetrate," others. Desire, however, is never innocent, and I believe that it is just as dangerous to always see these practices as beautiful. The noble savage is as much a construction of colonial history as is the brutal savage.

What I admire in Malinowski's vision is that everything that people do is *meaningful*, and that no one can truly appreciate what it means to be human without understanding the myriad ways there are of being human. Not all of these ways are beautiful. Human beings everywhere can be noble, generous, and compassionate, but they can also be petty, manipulative, and cruel. An account of Shuar culture cannot celebrate only the achievements of a warrior; it must mourn the death of his victim and bear witness to the never-ending toil of his wives and daughters. To understand that the warrior may be motivated by a quest for wisdom and honor as well as by a desire for power and wealth does not make him a savage. It merely makes him human.

The problem with much of the New Age and Native Spirituality literature is that it is less interested in understanding the experiences of real people around the world (whether Shuar or Euro-Americans) than in judging them. Although one cannot accuse it of ethnocentrism (for it judges Western culture quite harshly), it is hardly relativist. Perhaps we can call it *exotropic*, because it idealizes that which it sees as most different from itself.

However much this exotropism violates the spirit of Malinowski's vision, though, it is surprisingly true to its form, grounded in the assumption that cultures are radically different. In order to describe Shuar culture in its own terms, Perkins dismisses the experiences and views of Shuar living in Ecuadorian towns and idealizes the beliefs and practices of those living in the countryside. He thus helps us see a danger in the discourse of the West that may be more dangerous than ethnocentrism. This is a discourse—explicit in both ethnocentrism and exotropism and implicit in relativism—that threatens to undermine any humanism. This danger is essentialism.

Essentialism "is classically defined as a belief in a true essence—that which is most irreducible, unchanging, and therefore constitutive of a given person or thing" (Fuss 1989: 2). For our purposes, essentialism involves defining a group of people (for example, men, women, Blacks, Whites, Indians, Jews, Christians, Germans, hillbillies) by a small set of fixed properties, while ignoring the conditions under which such identities emerged. In the process, it discounts any possibility of change or variation within the group. Furthermore, it forecloses any real possibility of forging meaningful relationships between members of different groups.[24]

Westerners frequently use biological categories such as race and gender to essentialize human behavior. The first American academic anthropologists appealed to the notion of culture as a non-essentializing way to understand human behavior (and most anthropologists today argue that biological categories such as race and gender are themselves cultural constructs). Recently, Walter Benn Michaels (1992) has argued that people today simply essentialize culture, that "culture" has only taken the place of "race" in the popular imagination.[25] This is precisely what is at stake in Wolf's critique of ethnographies that abstract the

words and actions of people and reify them in such terms as "the Shuar."
Similarly, Stirling provides an example of how a historical narrative can
be deployed in the service of essentialization. I suggest that whenever
culture and history are kept apart, essentialism will be the result.

Malinowski's project allows us to construct myths out of ethnography
that stand against the nonhistory of colonialism by asserting a nonstate
morality. In other words, he allows us to oppose indigenous culture to
Western culture. Nevertheless, this project leaves people like the Shuar
outside of the state. Shuar (like the Trobrianders Malinowski studied),
however, do not live outside of the state. They live in its margins and
certainly have different lives and perspectives than those living at the
center of the state. But these lives occur in the context of changing
relations with different people, and abstract ethnographic descriptions
tend to obscure this. People are connected to one another not only
in theory but in practice, and thus these connections change. Euro-
Americans and Shuar are bound not only by a common humanity, but by
a common — if contentious — history.[26]

For example, most, if not all, Shuar shamans study with shamans
who live in different parts of the country and speak different languages.
Alejandro studied with Quichua living to the north and is as likely to call
the hallucinogen he uses by its Quichua name, *ayahuasca*, as the Quichua
are to call their darts by their Shuar name, *tsintsaca*. These shamans and
their clients do not believe that they are engaging in a strictly Shuar
practice any more than we might think that "Western medicine" works
only in North America and Europe.

Peter Gow has even suggested that "*ayahuasca* shamanism" first developed in colonial towns and Catholic missions in the 1600s and was
adopted only by those Amazonian peoples struggling against colonialism. He does not claim that shamanism did not exist prior to colonialism, only that its current form cannot be understood outside of
the colonial context. That is, *ayahuasca* shamanism is not a creation of
the colonizer; rather, it is a response of the colonized. In this struggle
against colonialism, "the Amazon" is a potent symbol as a source of
natural resources — which colonial authorities exploit for profit, and
to which shamans turn for healing. Consequently, shamans and their
clients talk of "the forest" as a place outside of history. Nevertheless,
this way of talking about the forest and shamanism has a history: it

developed in a particular context and has been put to different uses. Gow notes that *ayahuasca* curing sessions parody the Catholic Mass in the way the shaman blows tobacco smoke over each cup of the liquid before using it to bring life to the supplicant.[27] He suggests that this practice developed in Catholic missions, where indigenous peoples were more prone to epidemics because of larger concentrations of people, and it spread with the rise of the rubber economy (1994).[28]

Similarly, Shuar had a long history of trading *tsantsas* to Europeans and Euro-Americans in return for shotguns. Shotguns for hunting and machetes for gardening could be as valuable to Shuar men as women's labor, so it is not surprising that *tsantsas* took on for men a new function. Of course, men also used the shotguns to kill more Achuar and take more heads. Although there is no evidence that Shuar *did not* shrink heads before contact with Westerners, the intensification of this practice in the late 1800s and early 1900s was certainly a function of the expansion of the capitalist economy into the Upper Amazon. In other words, Shuar did not shrink heads solely to protect (or control) their families—they did it because Westerners wanted them to do it, and because they wanted Western trade goods. In short, the "essential outlook" (to use Malinowski's phrase) of the Shuar extends far beyond a vision of such persistent problems of the human condition as sickness and death, grief and anger. For Shuar look out on us, on colonialism, on the state itself.

Ultimately, I can neither understand nor effectively judge myself or Alejandro—or Chúmpi or John Perkins or Fritz Up de Graff—unless I consider the changing connections between us. Studies that assume a radical difference between history and culture, however, obscure or sever these connections. What is required is a move from essentialism to historicism, and from a commitment to relativism to a concern for relationships. I believe that the stories of actual individuals can dissolve the separation of history and culture and thus illuminate these changing connections.

"Only one tribe of American Indians is known ever to have successfully revolted against the empire of Spain and to have thwarted all subsequent attempts by the Spaniards to reconquer them": thus Michael Harner began his classic ethnography of the Shuar (1984: 1), and it was this sentence that led me to Morona Santiago and, eventually, to meet

Alejandro. But there I learned that it is not so easy to recognize, let alone distinguish between, conquest and rebellion. It is precisely because the Shuar were not conquered, at least not in the bloody way that the Inca and Aztec were defeated, and precisely because the Shuar have a reputation for bloody resistance, that their history provides an important insight into the relationship between colonialism and violence. For colonialism itself works through many different agents, and violence takes many different forms.

Chúmpi and Tséremp lived at a time when Shuar and settlers were struggling to define the political and cultural geography of these margins of the state. At the beginning of the twentieth century small numbers of Euro-Ecuadorians, lacking land or jobs, left their homes in the highlands to settle (*colonizar*) in the Amazon; when they arrived they took the name *colono*, settler. This movement of people was an effect of not only the Ecuadorian class-system in the highlands; it was also an effect of European discourses of the Amazon that portrayed the land and its inhabitants as wild and in need of taming. Within a relatively short period of time, *colonos* acquired considerable land formerly used by Shuar. Shuar could continue to occupy the remaining land only by harnessing it to the national economy, producing for the market. Those Shuar who could not finance the necessary investments have no choice but to enter the labor market. In order to survive under these conditions, many Shuar have turned against one another.

From the very beginning of Ecuadorian colonization, Shuar attempts to promote their own interests benefited colonial interests. Many Shuar welcomed *colonos* and entered into peaceful trading relations with them. Shuar men could use manufactured tools (including shotguns) to intensify production, which, in turn, increased their power over their wives, children, and one another. Moreover, Shuar believed that they were establishing a trading partnership, and that although their practice of shifting cultivation meant that they would move to another location, this new partnership would constitute an ongoing relationship. *Colonos*, however, believed that in offering the Shuar clothing and tools in return for giving up land, they were "buying" land.

Before long both Shuar and the government realized that this *ad hoc* process was leading to an untenable situation. While machetes allowed men to increase garden production, the flood of shotguns (along with Euro-American desire for shrunken heads) resulted in an intensification of warfare. Although some men surely benefited in the early stages of this intensification of fighting, the principles of blood feuding and revenge killing (arguably components of Shuar egalitarianism) resulted in what was effectively a war of attrition that decimated a generation. Gardening began to be more appealing than fighting.

Just as land was becoming more valuable to Shuar, however, it was becoming more scarce. Shuar soon realized that *colonos* believed that they owned the land, would attempt to use it continually, would not allow others access to unused land on their "property," and would not abandon it. Although some Shuar feared that they would be driven off of their territory, the government knew that *colonos* did not have the means to occupy the entire province. In 1941 Peru had conquered a good portion of the Ecuadorian Amazon, and the Ecuadorian state urgently needed to establish a presence on the frontier and to encourage the integration of the region into the nation.[29] Since colonization by Euro-Ecuadorians was not sufficient, the government supported Shuar land rights as a way to establish a permanent presence on the border.

In 1935 the Ecuadorian government, under José Maria Velasco Ibarra, delineated and reserved for the Shuar territory in what would become the province Morona Santiago. The government granted jurisdiction over this reserve to Salesian missionaries (but jurisdiction did not extend to settlers living in the province, nor did Salesian control supersede prerogatives of the two established Evangelical missions). It was during this time that the missionaries encouraged the formation of the *centros*, or nucleated settlements, to facilitate their work. Simultaneously, young Shuar who had been educated in mission schools realized that their knowledge of Spanish (and, therefore, their ability to work with missionaries and government officials) could be a far more effective tool in the pursuit of power than their fathers' more conventional weapons. They quickly assumed positions of leadership in the newly emerging organization. In the early 1960s *centros* began organizing into *Asociaciónes*, or associations, to defend their interests against *colonos* more effectively, and in 1964 the various associations united to form the Federation.[30] Salesian control over the reserve terminated in 1969, and by 1975 the government recognized Federation control over the reserve.

Initially, the boundary between Shuar and *colono* territory was little more than a blurry line on a poorly drawn map. Most of the region had not been surveyed, and few people had legal title to their land. In the years that followed, Shuar and *colonos* scrambled to occupy and thus define the frontiers. The Utunkus (in Spanish, Tutanangoza) River was one site of struggle. From its source the river runs east, and Shuar had long established occupancy on both its banks. But near Sucúa it bends south and runs parallel to the Upano for several miles. By the 1940s many *colonos* had settled in the plateau between the two rivers, and some were beginning to settle on the opposite banks. One *colono*, Filimon Lopez, settled in what was to become the Shuar *centro* Utunkus.

Alejandro, in fact, was born not in Utunkus but in Kenkuim (also called Santa Teresita) to the west of, and on higher ground than, Utunkus. His father Andrés was one of a number of Shuar who left Kenkuim to challenge Lopez and claim the east bank of the Utunkus for the Shuar. They sought, and received, the support of the *teniente político* (political lieutenant; the local representative of the state). Lopez, however, refused to leave, so Andrés and his companions chased the settler off the land at gunpoint. They destroyed his house and later built a chapel over its foundation. Utunkus thus came to consist of families forced together in order to block settler expansion. Conflicts among these families were at least in part a consequence of this process of relocation.

Conversely, such conflicts led to new relocations. After Tséremp's death, his son accused Andrés and Valentín of the murder, and the two had to flee to avoid arrest. The police came to Utunkus and removed Andrés's wife and children to Sucúa. The moral lessons of the fall of Tséremp thus go, for Alejandro, far beyond the dangers of power. Years later he would be haunted by the memory of the disruption in his life caused by these events. In his own words:

> Tsanchímp, the son of Tséremp, immediately accused Andrés of the murder. At that time we were afraid of the cops, or that someone else might avenge Tséremp's death. My father just took good care of himself: his brothers helped him hide in Utunkus.
>
> There are some men who, when they go after someone they suspect of murder, take advantage of his women. So this made me afraid, and we hid ourselves. We went into the hills, we left everything scattered—our dogs, our pigs, the whole house—we went into the forests far away, to Santa Teresa. Then we went to Antonio Nekta's, and he protected us. We ended up in Asunción.

Then the *teniente político* came with a group of policemen and other Shuar, saying that Andrés had to be imprisoned or killed because he was a criminal. That is, the police went to some Shuar's house and said, "You have to accompany us, you have to deliver this criminal"; then the police go to another house and say, "You have to accompany us," and so on.

Then the delegation arrived at our house—we were living in a part of Asunción. A delegation arrived to catch my father, accusing him of having killed Tséremp. I was scared of the policeman because he was of a very different race; it was very unbelievable to me. So because of him I cried, I was so scared. So I was very upset, my mother was crying, my little sister also; my mother was always crying, daily, frightened. They attacked us—they almost killed me!—they caught me and tied my arms behind me.

So then, this man said nothing. He was just angry and stood with his carbine, with his gun. Then he shot and killed our pig, and the turkey. "It's the house of a criminal," they thought, and in those days they killed to take the meat. The policeman killed that pig and killed the turkey and shared the meat with the other Shuar that were deputized.

But they didn't find my father in the house, so they took my mother. If my father were there he would have been killed, but my father wasn't there with us in Asunción; he was here in Utunkus. So there was a Shuar, Domingo Kúkush', the brother of Juan José, the nephew of my father. "Don't cry," he told me, "because nothing is going to happen, because I am here. I know the policeman, he's my friend, and I'm accompanying him so that nothing happens to you. But regrettably, they're going to take you away."

Domingo Kúkush' knew Spanish as well as Shuar, so he could explain among them. So Domingo Kúkush' said, "Don't do anything because the boy is afraid, and it isn't right, friend, to do it."

Then the policeman grabbed this *tumank* [a Shuar type of Jew's harp] that belonged to my father, and he whipped my mother with it.

She said, "It hurts!"

Mother hurts, so I cried and said, "Stop, stop, *eniesata, eniesata!*" and I didn't let go of my mother. So my sister came over, and I held on behind my mother, and we cried, and I said, "*Iniesata yajauch, iniesata mokosay!*" I insulted him.

"What does he say?" he asked of Kúkush'.

Kúkush' told him: "He says that 'You are really ugly and very bad, and I don't want you to hit my mother. I want you to respect me.' "

"Poor little one, we aren't going to do anything to your mother," he said. And then he said, "We have to take her; prepare meat, and then we'll bring them to Sucúa."

So they mistreated us. When the police pursued a fugitive, they often took the wife, or the daughter, the entire family, in order to make the husband appear. So they took my mother and my sister Imelda to Sucúa, and I followed. They sequestered us, but they didn't put us in jail. The *teniente político* was Carlos Olvera, and he lived with his niece from Cuenca and his wife. His wife said of my sister, "Why is a girl going to be incarcerated? She bears no guilt! It's better that I have her myself, to serve me." So from then on Olvera had a cook. And my mother worked in the house of the mother of the policeman, Ricardo Rubio.

Eventually the police found Andrés and Valentín, and they served five months in jail. In the meantime I got to know many more settlers. We went to Benigno Abarca's, who was a friend of my father's. My sister Sofia (the daughter of my aunt, the sister of my mother Teresa Suanúa [in other words, his parallel cousin] lived there, so we went there, and I came to know Benigno Abarca, Manuel Abarca.

One way to read Alejandro's tale is as a story of "culture contact." When the policeman entered Utunkus, he was imposing Ecuadorian law on the Shuar. From now on the Shuar would no longer be "left in peace to continue their customary fighting among themselves," as Stirling put it (1938: 4). Conversely, when Alejandro and his family moved to Sucúa, they left their own culture and entered the space of the state. Alejandro's mother and sister became servants, and his father and brother were put in jail. Here they became "civilized" Indians, as Rivet described them, "submissive, humble, cringing . . . servile." As a story of culture contact, it is really two stories: first a story about the Shuar and then a story about the state. When the story is viewed as two different stories, some people can express horror at the customary violence of the Shuar, and others can condemn Ecuadorian colonialism and the exploitation of Shuar women.

But the notion that any of this violence belongs either to Shuar or to the state is just another instance of colonial discourse, the same discourse that separates culture from history. In colonial practice, however, the violence of one side works through the violence of the other. Alejandro's story of what happened thus overwhelms any easy distinction between Shuar and settler vices and virtues. He was equally afraid of the police and Tséremp's family. Some Shuar cooperated with the police in the relocation of Andrés's family, while others helped hide the refugees; some settlers took advantage of the situation, while others offered aid. This is not a story about leaving Shuar culture to enter the space of the state. It is a story that simultaneously embraces and rejects different images of both Shuar and settlers. The geographical distance between Sucúa and Utunkus is clear, but the cultural boundary between them is not.

I therefore think it is important to read Teresa's account and Alejandro's account as parts of the same story, a story that takes place both in Utunkus and Sucúa, a story that involves both Shuar and settlers. For Alejandro, entering Sucúa did not mean leaving Shuar culture behind. On the contrary, it would lead to new ways of being and acting Shuar, and it is this possibility—that there are ways of being and acting Shuar that Rivet and Stirling could not imagine but that Alejandro can—that I want to emphasize.

So for me the significance of this account is not how Alejandro left Utunkus and Shuar culture, but rather how his story leaves the realm of myth: the Shuar myth that presents stories of how things are as stories of how things should be, the Western myth that presents Shuar history as nonhistory. Following Walter Benjamin, perhaps we can say that Alejandro is taking us out of the realm of myth and into the realm of fairy tale:

The first true storyteller is, and will continue to be, the teller of fairy tales. Whenever good counsel was at a premium, the fairy tale had it, and where the need was greatest, its aid was nearest. The need was the need created by the myth. The fairy tale tells us of the earliest arrangements that mankind made to shake off the nightmare which the myth has placed upon its chest. In the figure of the fool it shows us how mankind "acts dumb" toward the myth; in the figure of the youngest brother it shows us how one's chances increase as the mythical primitive times are left behind; in the figure of the man who sets out to learn what fear is it shows us that the things we are afraid of can be seen through; in the figure of the wiseacre it shows us that the questions posed by myth are simple-minded, like the riddle of the Sphinx; in the shape of the animals which come to the aid of the child in the fairy tale it shows that nature not only is subservient to the myth, but much prefers to be aligned with man. The wisest thing—so the fairy tale taught mankind in olden times, and teaches children to this day—is to meet the forces of the mythical world with cunning and high spirits. (1968: 102)

Fairy tales are literally "unbelievable" because they defy historical judgment. It is for this reason, perhaps, that children love them so—children who are forced to live in a world not of their own making, but who can still dream of other worlds. Similarly, myths provide Shuar with a sense of meaning and moral order, but they also imprison Shuar. And shamans such as Tséremp and Alejandro who attempt to control and exploit these myths also unleash their power to disrupt and confound.

What is important here is not where fairy tales really come from, or whether they are really believable, but rather how they may be used. For Benjamin, the fairy tale is a weapon against myth, against those myths that pose as historical judgment and conventional morality (see Taussig 1992). For me, they provide a more useful basis for learning Shuar history than Stirling's notion of history, a basis that can undermine the authority of colonial discourses—even at the risk of subverting my own.[31]

I began by asking Alejandro a simple question—"Did you ever know any shamans who were killed?"—but I was really asking a simple-minded question about the continuation of "Shuar" violence. Valentín, hardly a fool, returned from killing Tséremp in silence and lay on his bed saying nothing. Although he and his father initially fled, afraid of both the police and Tséremp's family, they eventually returned to Utunkus and were living there—more or less in peace—when I arrived almost fifty years later. And although I got off to a slow and difficult start, the younger brother eventually taught me how his chances to be Shuar increased as he left myth behind.

3

Life History

It is both hard and easy to justify my writing a life history of Alejandro. Hard, because I am currently working on two other books, both of which prominently feature Alejandro and some of the material in this book. Easy, because a life history of Alejandro is an obvious and necessary task. Of all the Shuar with whom I worked, he is the one I came to know best, and among my notes are innumerable details of his life. Despite the bulkiness of my record of our conversation (about a thousand pages) and the intimacy of our relationship, however, I am still often bewildered by his sentiments and actions. Although this confusion may express the unpredictability that is a necessary element of any friendship, I nevertheless hope that as I retell his life's story, I can come to a better understanding of the man and our relationship. But this confusion also expresses the paradoxes and perils of the ethnographic encounter in a colonial context. If we can read his stories in a way that takes such confusion seriously, not as a sign of his inarticulateness or our incomprehension, but rather as a reflection of a contradictory and conflict-ridden situation, we can also come to a fuller appreciation of what it is like to live and work in the colonial context.

The two other books on which I am currently working, both based on my dissertation, are concerned with politics: one through a history of the Ecuadorian colonization of Shuar territory and the formation of the Shuar Federation, the other through a reflection on the work of the anthropologist. This portrait of Alejandro reveals another dimension of these processes—that of the struggle of an individual, within and against his own culture and that of a dominant society, in the pursuit of economic security, social prestige, political power, and some sense that life has meaning and value. In chapters 1 and 2 I discuss how I became aware of these issues through my study of Shuar culture and my experiences among Shuar. In this chapter I review these issues through a discussion of the changing status of life history in anthropological theory and practice.

Life history, as I conceive of it, invokes an old tradition in anthropology that calls attention to the dynamic and changing role of the individual in his or her culture. In 1920 Franz Boas called attention to the dialectical relationship between the individual and society: "The activities of the individual are determined to a great extent by his social environment, but in turn his own activities influence the society in which he lives, and may bring about modifications in form." He therefore called for a turning away from "the systematic enumeration of standardized beliefs and customs of a tribe" to "the way in which the individual reacts to his whole social environment, and to the difference of opinion and of mode of action that occur in primitive society and which are the causes of far-reaching changes" (1940: 285).

This dimension provides an important alternative to ethnographies that focus on culture as that which "gives its members a definite vision of the world" (Malinowski 1922: 517), or that "web of significance" in which people are suspended (Geertz 1973: 5). That view of culture emerged after World War I and dominated ethnography between World War II and the Vietnam War. The writers of these ethnographies assumed that those beliefs and practices that endure over time are more important than those that are ephemeral. Of course, nothing happens exactly the same way twice—it is true that every year at Thanksgiving my aunt Gloria makes turkey and stuffing, and my cousin Andrew makes stuffed mushrooms. But each year the turkey and mushrooms are different; they might have been purchased at different stores at different prices. Moreover, the actual things that Gloria and Andrew do—the time they start cooking, whom they talk to while washing the dishes, what they talk about, and countless other things that occur before, during, and after dinner—are never exactly the same. On the other hand, it would still be Thanksgiving even if Andrew cooked the turkey and no one made the mushrooms. So ethnographers argued that the essence, or truth, of a practice lies in those parts that never change.

These ethnographies relied heavily on abstraction, emphasizing those elements that all instances of a particular practice have in common and excluding or minimizing those elements that vary. The most important abstraction was "social structure." At first social structure referred to the regular and enduring relations between different types of people (for example, between "husband" and "wife" or between "parent" and "child") and between different groups of people. If the social structure is an abstraction of what the ethnographer observes, it is merely a convenient way of *describing* social life. But some ethnographers argued that the social structure is in the minds of the members of that society. Thus, it becomes not so much an *abstraction* of how people *actually* behave but a *model* of how people *should* behave, and it is therefore an important way of *explaining* social life.

Both of these views of social structure had the same two effects (evident in the "Malinowskian myth" of Shuar culture in chapter 2). The first effect was on the mode of description. For decades the convention was to present general information in the present tense. For example, instead of writing that "when I went to Andrew's house in 1997 Aunt Gloria was basting a turkey and my father and uncle were in the living room, and when I went to a friend's for Thanksgiving in 1998 she cooked a turkey," I might simply write that "Every November Americans celebrate Thanksgiving. Women cook the turkey." Although any ethnographer would agree that such descriptions leave out a lot of interesting details, most would argue that it is nevertheless a reasonable and innocuous description. When an ethnographer describes every social event in the present tense, what we call the "ethnographic present" (see the composite ethnographic description of Shuar culture in chapter 2 for an example), however, the result is the sense that culture is unchanging.

The second effect was on the nature of explanation. Both views of social structure identify "culture" with "normative"—in the first instance, culture involves statistical norms; in the second, moral norms. In either case "culture" is presented as a given, as something that exists apart from, and has a deterministic effect on, individuals. Thus, if someone asked me to explain why Aunt Gloria was basting the turkey, I could answer "because it is Thanksgiving"; if someone asked me why she was basting a turkey on Thanksgiving, I could answer "because that is her culture." (This, of course, begs the question of *why* Americans have turkey on Thanksgiving. For Boas and many of his students, this sort of question—how to explain culture—is crucial). This emphasis on social structure furthered one of Boas's aims, which was to delineate "culture" as an object that anthropologists could study. However, it runs counter to another of his aims, which was to reveal culture as an accomplishment—the product of human "agency" (or, in Boas's terms, "action" and "activities").

As a document of the actions of an individual, however, life history has little room for the abstract and none at all for the ethnographic present. It should thus be a superb way to depict culture as changing. Many social scientists have been skeptical, though, of the value of life history as a historical document. For one thing, as one matures from child to adult, one's position in, and thus view of, society changes. Furthermore, life histories virtually never record the maturing person's experiences as they happen; rather, they are largely an adult's perspective on his or her own memories of growing up. Boas had mixed feelings about life histories:

> The better ones of these give us valuable information in regard to the struggles of everyday life and the joys and sorrows of the people, but their reliability, beyond very elementary points, is doubtful. They are not facts but memories and memories distorted by the wishes and thoughts of the moment. . . . In short the tricks that memory plays [on] us are too important to allow us to accept autobiographies as reliable, factual data. They are reflections of facts as expressed in the present mental condition of the informant. (1943: 334–35)[1]

Ironically, although Boas recognized that cultures change, he seemed to discount the possibility that our experience of change and our representation of history are necessarily cultural. In his search for "reliable, factual data," he dismissed whatever fell short.

However, such students of Boas as Paul Radin (1913) and Edward Sapir (1922) experimented with life history, not as an objective record of "what happened," but as a way of exploring the relationship between culture and the individual, and at the end of her career Ruth Benedict (1948) encouraged more life histories. But these anthropologists had different notions of the value of their work. For Radin, "reliable, factual data" simply is not enough. The problem with objective accounts is precisely that they are limited to what is observable. That is, because anthropologists are outside of the culture they study, they cannot truly get into the hearts and minds of the people they study (1963: 1). For Radin, then, life histories could complement ethnography by providing "an inside view of the Indian's emotional life" (1913: 293).

Sapir, on the other hand, suggested that the gulf between the internal and external life—the terms he used were personality and culture—was ultimately artificial. Indeed, for him the value of life history is not to complement ethnography, but to reveal the limits of contemporary theories of anthropology and psychology.[2] In the foreword to *Left Handed, Son of Old Man Hat*, written by his student Walter Dyk, Sapir argued that a life history that is equally attentive to structure and agency may overcome the apparent opposition between the individual and culture:

> What this singularly untroubled narrative does for us is to destroy all turbulent dichotomies of self and not-self. . . . Son of Old Man Hat, not by hinting at human likeness or difference but through the sheer clarity of his daily experiences, resolves all cultural and personal conflicts and reminds us that human life is priceless, not because of the glories of the past nor the hopes of the future, but because of the irrevocable trivialities of a present that is always slipping from us. (Sapir 1938: ix)

For Sapir, the value of life history is that it reveals what is meaningful in a person's life, and that such meaning cannot be reduced either to a public or a private experience.[3]

In pursuing their own projects, however, these anthropologists abandoned Boas's concern with the differences among members of a society and the struggle between the individual and the collective. In calling attention to the difference between "the insider" and "the outsider," for example, Radin risked minimizing differences *among* members of one society. In focusing on the meaningful, Sapir risked ignoring the conflicts and struggles between individuals and their social worlds—especially conflicts and struggles over "meaning" itself. As a result, these life histories are less vehicles for depicting culture change and more documents of one person's changing experience of a relatively static culture. Boas, however, felt that a dialectical approach to the relationship between the individual and society would lead to a new understanding of culture: "As soon as these methods are applied," he wrote expectantly, "primitive society loses the appearance of absolute stability. . . . All cultural forms rather appear in a constant state of flux" (1940: 284).

This book represents an attempt to return to Boas's project. Accordingly, I do not view "structure" and "agency" as different, opposing things. Rather, they are different ways of talking about events, and each term necessarily invokes the other. In other words, I do not treat "Shuar" as a structure and "Alejandro" as an agent. These words refer to identities through which a particular person presents (or is called upon or even forced to present) himself. But whether this person acts as "Alejandro," an individual, or as "a Shuar," a member of a society, he must be understood in terms of the play of structure and agency. I am interested not so much in documenting conflicts between Alejandro and his culture as in exploring "the internal tensions and incompatibilities" within his different identities, whether individual or collective (pace Joan Scott 1996b: 16).

Nevertheless, this book departs from some aspects of Boas's program. Although his view of culture was more historical than the views of Malinowski and Geertz, it was equally local (assuming, for example, a clear distinction between Shuar culture, Ecuadorian culture, and American culture). Alejandro's "whole social environment," however, is not. He makes his home in the Ecuadorian Amazon but has traveled to the highlands as both a healer and a patient. Like many Shuar men he has more than one wife, but one is German.[4] His children speak Shuar and Spanish, but he would like them to learn English. Individuals have a way of moving around that undermines social boundaries and strictly local notions of culture, and life histories by Simmons (1942), Mintz (1960), Lewis (1961, 1964) and Muratorio (1991) have called attention to the interconnections between individual biography and global history.

Ironically, however, by representing flux as an individual experience and history as a global process, even these life histories have reenforced the tendency to idealize "culture" as that which is stable and coherent (e.g., Shostak 1981). "Change" is not an aspect *of* culture, but something that happens *to* culture; "history," in this sense, is not a condition of constant flux, but a succession of different social structures (e.g., Sahlins 1981; see Fabian 1983: 56 for a similar critique). Life history becomes oral history in which the subject is more a witness to, rather than an agent of, culture and culture change. Thus, the promise of Boasian anthropology has remained unfulfilled. I believe that we cannot sustain a view of culture as dynamic and in flux unless we abandon the view that history is an objective account of "what happened." Fortunately, much recent work in ethnography has questioned just such a view and offers new approaches to "history."

Around the time that the United States was losing the war in Vietnam, and France and Britain were coming to terms with the loss of their empires, anthropologists became increasingly self-conscious of the fact that they usually belong to colonialist or imperialist states, while their informants belong to oppressed and exploited societies. Conventional assumptions about culture and history suddenly seemed inadequate, if not inappropriate (see Hymes 1969; Asad 1973; cf. Pels and Salemink 1994 for a review of the more recent anthropological considerations of these issues). Anthropologists, reviving some of Boas's prestructuralist program but also inspired by poststructuralist critics, questioned some of the commonplace ways of opposing Western and non-Western societies—for example, that modern societies are in constant flux whereas primitive societies are stable, or that moderns make rational choices and primitives are slaves to custom—as not only erroneous but dangerous tools of colonialism.[5]

But what kind of knowledge is possible when it is produced by an engagement between a member of a dominant class that wants to take the side of the oppressed and a member of a subordinate class who would like to join the ranks of the privileged? Recent works by such historians as Joan Scott and such anthropologists as Gerald Sider and Michael Taussig have tried to answer this question by challenging conventional views of history and culture. Central to these approaches is a shift away from viewing culture as an object (e.g., a set of beliefs and practices) to viewing it as a situation. Moreover, it is a complex and conflict-ridden situation in which people's beliefs and practices are often instruments of power—of domination, resistance, or, paradoxically, both simultaneously. Consequently, these authors have explored ways through which language may be turned against itself. In other words, they have argued that language is not a transparent medium through which they can simply describe and explain this situation. Instead, they have called attention to the ways language is an inextricable part of this situation—and the way their own language becomes part of this situation.

Joan Scott's recent work on the history of French feminism provides a model for using someone's life story to write against such power. She is skeptical of histories that tell of "the clash of opposing positions" or of opposing strategies in the struggle against patriarchy, as if one position could win or one strategy could be effective (1996b: 16–17). Instead, she focuses on the people who have had to live within and against these positions and strategies: "women (and some men) grappling repeatedly with the radical difficulty of resolving the dilemmas they confronted" (17).

Nevertheless, she does not present the stories of these women as "biography," which, like many life histories, is often either subjective or heroic. For Scott, the agency of the women about whose lives she writes is grounded in historically and culturally specific structures — and, moreover, these structures are fraught with contradiction, rendering such agency radically paradoxical. Reading their stories "in this technically deconstructive way does not work comfortably with linear narrative or teleology; it tends to undermine those stories that establish the truth or inevitability of certain views of the world by eliminating accounts of conflict and power within them" (1996b: 16–17).

Although many in the West like to imagine a great distance between themselves and those whom they have colonized, Gerald Sider has persistently described the situation of American Indians (in context Sider is addressing the situation of North American Indians, but his observations and arguments, at least in their more general form, apply equally to all American Indians) in terms that echo Scott's discussion of French feminists. According to Sider, theirs is a situation in which "no strategy against domination could achieve, for long if at all, the results it must minimally achieve, so there must be a profound dissent over its adoption and use, dissent that is both profoundly legitimate and profoundly destructive" (1993: 15). Moreover, when businesses and governments often use what people say (or what anthropologists report people to have said) to manipulate or control them, it does not make sense for people to express themselves clearly. Under these circumstances, the notions that culture is coherent and that history is an orderly sequence of events, or a transformation of some social order, are far from heuristic tools — they are instruments of power.

Against such power Sider invokes a different sort of history, an oppositional history that is lived by people and too often ignored in written records:

Rather, the disjunctions — the breaks and gaps that particularly characterize the history of dominated peoples (and in some ways form part of every history) — shape how history is imposed, claimed, and understood. And these breaks, these points where the past rubs antagonistically against the present, the past and the present against the foreseen future, are often the loci both of terror and of hope, of bitter struggles over meaning and over meaninglessness. (1993: 10)

Sider is especially interested in those moments of seeming inarticulateness on the part of dominated people—moments of confusion, tears, and silence—that in fact give full expression to these disjunctions. Rather than interpret what people say or explain why they act as they do (and thus claim the very power he seeks to write against), he asks: What situation is it that makes silence necessary, meaninglessness meaningful?

Michael Taussig is more interested in the ways people themselves talk about their situations. Although such talk often seems obscure or strange to anthropologists and their audience, Taussig, like Sider, does not believe that it is in need of interpretation or explanation. Instead he asks how such talk has been used (and by whom), and how it might be used against power. He has suggested that it is precisely through seemingly obscure and strange talk that people can reveal the disjunctions through which "history is imposed, claimed, and understood." Contradictory images or accounts conjure up, through their difference, a space that reveals what cannot be imagined or said. Thus, the record of fieldwork, whether ethnographic or biographic, is not data, not even biased data: the dialogues and interactions of anthropologist and informant constitute a "juxtaposition of dissimilars such that old habits of mind can be jolted into new perceptions of the obvious" (1992: 45).

Rather than try to explain the testimony of informants in terms of some broader historical context, Taussig has thus argued that it is precisely the "historical context"—the orderly narratives that we use to contain and sort out disorder—that must be challenged and scrutinized. It is in this context that he appeals to Benjamin's invocation of the fairytale, "because of what it may teach us about ways to deflate the heroism that is used by the state to invigorate if not invent traditions that make for a culture of nationalism—a culture, of course, that once set, becomes a powerful tool in the arsenal of social control, used not only by the state but also one which we non-heroes practice daily over ourselves too" (1992: 53–54). The tale of the fool, the naif, the adventurer, the wiseacre, may be the best weapon against the myths of the state.

In this book I use Scott's, Sider's, and Taussig's ideas to write a life history that will further Boas's project. This book is not so much "about" Alejandro Tsakimp as it is about his situation. This is a colonial situation that is too complex to be comprehended in its entirety directly, but that may be comprehended through its effects—specifically, as reflected by Alejandro's life. Alejandro Tsakimp is hardly a "typical" Shuar (I doubt that any Shuar would want to be thought of as "typical"), but in his life he has had to contend with all of the challenges facing any Shuar man today. His story, disjointed and at times obscure, often juxtaposing in strange ways ideas and artifacts he has picked up in different places or from different people, works against the easily ordered accounts of most histories and ethnographies. It is a story of a life lived simultaneously within and against culture and history, and I hope my telling of it sits neither still nor well.

Such a project is especially appropriate for a book about Shuar, who are currently contending not only with the pressures of colonization but with the concomitant intensification of inequalities within their own society. Alejandro lives at a time when Shuar identity itself is both a burden and a resource. Under these conditions there cannot be any simple lines of cleavage between a dominant, oppressive, and exploitative state on the one side and its long-suffering victims on the other. His story is that of one man caught up in these contradictions, and it illuminates the ways the internal complexities and divisions of native peoples and communities shape their struggles within and against the global economy, and how these internal divisions are affected by these struggles.

Shamanism has a way of persistently making problems for systems and practices of social control or domination—whether by Shuar or non-Shuar. When Alejandro first studied shamanism it was in the hopes of learning how to cure his father, who was sick, presumably from witchcraft. Alejandro's life as a healer has been punctuated by encounters with malice, sickness, and death. Many Shuar (and more than a few Euro-Ecuadorian settlers) believe that death is not natural and that illness has a social cause. Although a shaman can cure someone of witchcraft, the diagnosis itself often involves an accusation against another, which may be followed by a revenge killing. Moreover, even shamans who heal are always suspect of causing witchcraft because Shuar believe that the power to cure and to kill is essentially the same, and Alejandro himself has been accused of witchcraft. In the past, cycles of revenge killing had the effect of preventing the concentration of wealth and the institutionalization of political authority. Today such violence is shaped by new economic and political struggles. The present account of Alejandro's life hinges on two pivotal events involving witchcraft and murder that illustrate these struggles: his dislocation as a child after his father had to flee their home and his turmoil as an adult after his father died, allegedly of witchcraft.

These events are emblematic of recent colonial history. Alejandro was born in 1944, a time when Shuar were recovering from intensified intertribal warfare fueled by White demands for shrunken heads. Survivors welcomed efforts by the Ecuadorian government and Catholic missionaries to resettle Shuar into *centros*. However, the resulting increase in population density has precipitated new social tensions and has also led to an increase in disease, triggering new accusations of witchcraft. The institutionalization of *centros* through the formation of the Federation in 1964 created a new object of conflict: land. When Alejandro's father died in 1990, Alejandro and his siblings and children were confronted with an unprecedented dilemma: who should inherit what? And like Lear's children, they turned against one another and then accused one another of parricide.

Alejandro, like the majority of Shuar today, makes his living as a peasant, occasionally selling cattle, naranjilla (*Solanum quitoense* Lam.; an orange-colored fruit with green pulp and a tart taste), and lumber in order to pay for clothing, medical and educational supplies, and, increasingly, meat. Young Shuar who cannot acquire enough land to farm turn to wage labor and in some cases migrate to New York or Los Angeles in search of work, like many other Ecuadorians. Teachers and officials of the Shuar Federation, however, receive salaries from the state. Some of them have been able to afford to send their children to universities in Cuenca or Quito. Although the Federation represents "Shuar," it is also promoting the division of Shuar into economic classes.

The intensification of inequalities among Shuar, however, has not led to their division into two clearly opposed classes. Rather, it has led to the reproduction of instability at different, but closely intertwined, levels of Shuar life. Just as Shuar families have been breaking up in fights over land, the Shuar Federation has splintered over its relationships with colonists and the state. In 1983 one faction overthrew another, which left to form a rival organization. And just as fights over land often express themselves through accusations of witchcraft, struggles for political authority often take shape through accusations of corruption.

Whether Shuar can fight against colonialism without destroying themselves is perhaps the single most important question facing Shuar today. As Sider pointed out, this is a question that is not merely hard to answer, it is dangerous—and perhaps impossible. It is, nevertheless, a question that Shuar like Alejandro live out every day. Although this monograph does not promise an answer, it is offered in the hope that an examination and appreciation of one such life may help us pose the question more clearly.

4

Working With Alejandro

Although I moved in with Alejandro in the spring of 1989, I did not work with him in any systematic way until May of 1990. For one thing, I questioned whether I would learn anything of value from him until we had established a trusting relationship. Moreover, I doubted that I could formulate a meaningful question for him until I had learned more about the conditions of his life. In the tradition of Boas and Malinowski, I considered prolonged residence in his community a necessary precondition for any significant research.

When I felt comfortable enough to begin asking Alejandro direct questions, however, I quickly became frustrated. His answers often seemed evasive and sometimes abrupt. In the evening I would ask if we could set some time aside the next day to work together, and he would agree—but the next day he would disappear on some errand. He tried to teach me Shuar on an informal basis, but even as my vocabulary grew, my grasp of the grammar became more and more muddled. Suspecting that our relationship had reached its limits and afraid to confront him, I began spending more time in Sucúa interviewing Federation officials and colonos.

Finally, tired of the distractions and frustrations of working in Utunkus and Sucúa, I went to Santiago to visit Juan Mashu, the teacher I had met the year before. Santiago was, at the time, a small hamlet of perhaps five hundred colonos sandwiched between an understaffed military base and a Catholic mission. Nestled at the foot of the Cutucú ridge, along the Santiago River, it had formerly been accessible only by foot or plane, but the government was building a road, and I was able to hitchhike. Further south and at a lower elevation, the Santiago River dwarfs the small rivers around Sucúa and is larger than even the Upano. Juan lived in a small centro about forty-five minutes from the other side of the river.

Since Juan was a teacher, I hoped that he could help me with my Shuar. I had reached a point where most of the time I had a general sense of what people were talking about, and I could address people

71

politely and answer simple questions. But I realized that I would have to dedicate the entire year to studying Shuar if I hoped to participate even minimally in any conversation, and then my funding would run out. I was beginning to feel quite comfortable living in Juan's *centro*, but I was learning nothing about the relationship between the Federation and shamanism. So far, I had next to nothing to add to the books and articles others had already written about the Shuar. Janet Hendricks was right: if I wanted to pursue my project, I would have to go back to the Upano valley.

As I traveled back to Sucúa, I thought about Alejandro and our relationship. I recalled my attempts to interview him in his home; his younger children were climbing over him, and his older children were pulling at the hair on my arms and giggling. He was not the only person distracted in such circumstances. And maybe he really did want to work with me but felt uncomfortable talking about certain things in front of others. I decided to stay in Sucúa and to invite him to visit me.

Our interview lasted from May 1990 to July 1991. I recorded our conversations on cassette tapes.[1] Sometimes we met for an hour, sometimes six. Sometimes he stayed the night, and we continued talking the next day. Sometimes we met several times a week, sometimes we would take a break of several weeks. I continued to interview *colonos* and Federation officials in town, and I frequently returned to Utunkus, where I interviewed other members of the *centro* and Alejandro's family. In Utunkus Alejandro taught me about the life of a Shuar husband and father, and I learned about the work of a shaman by sitting in on healing sessions. When we wanted to continue the interview, however, we made plans to work in Sucúa. In the end, we recorded almost seventy hours of conversation.

We spoke almost exclusively in Spanish, although occasionally he spoke in Shuar, and we would pause to discuss the meaning of a particular word or issues in translation of ideas from Shuar to Spanish. Nevertheless, I consider this interview utterly useless for any linguistic analysis of Shuar. (I would direct readers interested in features of the Shuar language to the works of Janet Hendricks, especially *To Drink of Death*.)

Nor do I believe it useful for an analysis of how Shuar speak Spanish. I have invented nothing in the accounts of Alejandro's life; when possible

I have tried to hew to a literal translation of his words. I have tried to be faithful to the rhythms of his speech (at least, to the way he talked to me) and I have tried to capture his feelings as well as his ideas and recollections. But I have employed a heavy editorial hand in order to make both the language and the narratives flow more smoothly.[2]

This interview is thus also useless for a study of Shuar narrative or Shuar notions of history or life history. (Again, I would direct readers interested in Shuar discourse to Hendricks's study.) Renato Rosaldo has pointed out that "autobiography" has a recent history in European culture, and that anthropologists cannot assume that it is a sensible or useful category in other cultures. Rosaldo's own foray into this field of inquiry reveals how tricky a field it is. After one set of interviews, he concluded that his informant "Tukbaw . . . saw his development in linear terms, as steps along a ladder" (1976: 147). Rosaldo seems blind, however, to his own role in eliciting Tukbaw's story. Fortunately, he provides us with a description of precisely that which his analysis ignores: "One evening I asked Tukbaw to tell me the story of his life. He looked puzzled. I was perplexed; I explained it was really quite simple. He should tell me the first thing he remembered, then the second thing, and go on from there in chronological order" (133). No wonder Tukbaw's account is linear! I too started the interview by asking Alejandro to tell me the first things he remembered and what happened after that; I understood that the account he then offered was a response to my question, and not an example of how Shuar think about history. Life histories may be "insider's" accounts, to use Radin's term, but they are produced through ethnographic encounters (see Crapanzano 1980, 1984). After all, no one is an "insider" per se; one is an "insider" only in relation to some "outsider."

Like Tukbaw, then, Alejandro was responding to an anthropologist's questions. After that first question, however, I did not give him specific instructions about how to tell his stories, although I frequently tried to dictate the topic of conversation. My initial purpose in interviewing Alejandro was not to learn about Shuar forms of speaking, nor even to develop a life history as such. I merely wanted to learn more about him, and I wanted to learn more about the things I had seen, heard, or read about but still did not understand.

The first time I turned on the tape recorder I asked him to tell me about his life in his own words, and he spoke for perhaps five minutes.

I present this question and answer in chapter 5. I used this five-minute discourse as a basis for asking questions over the next several weeks, but as I learned more about shamanism, the Federation, and colonialism, I developed new questions. Although I started each session with a question, I always gave Alejandro as much control over the interview as possible. If he did not want to talk about, or tired of, a particular topic, I asked a new question. If his answer led in another direction, I followed it.

I have tried, through translation and editing, to present the bulk of Alejandro's narrative in relatively colloquial English, but in chapter 5 I present a more literal and unedited translation in order to give readers a sense of Alejandro's voice. In the life history itself I usually remove my questions and edit Alejandro's answers into a narrative. When I want to illustrate the dynamics of our interview or illustrate a point that cannot be made through a unified narrative, I indicate my questions with my initials (SR) and Alejandro's answers with his initials (AT).

Sometimes in an interview session we simply misunderstood one another, and one of us would have to explain to the other what he meant, as in the following interchange:

SR: No, I am confused. Once you said that the government does not care about the indigenous people, but now you say the indigenous cannot abandon the country? Why not?

AT: I am also confused with your question, because we have a country apart from the government.

SR: Okay, I am talking about the government of Ecuador.

AT: But I am talking about the country. Even if we Shuar get scattered among settlers, we have a country distinct from the government.

Other times, our interests were either fundamentally different, or I was simply incapable of communicating my interests clearly, as the following excerpt illustrates:

SR: Who were the candidates for president of the association?

AT: Miguel Minki was elected president.

SR: But who were the candidates?

AT: The candidates were Miguel Minki.

SR: There was only one; there wasn't anyone else?

AT: They were Ernesto Tséremp, Julio Saant, and Miguel Minki.

SR: Who did you vote for?

AT: I voted for Julio Saant but more voted for Miguel Minki.

SR: Why did you vote for Julio Saant instead of Miguel Minki?

AT: Some voted for the other representatives, but Miguel came out with the most votes.

SR: And those who voted for Julio Saant instead of Miguel Minki, why did they vote for Julio Saant?

AT: Because they wanted Julio Saant to be president.

SR: But why did they vote for one and not the other?

AT: Because everyone has the right to vote.

SR: But why did they vote for Julio Saant and not Miguel?

AT: Because they did not want to, they wanted Julio Saant to be president.

SR: Why?

AT: Instead of Miguel being president they thought it better that he be vice-president, he would be a lieutenant.

SR: But was this true?

AT: The majority voted for Miguel Minki.

SR: Why did they vote for Miguel Minki and not Julio Saant?

AT: Because the president has a position of authority, and you shouldn't have two people in that position.

Clearly, both he and I brought our own agendas to the interview, but these agendas changed over time, and the form and content of the interview itself reflects the contingencies of the circumstances under which it took place.

Nevertheless, I am not presenting this life history as a record of our relationship. There has been much good work on this dimension of fieldwork (see Maybury-Lewis 1965; Powdermaker 1966; Rabinow 1977; Dumont 1978), including an outstanding life history (Crapanzano 1980). I address my relationship with Alejandro in brief in the conclusion and hope to address it at length in another study. For the moment, I hope that the preceding introductory chapters reveal enough of my own background and bias to convince readers of the partial nature of this work. Although Alejandro occasionally refers to me by name (usually my Shuar name, Nanki), I have eliminated from the text my voice as interlocutor.

This is not to deny my role in writing Alejandro's life history; rather, it owes to my judgment that I have had a greater influence over the telling of this story in my role as editor than as interlocutor. The interview was

75

the result of a collaboration, of manipulation and compromise as well as cooperation. The life history, however, is not.

In writing this book my goal was to present a portrait of one man's experience of a culture in flux. It is not a "history" in the sense of an orderly sequence of events. Our interview did not follow a chronology, and neither does the life history. Alejandro's memory of dates was often vague, and the attentive reader will note persistent inconsistencies in Alejandro's age and the dates of events. This reflects the fact that in our work both Alejandro and I were more concerned with the many diverse issues, events, and people that illustrate the forces against which Shuar must contend. I thus selected from his stories those that cover three of the most important areas of his social life: his family, shamanism, and the Federation (these stories represent a little more than a third of the interview).

Alejandro's identity is as complex as his life. One marker of this is the fact that he has three names—a Shuar name, Yurank', which hardly anyone uses; a Spanish name, Alejandro (or Alejo), which his intimates use; and another Spanish name, Baudillo, which everyone else (Shuar and *colono*) uses. I should qualify each of these uses by adding "most of the time," for I encountered numerous exceptions, and no one, least of all Alejandro, could (or wished to) explain why some preferred one name for him over another. Identifying people by one name and one number is convenient for bureaucrats and police, but unnecessarily limiting to people who move through a variety of social relations. Even three names cannot capture Alejandro's various roles, and I have arranged these stories in chapters that highlight a range of his identities: as a son and a brother, as a student and a worker, as a shaman, as a husband and a father, as a member of the Federation, as a friend and an enemy, and as an orphan. Alejandro cannot be reduced to any of these identities, not because his sense of self is incoherent, but rather because his life is so complex. These identities are not so much "roles" that Alejandro "has" or "fills"; they are *situations*, within, through, and against which he must live. In Scott's terms, they are "sites—historical locations or markers—where crucial political and cultural contests are enacted" (1996: 16).

A persistent tension in all of these situations is that between autonomy and dependence. As Anthony Giddens's discussion of structure and agency suggests, this may be a tension fundamental to the human condition. In different situations, however, it takes radically different forms.[3] Among Shuar living on the colonial frontier, it takes the form of conflict between the desire for individual freedom and the need to act in union. Moreover, many of these conflicts explicitly revolve around, or come to involve, conflicts over access to land. When Andrés and his brothers first settled Utunkus, they were departing from the current Shuar custom of matrilocal residence in order to present a united front against colonial expansion. However, they secured their claims to land individually, through legal title. When the shaman Tséremp threatened the harmony of the new settlement, Chúmpi, Andrés, Valentín, and others united against him. Then when agents of the state (a far more powerful political union) acted to arrest Alejandro's father and brother, they divided to flee and hide in the forest.

At first, struggles over land may seem to be a simple consequence of colonialism: with more people living in the region, land necessarily becomes more scarce. But this scarcity is a product not only of demographics and immigration but also of the legal apparatuses of colonialism, especially the idea of private property. In the early years of colonialism this belief distinguished settlers from Shuar. But one of the major dimensions of colonialism has been to compel and entice Shuar to participate in and support this institution, to produce Shuar who not only accept the notion of private property as legitimate but find it unavoidable or even desirable. Consequently, whereas Shuar once competed with settlers for land, now they compete among themselves.

Alejandro was first exposed to these conflicts as a little boy, and it was through his family that he had to learn how to live with them. Chapter 6 tells of his childhood family situation. In many societies children experience contradictory desires and demands: they depend on adults for survival, yet they are expected to become increasingly independent. This contradiction, however, seems to me especially intense for Alejandro.

In Alejandro's childhood, this tension manifested itself in material and discursive forms. Hunger is a persistent theme in his stories, and he sometimes seems torn between depending on his parents and other relatives for food and his desire to acquire his own food. This creates tension not only between parent and child but also among siblings who compete for food. This may be a reflection of the turmoil on the colonial frontier. Since Alejandro's parents had moved into the area in order to block colonial expansion, they had moved away from many of the kin upon whom they might rely for support in times of need. Moreover, the increase in population owing to colonial expansion had led to a decrease in the amount of game available for hunting.

Another persistent theme in Alejandro's account is lying. In a world where children depend on adults for their material needs, knowledge is one of the few things they can seek to possess exclusively. From an early age, then, knowledge is associated with power.

These themes collide when Alejandro's sister Rosario tries to steal some of his nuts and he hits her. Their father, Andrés, forces Alejandro to take maikiúa, not so much as a punishment but as a remedy: Shuar take maikiúa to make themselves stronger, and Andrés felt that Alejandro's behavior was a sign of weakness. Maikiúa gives people visions, personal visions that translate into personal power. But Alejandro also relies on another kind of knowledge, as well as new objects and technologies, to become a man—knowledge of the colonial world. It was only when he grew older and came to realize how expensive soap was that he was able to appreciate fully the sacrifices made by his parents when they had to work in order to purchase manufactured goods for the family.

In chapter 7 I tell of Alejandro's encounters with the ambivalent features of colonial society: Spanish language, Christianity, and, most of all, money. These are instruments of Ecuadorian dominion over Shuar, and learning about them helps Alejandro better understand the situation of his parents. But they are, ironically, also means of establishing his autonomy from his parents. This is not so much an issue of independence from parents (as it is for many North Americans); rather, it means that he can begin to become equal and provide for others as others have provided for him.

Sickness and health present another dual legacy of colonialism. Colonization introduced new diseases to the region, and Shuar suffered from numerous epidemics. Conveniently, colonialism also introduced Shuar to allopathic medicine and surgery. In his youth, Alejandro was able to work for a visiting North American chiropractor, who would become for Alejandro a role model almost on par with his own father. On the one hand, Dr. Ferguson represented for Alejandro a man of relative wealth and independence. On the other hand, he represented a man dedicated to using his powers to help others.

As a North American, Dr. Ferguson was by law even more of an outsider in Ecuador than Alejandro and other Shuar. Eventually, the military concluded that he was a security risk and forced him to leave the country. Just as was the case with Tséremp, Alejandro learned that with power and privilege come conflict and danger.

In chapter 8, sex and affection take their place alongside food and knowledge as objects of desire. Nevertheless, another object of desire emerges for a moment: land. When Alejandro falls in love with a *colona*, his family fears that this will become a means for the settler and her family to acquire more Shuar land. Consequently, they arrange for Alejandro to marry another Shuar, Maria Tsamaraint. As a husband, Alejandro also becomes a parent—and learns that his own children can lie as easily as he does. As an adult, though, his lies have changed: now they center around sex and affection, rather than food.

Sex is not only a subject of lies; it is an object of conflict. Before Alejandro married Maria, his father had tried to arrange a marriage between him and a young woman from Cusuime. When Alejandro married Maria instead, the young woman's father became angry and, according to Alejandro, ensorcelled Andrés.

When Alejandro was a child, his father gave him *maikiúa* to make him stronger. Chapter 9 describes Alejandro's quest for knowledge and power through a different means—*ayahuasca*—in order to help his ailing father. (*Maikiúa* and *ayahuasca* are nonaddictive, and their use by Shuar does not indicate chemical dependence but rather moral commitments that are literally "embodied" and are achieved and expressed through physical acts.) Although hesitant at first, Alejandro considers shamanism to be his destiny. Besides being inspired by his father's work as a shaman and by the efforts of Dr. Ferguson, the North American doctor for whom he worked, Alejandro learned to desire *ayahuasca* while still in his mother's womb, when a shaman treated her to prevent a miscarriage.

After a long period of study, Alejandro believed himself ready to help not only his father but anyone who was suffering. Yet the first time someone asked for his help, he was afraid. If he were to fail, he might suffer the same fate as Tséremp. The fact is, shamanism is an intensely political practice, involving not only the power to heal but the power to kill, and thus linking the power that comes from knowledge over the supernatural to power over other people. The dilemma of the shaman is that with the power to help others comes a peculiar vulnerability.

Shamans help other individuals; leaders of the Shuar Federation seek to help their community. Chapter 10 tells of Alejandro's ambiguous relationship, as both an insider and an outsider, with the Shuar Federation. In Alejandro's experience, the Federation itself is the means through which Shuar have internalized and given institutional form to the ambivalent features of colonialism. These ambivalences are manifest in the organization's dependence on the state and foreign institutions (including the Catholic church) for financial aid and credit and its reliance on missionaries for political support and guidance. This paradoxical situation has fueled a variety of conflicts within the Federation. The complexity of this situation is evident in both the *centros* and the central offices of the Federation. It is most evident locally in the self-destruction of cattle cooperatives—although organized and financed by the Federation as a means to promote communal solidarity and collective action, cooperatives generally end up promoting individualism and local stratification. (Alejandro limits himself to a discussion of Federation-managed projects, but these problems plague all development work in the region, including projects organized by the Peace Corps and funded by the United States Agency for International Development.) Similarly, the Federation leadership is often plagued by accusations of corruption, which culminated in a coup, led by Shuar teachers, that replaced the elected leadership in 1984. Although the Federation survived that disruption, these tensions persist. They are manifest in Alejandro's own doubts about the Federation, which he fears may be helping enrich its leaders more than those it claims to serve—and certainly more than himself. At times the Federation seems to be the Shuar's defense against colonialism, but at other times it seems to promote the same political and economic inequalities as colonialism.

Shuar have to confront the challenges of inequality and difference not only in the offices and projects of the Federation but also in the homesteads and paths of the *centros*. In chapter 11, we see that Alejandro's experience as a friend and an enemy internalizes the ambivalent consequences of colonialism informally, through the psychic processes of identification and envy (in other words, through the competing desires to *be* like someone else and to *have* someone else's possessions). Alejandro's friendships with other Shuar are based largely on identification—the joyous discovery of shared feelings, ideas, and interests. Ironically, though, his closest friend is someone different and distant—an Achuar. The differences in their customs are reflected in the differences in their possessions, and this difference is overcome through the delayed exchange of gifts. Through these exchanges—both conversations about their respective customs and material gifts—Alejandro and his friend become more alike, while remaining distinct.

An enemy, on the other hand, is someone who has but does not give, or who does not have and so takes. Although this sounds like a fair description of the relationship between *colonos* and Shuar, Alejandro is most concerned with other Shuar, particularly those closest to him. Indeed, just as Alejandro had to compete with his siblings for food as a child, as an adult he has come into conflict with his siblings over land. Once he argued with his elder brother Valentín over land, but they resolved their dispute. His ongoing struggle with this sister Imelda and her husband Calisto, however, is tearing him apart.

All of these themes merge when Alejandro's father Andrés becomes sick and dies. Alejandro and his siblings are of the first generation in Shuar history to confront the problem of the inheritance of real estate. The effect of colonialism, which has produced a relative limit on the availability of land through an increase in the region's population and has produced an absolute limit to the availability of land through the institution of private property, is to force Shuar siblings to compete against one another. Adapting the new logic of inheritance to the older principle of matrilocality (which established a link between a father and son-in-law), Alejandro's sister Imelda and her husband Calisto wish to secure a portion of Andrés's estate. Alejandro, however, is concerned about providing a legacy of security for his own children. Some children will inevitably be left without land and will thus be forced to enter the labor market.

Andrés's illness and death raise the question of both probate and witchcraft. Alejandro is convinced that someone has killed his father, and Imelda is convinced that Alejandro effectively committed shamanic malpractice because he failed to save his father's life. Such accusations, and the resulting feuds, express in a local idiom the tensions created or exacerbated by colonialism. They seem to threaten attempts to unify Shuar and thus undermine the strength of the Shuar Federation.

Ironically, at the same time that shamanism threatens Shuar unity, it provides a stumbling block against all those who would like to govern the Shuar. The Federation has other effects besides representing the Shuar and promoting their interests—it is an instrument of colonialism, promoting the power of the state and capitalist development. It provides some Shuar with state-salaried jobs and capital to finance their children's college education and advancement in Ecuadorian society. It also supports the state's colonization policies that are producing a generation of landless Shuar youth who will have to look for seasonal and part-time employment in the margins of Ecuadorian society.

Alejandro is many things: a son and brother, a husband and father, a member of the Federation, a shaman. His stories illustrate the extent to which these roles are really complex situations, and they illustrate how the roles intersect and divide, how they work together and against one another—and how as one person Alejandro must negotiate all of these forces and tensions.

In editing Alejandro's stories, my objective was to present them in as straightforward a way as possible, in his voice. I do not do this because I think his words speak for themselves. Alejandro, of course, can speak for himself, to interlocutors whom he knows and who know him. But I have taken his *words* out of the context of our relationship in order to say something about the larger context of colonialism. In this complex context, how we listen to his words is not an easy question and cannot be taken for granted. In these introductory chapters I have sketched out the contradictory ways this context has shaped the lives of people living in the Ecuadorian Amazon, and how it has shaped the ways Europeans and Euro-Americans have perceived and talked about Indians. Now I return to Alejandro's stories, leaving it to readers to try to listen to him in their own way.

Part 2: His Stories

5

First of All . . .

On 5 May 1990, Alejandro and I began our formal interview. His remarks appear in this chapter as an unedited translation. I have provided brief explanations of unfamiliar terms in brackets; further explanations are provided in the glossary at the end of the book. I also include there a cast of characters mentioned in Alejandro's account and kinship charts of Alejandro's family.

This was my first question:

SR: What I want now is for you to tell me about your life—the first things you remember, your education as a boy, your relationship with your parents, a little bit about the history of your family, your father, your mother, brothers, and sisters, how life is in Morona Santiago and in your *centro*, when you were young, and all that stuff.

AT: Nanki,[1] first of all when I was around six, five or six years old, I spent my time at the Salesian mission in Sucúa; I remember I was in first grade.[2]

And then I went to the Evangelical mission when I was eight years old. From the age of eight I continued my education with Mr. Miguel Ficke, a North American Evangelical missionary.

And after fifth grade I went to a laboratory of the North American who was building it in front of the Evangelical mission, where Mr. Luis Trujillo lives right now. This was part of the laboratory that Mr. Enrique Ferguson, a North American, was building, and I worked there until I turned eleven.

Then I went to live with my parents, with my mother, and I spent several years there until I went to work with the brother *colonos* [settlers; non-Shuar, mostly from the highlands, who have come to live in Morona Santiago] in Macas for three years.

When I was sixteen, turning seventeen, I got married to my wife; her name is Maria Ines Tsamaraint. Kintanúa is her Shuar name, and we spent our hard life together with our kids for some years until we founded the *centro* [nucleated settlement] San José Utunkus. Coincidentally my father was *síndico* [trustee; the elected representative of the *centro*] during that time.

Later I was an auxiliary professor at the Fiscomissional School,[3] teaching literacy. And then my life went on, struggling with farming for three years.

After that my father got sick, and I tried to save his life. We went to Quito, to Baños, to Pastaza, and finally to a shaman whose name was Segundo Yasakam'. Then I tried to make my own cures with my father, and he got better. Since then, I knew about these traditions; it was our culture, and how to go to the jungle, and about our Shuar life. So I had enough of these brothers, and I kept working with our own community San José Utunkus. Then I studied more about natural medicine, shamanism, and progress.

Later, after some years, I had a woman, my second wife. Then, with much struggling, with all these problems—not because of love, nor letters, nor, as they say, civilization, nor for offers, but rather to protect, for the well-being of this poor lady who was a widow.

I kept up the shamanism, and the third wife came, this Marta; her family came and gave her to me.

My life went on, and I kept working for my people—whether apache [non-Shuar Ecuadorian] or Shuar, or inkis [non-Ecuadorian], the North Americans, so, the whole country. In that way I worked with brother Steven—"Nanki" in our language (so it is easier and for you to be part of us)—because as our brother *colonos* say, in front of God we all have the same blood, physiognomy, the same customs. The quality of life may be more developed, but we are the same race, we are the same.

So I kept struggling up to now. I am still working with my medicines in the *Sierra* [central highlands of Ecuador] and *Oriente* [the east, the Ecuadorian Amazon]. And that is how I met you, Nanki, and we are working for the well-being of the Shuar people and the Shuar nation.

I know the story of my mother and father, the myths and traditions, the customs and the work, the craftsmanship, Shuar folklore, the textiles, the drums, the spears—they are all Shuar handcrafts, all we have known, and for that reason we the Shuar are how we are. And we want to progress for the sake of our communities, the Shuar towns and the Federation, which is united with this year's president, Miguel Puwáinchir.

Nankichi [the diminutive for Nanki, my Shuar name], let me tell you what my parents told me, "You have to work, you have to go along with the people; be a person, have a position. You cannot sell your land; keep it and protect it because it is your base; you don't have to be a trader of land. Don't be a wanderer, but a hard-working person who helps apaches and Shuar brothers as well, Achuar, Huambisa,[4] any kind of person who gives you a hand. You have to be their friend and help them." These were the counsels my parents gave me; they are already dead. So we have been working on this, Nankichi.

Then a religion, named Father Juan Shutka, and with Father Albino Gomez, came in 1962. It has already founded San José Utunkus, and we have worked there; my father, Andrés Tsakimp, was the first *síndico*, the first Shuar adviser. He worked for the benefit of the community and fought for the Shuar nation in my country, Ecuador. That is why we know the Shuar lifestyle, how to work, to live, how to fish (we have barbasco [a plant that is mashed and placed in shallow water, releasing a poison that stupefies fish]), what to plant and to harvest, and we get our own food for us to have at home.

This is my story, Nankichi. So, I have had a wondrous life; my wives are not jealous or bad. On the contrary, they have given me the strength to live, to work, and to accept what I am, my luck in life, in my forty-four years, forty-five years right now. In this way we have struggled, and I am struggling for the development of my Shuar people, just for us to develop.

And I hope you, my North American brothers, will give us some directions, or something of yours, for example, about commercialization, and how to improve our work, and about medicine, as health is the very basis of the community. Because the people function better if there is health, because when you are sick, brother Steven, you are never happy, and with health you can do everything.

So, for the meanwhile, and first of all in name of our Shuar Federation, the organization of my nation, the Shuar, how do you say it in big countries, I want to keep progressing forward and with all the medicinal plants, the apothecary medicine, and all the doctors who really want to work against the diseases. But not to play "who makes more surgeries," because I have seen in my country, the provincial chief of the doctors of Morona Santiago has said that whoever makes more surgeries makes more money. This shouldn't be. I would really like the doctors of the Shuar people to be doctors that really fight against the illnesses there are in this place in the province of Morona Santiago.

That is all I want to tell you for this moment; thank you.

6

Son and Brother

Independence

My daughter Herlinda wants to nurse from my wife Maria all the time!
I was like that, too, when I was her age. But when my mother was busy
at the garden and I wanted to stay with her, she told me that she was
busy at the garden and that I was old already and could wait longer. So
she gave me a little bit of *chicha* [fermented manioc beverage], very sweet
chicha, and tied me with a sash so I would not fall from the bed. She
left me there every day, until little by little I learned to be away from my
mother's breast.

Lies

When I was around seven years old, my brother-in-law Pedro Tunki told
me he was going to separate from my sister Teresa, and I believed him.
I asked him why and asked him not to fight with her any more, saying
that my father might be upset.

"I was lying," he said; it was just to see what I was going to do.

But to know the truth I asked my sister if it was true that Pedro was
leaving her. She asked, "Who said that?" I told her it was Pedro, and she
said that he was just kidding me. Then I asked him why he had said that,
and he told me that he didn't say anything—he denied it!

When I was a little boy, I sometimes lied. The first time that I lied, it
was a joke; I was three or four, and I remember that I wanted to steal
the meat that my mother had. They had hunted an agouti [large rodent]
and had eaten some of the meat for breakfast. They said, "Here's some
in the basket. You can eat from this, but not from the pan."

I said, "*Ayu, ayu*" [right, right].

Then they all left to work after breakfast, and I waited some time to
make sure that they were gone. They were working—my mother was in
the garden—so I thought they were not coming soon.

There was no dog, and I wanted to be very smart—I was four years old but a clever kid. So I took a piece, a big piece, but I left some in the pan.

My mother used to leave some ashes on top of the lid (we used a leaf as a lid, and the pan was an *inchinkian* [clay pot], so when I took the meat the ashes fell down . . . but I put them back.

When my mother came back she went to heat the pan, and she saw it and said, "Hey, Yurank', why is the soup different? Did you touch it?"

I said, "No, it was the dog."

And she said, "There is no dog—the dog left with your father!"

So I said that the dog was there, but it had left.

Then she asked me where I had been. I said that I had been making a house and showed it to her. I asked her, "Now you want to blame me because the dog dumped the ashes?"

So she said, "Okay, okay," but then she saw the leg of the agouti. She said, "You, rogue! How can you tell me you haven't stolen it and that it was the dog?"

I said that the dog was there!

Then she asked me, "The dog wouldn't save the leg, would it? Was it the dog or one of your father's *pasuk*" [shaman's familiar]?

So I said that it was the *pasuk*—that my father was hungry and sent one of his *pasuk*. "I was making my house—I'll show you!"

She was sweet with me; she said she was going to ask my father if he had sent a *pasuk* for the food. She asked me if I had seen the dog, and I said yes. It was the first lie that I ever told.

Later my father came. My mother served the food and waited until he was done so he wouldn't be mad. Then she said, "Andrés, you know Baudillo did something today. Did you send your *pasuk* to pick up some food? He says you sent for the food because you were hungry, and now he is blaming the dog!"

I was ready to run! My father laughed and said, "This lie has to be paid for today. Bring him here so we can burn him."

It is a tradition here that when you steal something, they bandage your eyes so as not to hurt your vision, and they burn hot peppers until they smoke so much that the smoke gets into you, and then they put the peppers in your face until you get burned so people can tell who the thief is.

But I had already climbed up the guava tree, hiding so they wouldn't get me!

I was thinking, where was I going to sleep? My aunt was dead, so I couldn't go to her house. "Now the *iwianchi* [demons] were going to get me," I thought. So I decided to go back to the house when my parents were sleeping.

It was already late, and my mother called me, "Alejandro come, come," but I didn't answer. It was getting dark; I went behind the henhouse and heard my parents arguing. My mother said, "Now we are going to lose our only son! The *iwianchi* are going to take him! Call him!" She came out with an ember from the fire and found me watching the hens. She said, "Here you are, so quiet . . . come in. Your father is very mad."

I kept lying, "I just ate what was in the basket, nothing else."

I went to bed, but my father woke me up. The adults have the tradition of drinking *guayuza*[1] at midnight while giving advice to the kids; they wake up everybody and drink *guayuza*, and the whole family vomits. We do this so you have good digestion and good health.

So he came to me and I cried. "What *pasuk* ate the food? Did you see him?" he asked.

I said, "Yes," and he said that he was going to burn me with hot-pepper smoke, without a bandage to protect my eyes, so I would get all burned, even in my mouth, because I had eaten the food. He would punish me in this way so I would learn not to steal.

He quickly put the hot peppers in the fire, and my mother cried and put more hot peppers in the fire. He said "Quickly, because he has to be punished."

I said that I was going to die, and finally, just when the smoke was too much and I couldn't take it any more, I said that I had eaten the agouti.

I will tell you, Nanki, another time I lied to my father. I said I had killed a big bird, a turkey, with a piece of *nanku* [a papaya stick, like a little pipe]. I was young, maybe three or four, a little bit older than my son Sandro, and like him, I was not good at lying. Sometimes he would say, "Gosh, I killed that animal with a rock." The joke was that I said I had killed the turkey with a rock, and the bird had fallen but it left.

My father said, "But if you hit it on the chest, why did it leave? Why do I think you are lying?"

I said, "Yes, I killed it with the papaya stick. The bird was in the cacao tree and gosh, I caught it. I had another, but it escaped. Then I hit one with an arrow in the middle of the chest, and I gave it to my aunt and she is cooking it."

He asked me if I was lying. But I wanted to go to hunting with a gun, so I said that there were many turkeys in that cacao tree. "There they are, the birds I was teasing with the papaya stick and my little arrows." But I lied about it. I wanted to go hunting turkeys with my father, that was my idea, so I said that I had killed one and that there were two others I injured.

It was not the truth, I was lying, so he asked me where the turkey feathers were, and I said that I had given it to my aunt with feathers and all.

He said he was going to say to my aunt: "Let's go, I want to drink *chicha* at my brother-in-law Yankúr's house."

I stayed behind and then ran to her house, so I got there first, and my father came later. I said to her, "Isn't it true that I brought a turkey for you?"

But I knew that my father loved me. I knew this when I was maybe four or five and broke the *pinink'*. *Pinink'* is like china, like a big cup, where we keep the manioc, soup, and all that. I broke that *pinink'*, and my father asked me what I was doing. I told him I was playing with my little dog. He asked me in Castillian why I had done such a thing, since I was very strong.

I told him that my little dog was playing with me and bit me. I was bringing some water; the dog grabbed my hand, and I dropped the cup. I told him that it was the truth and that if I was telling the truth he could not hit me, but if I were lying he could hit me.

So he told me that it was right to tell the truth, and he would not do anything as long I was telling the truth.

I was happy because I always told them the truth quickly so I would not be punished.

Death

But I was sad when my aunt Luz Pakésh died. I was very little when I saw that. I was five years old. I saw her crying when she died, so I was very sad. I said, "Is this how you die?" I had never seen somebody dying. I saw my aunt Ines, and she died in my presence, too. It was in their house in Asunción. People called us when she was dying. We went to her house, and she was dead, she was dying. Those were sad moments.

I recovered from that sadness when my mother told me that if you think too much about something, you might have bad dreams. She said that everybody dies someday, and we could be next. It was the first time I saw my aunt dying, and I was sad.

I asked how people die.

My mother said that the blood just stops . . . there is a breath, and then it stops and does not flow anymore, and you are dead.

I was sad, because she loved me; she always gave me food.

Duty

I remember, Nankichi, that my parents were proud of me when I was doing my duties, even those I did not have to do, like when I did some work at home or took care of the birds.

Once when I was a boy, around five years old, my father was studying shamanism, and there were times he could not do some things. So I helped him, like by preparing the tobacco concentrate: I gave him water and the little cup to prepare the juice—the one that is used in shamanism—and then I rolled the cigarettes.

My father was very proud of me during that time. My father was so happy that he wanted to cry, because I had woken up three times because I thought he was cold. I told him that I was worried because he was away from my mother for a very long time (she was away from home because my father was studying shamanism and fasting).

He told me, "Little boy, I know you are worried about me. Other little kids do not do this job that you have done so well for me—you made the cigarettes for me to smoke; you brought the kaonak [dried plantain leaf]; you woke up three times during the night to light the fire because you thought I was cold, because I was alone in my tankámash² bed. You were very brave and very worried about me, and that is why I am very happy with you."

He hugged me and told me that my sons would do the same for me one day.

"People will love you very much, and you will care about people and your brothers. You have to help people when you grow up," said my father.

I said, "Thanks, Dad. I am sad because you are away from our bed, and I always have to visit you to sleep with you. . . ."

Then he said that it was not good for him to sleep with me and my mother because he was fasting. We talked all afternoon about me being a father one day and how some day my kids would do the same for me.

But once, when I was five or six, I broke his *tumank* [jew's harp] when he was bathing. I put it back on the table.

When he came at night and took the *tumank*, he noticed that it was broken and said, "Yurank', who broke the *tumank*? Did you come to play here?"

I told him that I had left the *tumank* on the bed and that it had fallen down and gotten broken because I had misplaced it.

So he told me that I had to help him the next day and look for *nakuchim*, the reed, to make another *tumank*. My father loved to play the *tumank*, but because I told the truth I was saved.

At this time, when I was five or six, my mother always went to work with my father, so I stayed at home alone. I had a little hen with chicks and a little pig that was mine. I fed them together, and my mother was happy.

When she came back from the garden she would bring some water to drink. She told me that because she was coming late at night I needed to close the door for the chickens. She told me that the jar for the water was ready, but that I did not have to move the water.

But I did move it for her, and she told me that I was a good husband because I carried the water, and because I made chicha for her when she was tired.

I told her that I had made it for her because she was coming late and that I was there to help them.

She told me that it was nice that I was thinking about that even though I was very young. She was very proud and happy because she had carried wood and manioc in her basket, and I had the water ready. It was getting late, but I had gotten things ready for her.

When I was five or six years old I loved to hunt animals, like the agouti. After my mother cooked them, I always got the head, but never a good piece.

One day my father gave me a whole head of a peccary [a piglike animal], and I told my sisters Imelda and Teresa that they hadn't gotten any.

They told me that the head was for women, but I told them that I was not going to eat the brain because it was worthless—you'll become as dumb as the animal—and I was going to eat the rest of the snout. My father told me to save some for the next day, and I hugged and kissed my father.

I wanted my parents to be proud of me. When the president Velasco Ibarra came in 1954 or 1955—I was about six[3]—they sent me to the airport to see him. Yes, I saw José Maria Velasco Ibarra. When I got home I told my father that I had seen him, that he took me to his plane, and we flew together to Quito. I said that, and my father never found out the truth.

Also, I once told my mother I had seen a jaguar. It was a lie—I didn't even know what a jaguar was like! I never saw the jaguar, but my mother believed it until her death. I wanted her to believe that I was brave, that I was not afraid of any animal, even a jaguar. I wanted to look good, but it was a lie.

Years later I asked my father: "The jaguar is very dangerous, but it stays on the trees. If it is so brave, why is it on the trees? It is a coward because it is not on earth." I asked my father how he could believe the jaguar was so fierce. I also asked my mother why it was alone on the trees if it was ferocious.

She Really Loved Me

I was losing my teeth when I was seven, and my father wanted to take them out. One time he grabbed a little nail and picked at it and—pow!—he took the tooth out. So what is it going to be like after all this? Then my mother said, "Come here; I'm going to help you with your tooth. Let's tie it with a little string from a tumank. Now wait, I am going to pull it." So my mother did the job, and I was very happy because she did it in a softer way and didn't hurt me. I told her I was very thankful.

I was very happy with my brother Francisco [Valentín] when he made me a headdress and a basket. He had been hunting and saw me making a kunam [headdress made from a squirrel]. He made a little headdress for me because I was already a man. And he made a basket for me to carry when I wanted to participate on any occasion, like fishing or hunting. I always carried it because I felt so proud that day when he gave me that. He gave me the basket so I could carry manioc or whatever. Every time my mother went to the gardens I took it so I could carry my manioc, and plantain, and "Chinese potato" [taro]. I was very happy that day.

When I was eight years old I was interned in the mission studying with the Evangelicals in Sucúa, but I came home every Friday. And I put up some warm water for my stepmother because she did not like to bathe with cold water . . . this was Mama,⁴ the one who died from measles. . . . She said, "Gosh, am I tired, because you were gone and your father is helping his brother Antonio Akachu to clear a garden. I am tired."

I told her that the water was ready for her to bathe, and she said that she loved me more than Navira, her older daughter. I had everything ready for her, even a stool for her to sit on. She was very happy and proud of me. She told me that if I was thirsty there was *nijiamanch'* [fermented manioc beverage] for me. She really loved me.

It Was Funny

The funniest day in my life was when I was seven years old. My brother, the oldest, Francisco—that's Valentín, it's the same thing—brought an armadillo, *shushui*, to show to my parents. He brought the animal tied up and said he was going to domesticate it. He left it in the kitchen, blocked in the corner by a stick—he was going to build a corral. During the night the animal burrowed under the floor and left. In the morning my mother said she was going to feed the animal, but when we got there the animal was gone. I ran to my brother and told him, "*shushui*, it is gone, *shushui* left!"

He said that he had put him in the corral already.

I said, "Francisco, the animal is gone," but he was asleep.

My mother was dying of laughter and said, "And you were going to have thousands!" It was funny.

Another funny day was when I saw a mute man, a Shuar named Wisúmp from Asunción. I was around eight, living at the mission. He just said, "Ah, oh, ah." So to bother him I always followed him and made him speak. He always cried and said, "Fu, fu, fu." He used to blow on the fire in a funny way, and I imitated him. It was funny.

My father asked me why I always made fun of Wisúm; he said that he was going to reprimand me. But I kept imitating him. I gave him a torch, and he blew it and looked to the sky, and I laughed so hard! My father scolded me and said that I could be like him one day, but I kept laughing.

To Make a Man out of You

We Shuar have this punishment: The parents do not give the child food for three days, until he has surrendered to fatigue and hunger; then they give him *maikiúa* [plant infusion] and he lies down as if he were dead. There are different kinds of *maikiúa*. We take *waimiatai maikiúa* when we want to see our *arútam*. We take *maikiúa tsuákratin* for healing. But when we punish a person, we use *unkush maikiúa* so that the misbehavior won't come back. When you take *unkush maikiúa*, you lie dead for one day, for twenty-four hours, into the next day. And phantasms bother you: *maikiúa* gives visions like spirits of snakes or more fantastic things, and you cannot rest. It's as if you were dead but had no peace.

I've tried it. I did a bad thing to my sister Rosario, the daughter of my dad and his second wife (she is not Mama's own daughter; she is the daughter of Mama's classificatory sister,[5] a widow; when her husband died, my father and Mama adopted the daughter). I was about nine years old, and she was about eleven. I was grilling nuts, what we call *nampi*, and my dad went to hunt. And just as my dad was coming back Rosario began crying because she was trying to get the nuts from me.

I was saying, "You are eating my *nampi*! But you didn't grill it, I did!" and she protested with rage.

She hit me, and then I hit her with the ember in my hand—just when my father was coming back!

Well, I cried then, and he asked me, "What happened?"

I didn't say anything. My stepmother, Mama, said to me, "Let go of her, let go of her. You don't have to hit her—I will do it myself! I will punish her!" Then she told me, "You are a man. You don't have to do women's work; they are the ones who cook. They have to take care of you, because as a man you don't know how to cook."

My stepmother was angry with Rosario and hit her very hard. My stepmother said, "Why are you blaming him? You are a woman, and you specifically must grill the nuts. He is the man, and he will take care of you."

Then there was an argument with my dad, because my stepmother was defending me, and my father was defending my sister. "It is worthy to be nice to orphans." He told me that I have to love them; my dad was saying, "You have a mother and father. Now, her mom lives, but her dad isn't here; that's why you shouldn't have done that." That's what my dad was saying.

Mama said to Rosario, "As a man, he'll defend you. And when you grow up, you'll say to people, 'He is my brother; his mother took care of me.'" She went on: "So why do you get angry with him since, when he grows up, he'll bring the food, he'll defend you, and he'll do small jobs for you?"

She was saying all these things, and my father went quiet. He didn't want more problems because he had killed a peccary that morning and had to prepare it.

Then my dad said, "It would have been better that nothing happened, and that nobody got punished, neither one nor the other. But you have already punished Rosario," he said to my mother, and then he turned to me, "yet I haven't punished you."

My stepmother was defending me because my own mother was not there. "You should hit him instead. Why does he have to fast? He has to eat meat—that is why you kill meat, to give to your sons. So now why does he have to fast? Why give him maikiúa and not her?"

"No, she is a woman. I won't do that because she is a woman," my father explained. "She must be taught to respect men, or when she grows up the girl won't be able to respect her husband, so I'll punish her with the whip."

I myself prefer the whip; the maikiúa is too much! I would prefer to be whipped rather than two days of fasting. I wanted to be eating the meat with my dad, so I was a little bit angry with Rosario because she was eating and I wasn't. And she had eaten my nuts!

Well, whatever—I was already fasting.

My father told me that I couldn't cook. "You are not for the kitchen. You must respect this little woman. If you don't, when you grow up you won't know how to respect your wife. That's why when you are young you must learn to give respect to your sisters and little sisters." Then he told me that I deserved a punishment; since I was brave enough to hit my little sister, "therefore you must be punished."

Then my father gave me the punishment of maikiúa for hitting my sister. I was afraid of the punishment, but my dad told me that I have to appreciate it because it would make me stronger. "You have to be like a *kakáram aishman*," he told me. "You have to be like a powerful, brave man." So they made me fast for two days since I was a little boy, and then at five o'clock in the afternoon they make me drink the *maikiúa*. And then I didn't know where I was, neither that day nor the next; it was like I was dead.

After the effects of the *maikiúa* passed, my dad got up at midnight. "Wake up, wake up," he said and started giving us counsel. He asked, "What do you think about your mother, who is the one that gives the orders? You are young. Who gives the orders, who? Your mother and your father, that's who. Look at your brother. You should feel sorry for him. You make a coward out of yourself when you hit a small boy. But when you have a child of your own, you shouldn't be ashamed to punish him. The mother has the right."

To me he said, "And when you have a son, what will you do? I hit you to make you feel, you see. If your older child hits your child, you'd better think well. If not, you'll have problems, you'll get angry at your son.

"I'm not angry at you. I'm punishing you in order to make a man out of you. That is all; and you won't misbehave again, or I'll give you more of this punishment again."

After that my sister asked forgiveness from my father and mother. She said, "I won't do this again to my brother, and I won't talk back again to my mother."

I was still angry, but I said, "I hit you because you hit me, but anyway forgive me." Then she had to get on her knees to ask forgiveness, and I said, "You are forgiven, but don't come back again."

But my father said, "Hug your little brother," and she grabbed me and said again, "Don't cry, I won't hit you, don't be afraid of me."

Since then we had peace—this is how it was, Nanki. After that I was like a saint. I wasn't angry again because I didn't want the punishment from my father again. And it was shameful that he punished my sister. Right now I have put all that behind me; right now my sister loves me, she loves me.

Taking

Once I wanted to steal something. I was nine or ten, and I liked the neighbor's dog (Juan Gutierrez was the man's name), and I played with him after I finished my duties. I thought, I don't have money to buy the dog, so I told my friends that I was going to steal it while the old man slept. So I was close to the dog, and my friend says, "Okay, okay, okay—no more! Let's just steal the dog, and if he wakes up we'll tell him we were playing, and we can give it back to him." It was wrong, though, and I was conscious that it was wrong. So we didn't take the dog.

Giving

One day, when I was nine or ten, I went fishing and caught several fishes. My stepmother didn't have anything to eat, but she didn't want to tell me that. But I gave the fishes to her, and she told me that I was very generous, not like the other kids that fished for themselves and never gave her some. I told her that the fishes were for her, and she cooked them for me.

She was very proud of me then. She said, "I really appreciate it, little boy. You went fishing with your neighbors, although they didn't invite you. But you still went and brought food for us. I don't know what we would have eaten without you! I wanted some meat to eat tonight, and now we'll have meat because you're brave. You won't be immature; you keep going on like this, and you'll be happy in your home." This is what I remember the most from my stepmother.

Once my brother-in-law Pedro Tunki was sick with what we call "a grave flu," with fever and all. His wife, my sister Teresa, was not at home, and he was very sick and needed me. They did not have any wood so I brought wood and made a fire; in order to ferment the chicha I tied the lid on the pot with rope so it wouldn't fall. It was raining, so I knew Teresa would be wet when she got back. When she returned she asked me if I had made that big fire.

I told her that there was a dried tree, and that I thought it was going to rain all night, and that she needed the fire for the chicha, and that she should give me some, too.

So she told me that I was like an old brother and that she was very happy.

When I started going out with my friends to drink she used to tell me not to do that, or to drink just a little bit so I wouldn't get drunk. She told me she loved me and she appreciated what I had done for her when her husband was sick. I also caught some fishes and gave her the biggest and took the others to my mother. She told me that I should act this way when I got married.

Freedom

But I didn't like everything about me back then. When I was a kid, around ten or eleven, I liked staying at my friend's house. When my mother called me, I didn't pay attention to her. There was a neighbor, my uncle Manuel Tankámash, and I went to his house to see what I could do, like cutting the trees down, or planting plantains, or whatever—but without my parents' permission. "Where is Baudillo? Go look for him, Teresa," my mother would say.

She was *always* looking for me, and she would ask why I didn't let her know where I was going. I told her, "There is nothing wrong with going there, and I don't have anything to do here."

"I'll find something for you to do," she said, "so you won't bother anyone there. Go help your brothers," she said.

When I was twelve I liked to play with a ball. I was late coming home, and my mother waited with the food. Finally she gave it to someone else! When I asked her where my food was, she said that I was late, and if I wanted food I had to cook.

Later, Maria always asked me if I was still a boy, because I was always playing with a ball. She said that I should have been thinking about working instead. She teased me until we got married!

She teased me like my parents never would. I knew that my parents treated me as if I were an only child, because they lost so many—I was lucky to be born, thanks to the help of my grandfather Tsakimp. So my mother and father did not make me suffer much; they gave me all the freedom and happiness I could want.

Almost all of my own kids are like this—except Esteban; he is the humblest, he is very calm and serene, ever since he was a little kid. He takes care of his things, like his clothing. When I was young, maybe being naked represented my personality! When I was five or six, I was always naked. I would drop my clothes, and I showed up like that when there were people around. When I went to the visiting room when my father was there with people, my father would ask me not to be there. Even when I was eight or ten years old, I did not care about my clothing. I was dirty and wet all the time; I tore my clothes; I climbed the trees; I tossed them wherever; I did not wash them.

But as I grew up I came to realize that soap is expensive. And I thought, "Now I have a wife, and she has to do all the work for me and her own duties. I better take care of my clothes now." If I tear my clothing I sew it myself, so it is easier for Maria; she doesn't have much to do for me. I have realized it myself, that is how it is, Nankichi.

7

Student and Worker

Like a Domesticated Parrot

My mother was really a fine person. She worked hard to take care of us. She worked making ceramics, those jugs—*pinínkias*—so she could buy us clothing and take care of us after Daddy had fled because of those problems over Tséremp's death. My brothers and sisters and I were separated: one stayed at the mission; one lived with the *teniente político* [political lieutenant](this was my older sister Imelda, the widow; she worked for the *teniente* and then married a *colono*). I lived with the family of Ricardo Rubio, there in front of the mission.

I was a small boy; I remember Mr. Monticone, Francisco Monticone, a Salesian acolyte from Italy, would take me for walks and carry me on his shoulders. So my mother left me at the Salesian mission to study. My dad told me, "You go there and study, because your brother and I are in hiding and cannot be with you. You've got to study and progress, so one day you can help us." I was around five years old when I boarded at the Salesian mission school.

We learned to read, to write, to count—math, as they say—and grammar, to be able to speak Spanish very well. The priests taught us to pray in the right way to the Virgin and to Jesus Christ and God. That's what they used to say, that God lives, that God is in Heaven, and you have to ask and be thankful and pray to the Virgin, the mother of Jesus. They taught us the rosary, to pray to the saints with the rosary, every day more rosaries, and every night we would go to the chapel. I don't know what to tell you about these lessons, since we were just learning there like a domesticated parrot. I don't know—I thought, "All they say is that I have to pray, so I will imitate them." That's all that I remember, Nanki.

Only an Image

The first time that I went to church was when I boarded at the Salesian school. I didn't have enough clothes; I had only a pair of pants. I also had an *awankim*, a kind of fabric that my father got from a niece that he had healed. So I wore an *itíp'*, a Shuar skirt. I also made a shirt from this *awankim*.

I remember that I went with Mr. Monticone. He took me to church, and that's how I saw the priest giving a service. Monticone told me that I had to go to church, or the devil was going to get me. I was convinced! I imitated the prayers, the rosary, I wanted to believe in all of it. I had seen some pictures inside the church and liked the priests and thought they were gods.

But when I started to become a man, I started to learn, and I knew that it was only an image. They were only teaching religion. I started to ask about the truth, the reality, of what images were, and they told me in Spanish that those images were of events that had happened centuries ago in Egypt and Judea, things that had happened to Jesus, Jesus Christ. God is in heaven and is all-powerful and protects us from danger and saves us from death. So this is what they preached, that the images weren't of gods but of people in heaven. I realized they were people just like us. That's what I learned in church the first time I went there.

Around 1962—let's say 1957 to 1959—those ideas came back to me. You had to believe that—there were all these priests. A priest took me to pray and to bless me. And in the Evangelical mission you had to close your eyes and talk to God, and this made me believe. But now I see that it did not turn out well. I said, "No, this is not my religion." There are Catholic and Evangelical Shuar, but it is not my religion, my mother religion.

When I was twenty or twenty-five years old, I talked to Teresa Suanúa, my mother, about Shuar religion. I asked my mother how we did before, and she said, "Our God is Entsa." She told me that many years ago our ancestors believed in Etsa, Nunkui, and arakmatin. I was curious that day. I had been studying the sacred Bible, its scientists and prophets. I mean the people that lived during Christ's time, and before Christ, like 14,000 centuries ago, there were people. So I asked her how the Catholics, the Salesians, can say that once there wasn't anything and then God made Eve and Adam? Where did they come from? So I asked my mother, and she said that people in the Sierra used to worship the Sun. She said they believed in the Sun and made gold from a yearling calf and adored it. All natives had their own beliefs, so I figured that religion was just an idea.

In Loco Parentis

I was fine during my first year at the Salesian mission school, but I always felt guilty because of my mother. Since my mother was living right there at Ricardo Rubio's mother's house, I always visited her on Saturdays. But the mission didn't like me to visit my mother. They said that I should always live within the mission, because that was their tradition. "The Salesian students must be confined, they cannot go out without permission, so they won't go hanging around with others or their mothers. They must live apart because it's better to study and learn catechisms and pray, because there with their moms they won't pray." That made me very uneasy and I didn't like it; that's why I had to leave the mission after one year.

I left the Salesian mission school because I fought with a kid. He started to hit me! But he was older, and since I wasn't able to hit him back, I took a ruler and hit his head. The kid got an infection, and scabs, and blood came out, and it scared me.

After that Mr. Monticone came and told me that I shouldn't have done that. He asked me why I was bothering the kid, and then he took me. I was afraid of all this, so I said to Mr. Monticone that I was going home with my mother and that I wasn't going to study again. I didn't want it and I didn't like it. So I left quietly.

Then my parents came to talk to them and told them that I didn't want to go to school anymore. Then I was by myself.

This Is What Your Life Will Be Like in the Future

But that very same year another *apache* professor called Gustavo Molina came to the Evangelical mission.[1] "We are not bad," they said to my mother, "We are not bad, we are Evangelicals, we are good, we will care for your little ones, so they may study," this *apache*, this Gustavo Molina, said.

So when I was about seven years old, I switched schools: "La Union #52"—it was an Evangelical mission school for both sexes; boys and girls studied together. Miguel Ficke, the North American, was the director, and Gustavo Molina was my teacher. They said, "We do not treat our interns like slaves, as the priests do." It's true, totally true! The interns at the Salesian mission couldn't leave without permission, never. Those Fathers were like the military! "You have to come here. If your father wants to take you away he needs to get permission. If the Father or the Mother [nun] didn't want it, the parents couldn't take their children home. But the Evangelicals weren't like this at all. We could leave whether our parents came or not. When Friday came around our classes ended, and they said, "If you want to go to your mother you can go! If you want to stay, stay here and rest, or study." And if we worked, they paid us. They paid the older children a *sucre*,[2] and the smaller children two *reales* or one *real*. "Well, this is what your life will be like in the future, boy."

Laughter and Tears

At this time I had just a little piece of material that we used for the itíp', the kilt—we were practically naked. Dr. Miguel Ficke, the missionary, called us on Saturday and gave a shirt and pants to each of us. He said he was happy with us because we were working hard. He gave us clothes in our own size.

There was one kid crying. Dr. Miguel came and told him not to cry, that he could save the clothes and wear them when he wanted. I was very proud every time I wore my pants. I was happy; it was the first time I wore manufactured clothing. I kept my itíp' so I could wear it when I wanted, but I didn't buy more material, and eventually, maybe when I was nine or ten, the itíp' became old and ripped.

There was this kid who didn't pay attention to the teacher, Gustavo. For example, when the teacher was explaining something at the board, the boy used to make faces, imitating him behind his back, and this boy teased the girls, sending them notes. That is what I saw, that my classmates didn't pay attention in class.

Sometimes the kids made fun of the missionaries by pretending to be pastors, too; we played like this. For example, one boy pretended he was Mr. Miguel and was pastor of the church. He took the papers to sing, as if they were a hymnal, or he pretended to read the Bible. He would say, "Close your eyes and bend down; we are going to ask God . . ." then he would say like Mr. Miguel, "Pray to God then, holy God that are in heaven, you are our holy kingdom, bless the world, you are the only one that has given us life, health and in this day protect us." But everyone laughed at him because this was a kid that didn't know how to sing. Since Mr. Miguel didn't laugh when he preached, the boy would ask us why we were laughing.

Privilege

When I was in ninth grade, when I was around nine, my classmates did not like my personality. I was assisting the Ficke family while they were away. They said, "We are going to Quito. You take care of the older workers here from the start of the day." I stayed at their place one week while they were in Quito (because their kids were coming for vacation). I stayed with some girls—Maria (now she's my wife, but she had been a classmate of mine) and Rosana, my cousin who was raised by Mrs. Ela (Miguel Ficke's wife) since she was a little girl; Tsunkínua was her Shuar name. So I was there as an assistant coordinator. Then, Dr. Miguel did not come back, just Mrs. Ela, and I was taking care of everything. My teacher, Gustavo Molina, looked in on the house at night. I was managing the workers, telling them what they were going to do after classes and all. Some of them would cut the wood, or cut the trees and break them.

Well, they didn't like my personality, and they started complaining. "Alejandro, are you a missionary whom we have to obey?" they asked. I told them that if they didn't want to work they didn't have to come back. I said, "Me neither." I didn't have to suffer with them!

Then I had to go with my brother Antonio (Antonio Tankámash who lives in Makuma, Patricia's brother) to bring the wood. We were using the car, and they said that I was having fun while they were working. I was directing them, and they were older, they said, and that it wasn't fair. So they didn't obey for a long time.

I told them that nothing was a secret for me and that I was going to tell Mr. Miguel when he got back. He told them: "You haven't done anything! You are devilish! And if you are Evangelical, you should follow what's said by a brother, whether he is older or younger. Alejandro was here to take care of these things, as was Rafael. But you haven't done anything, so I will punish you!" Well, the punishment was more duties like cleaning the back yard—he didn't hit them. But they didn't like me after this; they all said that I was a bad boy because I told Mr. Miguel on them, and they said that I wasn't their friend.

For my part, I didn't like the personality of Tsunkuman Kashíjint. He was my classmate in 1954, and he used to be quiet whenever he was hit, and quiet when we invited him to play or swim. I asked him why he was so quiet and dull, why he wasn't happy and quick. People used to hit him, and he just took it. When there was lunch with milk and bread, people took his, and he didn't say anything! I told him, "Okay, Jorge, your personality should be more aware and rapid with a strong way of thinking." I didn't like the personality my schoolmate Jorge had.

Death

In 1954 there was an epidemic, and I had measles. We all had it. There were many deaths in the Salesian mission and among the girls at the convent. It was probably due to some negligence; the kids drank the water, and the doctors were careless. The Ficke family had medicines, so nothing happened to us, none of my companions died, but my older brother Valentín caught it, and his wife, my sister-in-law, died, as well as my stepmother, Mama.

I was scared; I ran away from home. By that time we knew there was an epidemic. Mrs. Ela said that Etsinka had it because they had taken him to a clinic in Quito, and he got the disease there. The cook, my aunt, told me that I was going to be next, that I was going to die. So I packed my things and left the Evangelical mission to go home to San José on Thursday afternoon.

My parents asked me why I had come back, and I told them that I was scared of the measles.

"You left during the day! Never leave during the day, son. I see that you are already sick because measles is very contagious," my mother said. My father said, "Poor boy, you have caught it and are going to die." Then he said to me, "I am telling you, Teresa took you to the mission, and now you are contagious. If you had come back during the night just after having had a bath, you wouldn't have caught it."

Then I thought, "Damn, how stupid of me. I should have thought about it. I could have left at night with a friend, so the measles wouldn't see me." I asked my father what I could do so the measles wouldn't find me, but after two days I had a fever. We were sick, my friend Shimpiu (he is the son of my aunt Tsapik', the one who died in Yaap', my father's sister) and I. I had a fever for six days; blood came out from my nose; and I had a cough that burned my throat. Then I had an infection in my mouth, on my lips, and there were red spots. And what a thirst I had!

My mother gave me remedies; *ajija* [ginger] is good for measles, and a good, very smooth *chicha*. I chewed on the *ajija* leaf so the measles wouldn't stay in my body. I cried while I ate it. But the fever was gone, and I wanted some food. My father was gone, but he had dried a fish; I ate it, and I was okay. My body had broken out and peeled all over—measles are like that, everything is peeled and burned because of the fever. But my mother healed me with *ajija* drink. Then I went back to the mission, and they told me many families had died, that the measles killed many people.

I Would Give My Life

I left the Evangelical mission school when I was nine or ten years old and went to work for Dr. Ferguson. My mother met him during the measles epidemic. He was a North American who had a laboratory in front of the mission. He was working on a project with medicinal plants like *cascarilla* and *ayahuasca*. He also made films about the Shuar, with people from France and Switzerland. He had a lot of money! So I left school to work with him.

Once, when I worked for Dr. Ferguson, I saw the surgical operation on a man from Huambi, and it made a big impression on me. The Fergusons told me to look and not to be afraid, because when I go to the United States they would let me study medicine. I thought, "I would give my life, my soul, my heart, my blood, for this man to live"; this was what I felt when I saw that man.

I was at the clinic, and they brought in that man, and his relatives were begging for him to be saved, and that impressed me. He was all swollen, and part of him was burned. When I washed him and changed his clothes to put him to bed, I saw that he was just swollen up, as if with tumors. I thought, "Is he going to die or live?" I had that feeling. And when they were operating on him they gave him an anesthetic so he would be sleeping for hours, until they finished the operation on his groin and his leg. Then they closed him. And this was the first time I saw that.

One day a North American friend of Dr. Ferguson's, Roberto, came to make a film about the Shuar world. I was very happy because he brought gifts. We organized a *tsantsa* party, because the doctor had bought many *tsantsas* and wanted to see how they were made, so we pretended to make a *tsantsa* so the North Americans and French could film it. I said to Roberto, "Listen Mr. Roberto, what can you tell me about the United States? You are recording the film, but how does it work? How do you get the soul of a person?" I was trying to find out about film.

He said it was like a diamond, a special instrument that takes the shadow of the body and turns it into a film.

"Very interesting," I said. "This is the first time I have seen this instrument. We, too, would like to make films, but we don't know how. I thought someone was inside the camera!"

But Roberto laughed. He said, "No, Alejandro, there is no one inside. It is the shadow that goes through; this light enters, and the shadow stays there.

"Ah," I said, "And what else can you do with that camera?"

"It films landscapes and movements, and records everything, even the conversations of the Shuar," he said.

And I said that it was good, that he would leave with something of this country, including books, histories, all about Ecuador. It was good for me because I was curious how they did that. He said they were going to take it to the United States, where he would develop it, prepare it and a lot of things, and after that he would see if they could make more films. This was my first meeting with this North American.

I talked to a Frenchman, too. They had good guns and had brought many. And I said I wanted to shoot; I said that we could practice with those vultures.

But he said it was prohibited to shoot animals that were not attacking. Then I said, "No, here you just shoot at them, so let's go!"

So the French killed the king of the vultures, we call it *yápu*, that white one. What an aim he had! He killed it from far away, with a 30-caliber rifle. I retrieved it, and the Frenchman was excited. I said that we needed to put it in an antiseptic solution so it wouldn't spoil, and then in Quito we would embalm it and fix it up nicely with wire.

Then we talked about how nice it was that when the Ferguson family was tired of the city they could come here, and how they appreciated that we were working for them. That was what the Frenchman said. It was nice, and I was happy because we would talk at night with the girls, and they played ball with us.

My Best Friend

José Chau was my best friend when I was a child, around the age of ten or eleven years. We met at the laboratory of Dr. Ferguson. It was about November 1957, and we got to know each other because we both worked in the laboratory. He is older—I think he was around sixteen or seventeen by then, and I was eleven or twelve. But I knew a lot, so he was generous with me. We were working, and he said he was going to help me. We met on a Sunday, and we took our money to go to the grocery shop. I said, "When I need money for cloth, you help me, and I will help you. We will be friends from now on." He was my first friend. The friendship broke up in the year 1963.

My father had a friend, Achayat', who was his first friend, and I had a friend too, this José. Achayat' was my father's friend, and I learned about friendship from my father. I told my father that I had a friend. He asked me who he was, and I said he is José Chau—he is a relative of ours (his father is our "uncle," a saich [affine; one who is or can be related through marriage]; but they are a different family: they are Pinchupa, we are Tsakimp), and he is my friend. So I was telling my father I had a friend, and he asked me what I had given him. I told him I gave him shoes and a shirt, and he gave me a belt and once in a while he brought meat and also helped me with the food. José worried about me, and we were very loyal. I always loaned him money for his necessities, and he did the same when I didn't have any money. He gave me advice on how to behave, how to work or to live. He used to say that we would remember our friendship when we got married. Indeed, we were friends even when I got married and had kids, when I was around sixteen or seventeen. We still shared drinks and food. But everything changed during 1962 to 1963 when I studied shamanism.

One day in 1957 he took me fishing in Asunción. He said, "Friend, let's go fishing, because a family from Asunción has invited me." We went fishing, and they gave us food, because it was Asunción's holiday, the 15th of August. I felt so happy because it was the first day I was going to drink and eat with my friend. I would drink chicha and dance with the girls who were coming. He said, "My tsaniri [girlfriend] is coming."

So I went fishing with José in Asunción; we helped uncle Kukush to dry the fish. José and I put a washim [wooden grill] on the fire, and we ate the skin. We were very happy; we caught fishes, and Mrs. Ana Luisa cooked for us. Later there was a party, and José Chau danced with his girlfriend. I told him how happy I was because he was with someone that loved him, and I wished him to be happy forever with her. That day I was happy because as he was eating, he gave me food, too.

When we got to his brother-in-law's house, he bought a chicken. He gave me half of it, and I thought it was nice that he cared about me. I mean it is nice that he was worried about me because my parents were away; his mother brought meat, and he always saved some for me. Besides eating we were happy doing sports. We ran, and the boys of the mission, our Evangelical friends, joined us.

When we were friends, he told me how we could help each other when we were fathers. He told me who was going to get married first, either him or me, because he had a girlfriend by that time. It was, in fact, he who got married first. He told me he could get married to that woman because he loved her. She was from Saip, and he was in love because she was in the mission. He said he was going to see his girlfriend and would marry her because her mother had agreed. He also said that the girl loved him, and that's how it should be to get married. He said that he could support the woman because he was older than I was and that I could not marry yet because of my age.

But sometime around 1955 or 1956 his girlfriend betrayed him and married somebody else (but then she herself was abandoned). He had to forget about her and get engaged to another girl. He said it was a sad thing that life had given him. He was sad, but even so, he said he would hold on and carry the pain.

But he wanted me to know a girl that was still unmarried. I told him I did not know about life and women. He said that I should not shy away from women. I still did not know because of my mundane life, but he invited me to go out that night. That day we went to see the movie at the Salesian mission (it was about one of those wars between the United States and Germany), and he introduced his girlfriend to me. I was very excited. This was around 1957. He also introduced me to another girl, a relative. She talked, but I did not answer much. She asked me if I wanted to go to school at the mission, to be interned there—because she was an intern. I told her I wasn't used to it and that the work that they did was too hard and that I had an easier job, more comfortable.

José asked me if I had had a woman—not a sister or a mother. He was already mature—he knew about sexual unions, but I knew nothing, nothing of love and sexual relations. He used to say that we could play with the women at the mission, but I was scared because my father and my mother told me not to get involved with a woman. They said that when I did that I would be bringing myself close to death, because women take out your penis and use you, and it is not worth it. They told me I was not old enough, and my bonds were not strong yet; I had to take *maikiúa* before I could do that.

So every time José talked about his girlfriends he said that I was still happy and that I did not have the pain he had. He asked me how I was feeling, and I told him that I was okay, that I did not have to deal with fights. The girls always teased me, but I didn't pay any attention. When my friends brought their friends, I always said good-bye, and they told me not to be a coward, not to act like women, but to talk. I said, "Some other day, because my parents would punish me, a strong punishment," because, as we say, I was just a snot-nosed kid, and I wasn't supposed to be with women. My father would punish us if we talked to the daughter of some man, because her father would talk to my father and then he'd be mad.

José and I were never jealous of each other, because we shared everything that happened to us. He told me about his girlfriends, and when I told him that I had not paid attention to a girl, he said, "Okay, I'm not going to force you to do anything, just like you don't force me." We never had an argument. When there were arguments among the workers in the lab, we supported each other.

One time some people fought with José. We had bet on a volleyball game, and we won (this was the 24th of May in 1957). We went to this game, and they said, "We won." But we said, "You won because you were playing dirty, lying, and cheating, and if you hadn't, we would've won." That is when somebody threw a punch, and we began to fight. Ferguson came and said, "What happened?" and separated us. But I defended José and said, "Fine, here I am—punch me!"

Another time, when I was working for the Ferguson family, I told Miguel Pilico, a *colono*, to go with the cattle. I was his boss, so I told him to clean the stable, move the cattle, cut the grass, and all that. He said, "Cunt, you don't order me around—you are a kid!"

I told him that he was paid to work, and we started to fight. José Chau backed me up, yelling, "Get him, get him, don't let him get you!" But the *colono* was an old man, and I had to respect him. But when we fought, it was fantastic. First he hit me, and I was afraid, but then I started fighting, and I liked it and wanted more! I was mad! I was fifteen, yes fifteen, because in 1959 I was already sixteen; that is when I fought. After a while, José grabbed me and told me to let the old man go.

José helped me when I was told to do something like milking the cows, moving the cattle, taking care of the birds and billy goats. He told me that he was there for me; we went shopping for the other boys together. Those were happy days. This lasted until he became an intern at the mission school. Then when we saw each other, we greeted one another with "Hi, how are you?" but that was all.

A Day of Tears

We would have been very happy if we hadn't had arguments with the Ministry delegates. Unfortunately, the delegates accused the Ferguson family of having come to spy on Ecuador for Peru. The saddest day was when the problems with the Ferguson family began, and the police and the military came. The laboratory was well equipped, and we had radios. That's why the people from the government said that Dr. Ferguson was in contact with the Peruvians and that this North American was going to betray our country. That was the rumor in the armed forces. So a captain came from Quito to see where we had the radios. Well, they treated him with a lot of respect; they just came to investigate where the radio was. And then the priest, the Salesian, Father Loba, came to speak in his favor. There were some *colonos* that were against them, because they also helped the Shuar, but most of the *colonos* were also in his favor because he had a clinic here with medicine and performed surgeries. They were well known, so almost all the *colonos* helped the family.

Well, they did not find anything—it was just a rumor. He only had a radio in case he had to call a plane in an emergency. Dr. Ferguson talked to them, and they gave it to the police to guard. I asked him, "What are they doing? Why are they bothering you?" I felt sorry for him. "Are they going to kill you?"

"No, nothing is happening. They're really just investigating those machines. But we are not betraying anyone; we are helping people, looking for medicinal plants. We are not betraying Ecuador," Dr. Ferguson said. "Son, it is almost over. Tomorrow I am going to Quito to talk to the government. And this is the last year of our project, because the contract with Life is almost over, and then we are leaving," he said.

Those were my saddest days.

The Fergusons told me that I could stay at the laboratory because I'd done a good job there, but that they didn't have more money. "Maybe one day we'll be able to come back to visit you. Jean [son of the Fergusons] has to come back, because he is like a father to you."

So I said, "All right, thank you, Doctor, but I want you to leave me some of your pamphlets, so I can continue studying. Because I like medicine, and natural medicine, so leave me these pamphlets so I can orient myself." That day of our good-byes we agreed that one day I would have the good fortune to be friends with fellow North Americans and people from countries in Europe. Up until the day they left we worked together: "What is this bark?" and "What is that bark?" We said that although it would take a long time, they would come back to visit and would buy more medicines, like *natém*.

I was upset one day when I didn't have enough money, and I was tired of working. I was twelve or thirteen, and I was sad when the Ferguson family left. I was sad and said to myself, "Gosh, I wish I could leave too," but I couldn't.

So I was asking people for money, practically begging. I thought it was a horrible day, it was a day of tears. I thought I wasn't going to have another happy day working with them again in my life.

Happiness

When I was young I never believed in happiness for my life; I thought I wasn't ever going to have a woman. After I worked for the Ferguson family, I worked with a *colono*, an *apache*; I went to work for Pepe Narvaiz. I worked as a carpenter. But sometimes when payday arrived, Pepe didn't pay. Pepe and I had problems because he didn't have the money. He kept saying he'd pay me next week. I talked with my father and my mother about it. "I don't like those people. They're not like North Americans; I'd better go and find another job."

And he used to mistreat his family; when he was drunk he hit his wife, Mrs. Lupe, and I told him not to do that. It was hard for me—I had not seen that before in the Ferguson family. So I was thinking, when I got older, when I became a father, I would probably be like that, I wouldn't be happy with a woman.

I left Pepe in 1957 or 1958, when I met the Jorge Lopez family. One day I was coming down to Huambi, and there was a girl coming toward me. She was Judith, the daughter of Jorge Lopez, and she asked me if I wanted to work for them. She asked me what I could do, and I told her that I could do farming and could work with a machete.

She told me that her father could teach me how to work with a woodcutter.

I told her that I was ready, but I had to get my mother.

She said that it was okay, that they were going to take care of me.

I told her that I was sad because the Ferguson family had left, and they were like family to me.

She was sorry for me and wanted to talk to her dad. She told me that her father was looking for a worker. "You can work for us," she said. Then I was thinking since I liked to serenade people, I would sing to her to get her to talk to me some more.

We went to her house in Huambinimi where her father was. He said, "Boy, we're going to work just fine here. What's your name?"

I told him my name was Alejandro, and he asked me if I wanted to live with them. They were Evangelical, and he said they weren't drinkers. She said, "My father works on projects to make sugar mills, so you can also work on a machine."

He told me that his children were going to teach me how to use the woodcutter, and I told him I already knew how to do it. Well, I liked to mill wood on a machine, so he installed a woodworking machine. I worked for them for three years, and it was another life. No one bothered me. They were good people; they didn't drink. I spent all my time there, until I married and returned to work in my own fields. Little by little I was feeling better. When I got married I saw the happiness that was there, and everything was okay.

8

Husband and Father

Temptations

When I was fifteen I met this girl Isabel—I still have a picture of her—and she was smiling at me all the time. I thought, "I am going to play with her when she is milking the cows. But I won't just play, I am going to ask her to have something with me, to let me do something to her." Then I got there . . . and thought that I better not do anything. So I helped her with the milking of the cows, and went back with a better conscience, because I did not give in to temptation.

But when I was sixteen, at Christmas of 1958 or 1959, my cousin Juan Pinínkias Chiríap told me that girls from other places were coming for the holiday, and we had to be there. "Ñañito [brother], come on, let's go, you are good-looking and strong—you are a real lover boy! I am ugly and dark, but I have my dates—so let's participate there," he said.

It was a good temptation, but I thought, what if their families get mad and hit us? So the next day I told him, "I am a man, too, but I will never, never give in to these temptations."

But one day we went out. "Let's go, let's go," he said. "Don't be a chicken! You have to be a man; you are going to get to know a woman."

And I knew that I would get to know a woman, and precisely for this reason I didn't want to succumb to temptation. All right, every time I was thinking, "What's going on with me?"

Anyway, one day we were out walking and ran into this girl. So he said, "Look, since you are younger, and I am corrupting you, you have the first chance: you have sex with her first."

So I did it. We began to fuck. She brought us to her house. She was with her little brother who was asleep, and Juanito took him so he wouldn't bother us. So she said, "Let's go, so they won't bother you here. The *colonos* are going to bother you, so let's go down to the FAE" [armed forces base]. So we took her there and did our pleasure.

Then Juan told me he was not going to have sexual relations with her because he tempted me; she was for me, and he was feeling guilty because he made me do that in my youth. The sunrise came, and I took her to her house. She was a Shuar from Arapicos. Her name was Nusuínkiur and she was the daughter of Pítiur.

When I meet her now, nothing happens. She says "Hi," but she has told me that I am a bad man because I cheated on her and I hurt her when she was young. She told me this around a year ago, because we met at a saloon at Christmas time. "You are ungrateful! Now you live well," she said, "with all those women you live with. But you cheated on me! You went to Taisha and got married!" I told her that it was not my fault and that if she were single now I would marry her, too—and that's where we ended the conversation.

The first woman I flirted with was Elena; she was the daughter of Don Antonio Nekta, and Maria's classificatory sister. We used to flirt, but at first we did not have sexual relations. We played and slept together but just fooling around. It was December 25, and they invited me over for Christmas. José had already left by December; I went alone, and the girl flirted with me.

She said that I was good-looking, very pretty, that if I were a man, why was I afraid . . .

I said that I didn't know these relations, and we could be caught and punished. The punishment scared me—what if her parents found us and threw me out of my job?

She said that nothing wrong could happen because she knew. Then she told me to go to bed just for playing, that nothing was going to happen to me.

I said, "I do not like those things, sexual relations." Sometimes she teased me, and it made me a little bit angry. (But I changed my way of thinking when I met this *colona* from Macas!)

But Elena Nekta and I had a falling out. I loved her, and her parents agreed that we could get married while the Ferguson family was still here, so they could celebrate for us. But there was a problem; she was giving her love to another man.

We Are All the Same

Then I betrayed a woman. I had a daughter with a *colona*, and I felt very bad. This happened the very year I married Maria. Before I married her,

I had a girlfriend who was a *colona*. Judith, my first girlfriend, lived in Macas. When I was working with her father, he loved me very much and treated me like my father treated me. He saw the way I behaved and told me that I was more obedient than his own sons. This was Jorge Lopez. So he said to me, "All right, I have decided that if you want to, you can marry my daughter Judith. It doesn't matter that you have relations with my daughter, for we are all the same."

Well, I was a bit scared to tell him that we had in fact been discussing our marriage. Now we could marry. But I was very apprehensive. In the meantime, unknown to the family, the girl got pregnant (she missed her period) by me. Well, she had to go to Limoncocha [a town in the northern Amazon] to work on a mission, in order to escape her father, so he wouldn't know what I had done to her. (She gave birth and is now married to a *colono*. I think they live in Tena. Her husband's name . . . I don't remember . . . it's too hard to remember.)

Either Way . . . Your Mother Will Die!

So I went back to Utunkus, where I had a really fat pig to care for. And I talked these matters over with Antonio Nekta, Pedro Tunki, and my sister, Teresa. They wanted me to abandon Judith.

"You say you are going to marry a *colona*, that you are engaged?"

I said, "I don't want to have to lie about it. . . ."

So Antonio Nekta said to me, "You are young. You don't have to do this. It would be better if you married my niece, or one of my daughters, but anyway a Shuar." Antonio Nekta was Maria's uncle. She was orphaned as a small girl, so he was looking after her.

So I said, "Why?"

And he said that if I married an *apache*, they would come to live on my land.

"I know this," I said.

"Well, you're mistaken. You'll see. If they don't take our land, you'll leave and go away. Either way it will create problems with your family, and your mother will die."[1]

Well, as I had a lot of compassion for my mother and my father, I said, "In that case, what can they do to me? But I'm not going to love your daughter, or anybody. I am not interested in this." I still thought

I couldn't marry his daughter because I was engaged, that Judith and I would get married when I turned twenty.

"No," he said, "I married when I was a lad, and my niece Maria Kintanúa is older than you[2] and is already experienced, and she can make a good life for you. I can assure you of that. Don't go over to marry a *colona*."

In response I said, "She is pregnant and is in danger. I—what can I do?"

"Nothing, just let her go. Your mother will die if you go far away. It isn't right to abandon your people." He said this because Judith and I were thinking of going to Tena[3] together.

Pedro Tunki, my brother-in-law, married to my sister Teresa, and the brother of Antonio, talked to me about these things, too, and left me thinking.

Then I was going to go down to Sucúa with the pig, so Mrs. Carmelina would take it to Puyo[4] to sell the lard for a good price. I stopped off at the house of Antonio Nekta, and Maria was there. But I was always bashful around women and girls. Well, Antonio said to me that if I married her and obeyed him, he would give us cattle and land.

So I said, "I don't have to marry out of self-interest! I have to marry for love. Because if I marry for self-interest, and she marries for self-interest, the marriage will come to a bad end."

But I came to understand that I could marry, and that if I loved her and she didn't love me, I could pursue her until she would want to marry me.

So this is what happened. Out of compassion for my parents, and because we hadn't reached an agreement with the father of the *colona*, and the girl had already found work in Tena, in Limoncocha, and was happy, I said: "All right, I accept. I'll talk to Maria, and we'll see what she says."

A Jaguar's Roar

So we went to Antonio Nekta's property in Wakán and spent about a week there, and something sad happened. One day I was in the hammock that my patrons, the Fergusons, had given me,[5] and Antonio Nekta said, "I saw a circle in the sun. This means that Aunt Teresa Suanúa is going to die . . . she will die because this is a bad sign, like a rainbow encircling the moon." So it made me feel very sad.

So I said, "Well, I am going to leave."

"No, you stay, and I'll go, and then I'll come back. You stay here to help clear that garden until I come back."

I had been working for him as a way to conquer Maria, as a way to befriend her. So Maria's aunt Chinkiásu was supporting me, and she said to Maria, "Get married! You are an orphan. If I were young I would marry him, because this guy is good, he is calm, he could make a good life for you. Because if you marry a bad guy, he is going to do bad things to you. But I will give you good luck; this is a good man, a good guy; he will serve you well."

But Maria didn't want to come near me; she didn't want to know anything about me. And one day when we went fishing, I said, "Take my shirt, my clothes," and she didn't want to even touch my shirt. She was very mistrusting. She said, "I don't like to have men's clothing. Elena," she said to her [classificatory] sister, "you like this stuff, you take it. If you want to marry, you can marry Alejandro. I don't want to marry; I don't want to be married."

Well, one day, a jaguar's roar brought us close together. A jaguar came very close to the house and screamed, and it was tremendous. Maria was terrified—even now Maria is very scared of jaguars. I was lying in my hammock and Maria was sitting on her bed, and she said, "Alejandro, come here. Come, because we are going to be together. If we die, if we are finished off, we will die together. Come here quickly, come!"

So I lay down very close to her, and I said, "Look, I'll protect you," and she embraced me, she grabbed my back and trembled in fear.

And the next day we talked. I said, "Truly, your uncle has to decide whether or not we marry, Maria. But we are buddies, we have known each other since we were kids. You are older than I am, but it doesn't matter to me. We can make a life together. I cannot offer you marvels, but we can make a slightly better life."

So we returned to the house in Huambinimi, and we talked, and she accepted my proposal. She said, "All right, we can get married. But what will your father say? You have to go and ask him."

So I went to my father to ask if he would accept my marriage to this woman, Maria. But my father didn't know her; he had met only her older sister Mercedes. So he said to me, "You are just a kid; why do you want to marry this widow, this older widow?"

I said, "No, Dad, I want to marry the younger sister, the one who was brought up in the Evangelical mission by Miguel Ficke."

"Ah!" my dad said, "But I want to see her." So Dad went and spoke with Antonio Nekta, and they said, "Right, we accept."

So we got married in a civil ceremony in 1959, on August 2. We went to our house, we went to our property, and began working.

A Little House

When Maria and I first got married, we had a little house. When the kids were older we moved to a bigger house with more gardens that I built to make my wives happier.

After I got married, for three years I had the custom of playing the guitar and serenading at other houses. But people complained to the síndico, saying that I was disturbing their sleep, because I did this at night; I started around 8 or 9 P.M. and I serenaded here and there, singing and asking for an invitation to come in—I went to the girls' houses serenading, and people did not like it. They thought that if I was married and I was doing that, there could be a problem. So I said that I was not going to do it anymore because otherwise people would avoid me.

I remember when my little woman, Maria, was very happy with me. We had been married for a good seven or eight months. I bought a mare for our trips. She said that it was a good deal, because it was going to carry all the weight while we walked and because I had not spent the money on other things. She was happy, she kissed me and hugged me, and she said she loved me. Maria was twenty-five years old, and it was for her birthday. I told her that it was because she helped me, so she said she was very thankful and that I was like a second father for her.

What Am I Going to Do?

I also remember how happy I was when we had our first son. I told Maria that she had given me a nice surprise because we wanted a boy. I told her that I loved her because she was going to raise my son, but she had to love him, too. She said, "Okay, but kiss me," so I did when she was in bed with the baby. I always came home and hugged her, and she used to tell me that she would clean or cook for me. She was also very proud, and I was, too.

Well, I remember when Maria missed her menstrual period (*nantu wanawi*, that's what we call the period; it means "when we see the moon"), and the next one, too. So she asked me what had happened to her, and I told her that she was pregnant because she did not have the period.

My parents explained all this to me when I was twelve or thirteen years old. Okay, Nanki, this is what my father told me about home. He told me that I should not think of getting married at that time because I was still too young. I told my father that I liked a girl, and he asked me if I had done something yet.

I told him, "No, but I like the girl."

He told me that I did not know about this, but if I was with the girl and she missed her period and got pregnant, that her parents could blame me for that. He said that I should not get involved with girls who are menstruating.

I asked him what it was and where it came from.

He told me that it was because they were ready for that stuff.

So I asked him how one could be careful about it? I asked him if he had helped my mother when she had me?

He told me that I could know it because I was old enough, but when one is still young it is prohibited. When you are young you think about candies, but because I was a man he was going to tell me everything. When my mother was pregnant he gave her fruits and she had moles, so she would have a bad birth. He said that he knew about it because he was already married, so I was sad and thought about how life was when one has a woman.

He told me that when they are pregnant the pains come more and more frequently as the baby comes down, but it is because they are having the baby. You should leave them alone, and when the baby is coming down you push—but not hard—and you take your arm and hit the stomach.

I asked him if you should clean her, and he said that you still need to cut the umbilical cord. Then you take a leaf—he was going to show me which one—and you burn it and put it in the baby's belly button so the blood stops and he does not get an infection. Then you need to have your wife's bed next to the fire for her hips to get warm, and you should not get near her within thirty days because you might hurt her. She can have a hemorrhage if you are fooling around with her; she might die, and then you are in trouble with her family. "That is why you should be careful when you get married, I am warning you," he told me.

I wanted to know what the mothers felt when they were pregnant. I was sixteen and told my mother that Maria was moody and did not want to eat.

Then she said that Maria was pregnant, because that was how pregnancy was. That pregnant women do not eat or drink; they just want candies or little cravings, like fruits, but not meat because they have nausea.

I was a little bit timid to talk to my parents about these things, because I was afraid they wouldn't tell me. But I have always been very talkative and say what I want.

When Maria gave birth to Lorenzo, I was wondering if she was in pain because of all the screaming. She stood up and cried, and I was thinking, "Golly, why did I get married? What if Maria dies, what am I going to do?"

I asked her what I was going to do without her. It was going to be difficult to find somebody else.

She told me not to talk about that.

My mother and I made her give birth on the floor. It was at night, very early on Saturday, July 31st. Maria had been rolling around in pain for four days, because it was the first child, and it is always like that. Maria asked my father to help her (we have a tradition to give a pregnant woman a warm egg, to make her stronger).

My mother told me that these were the consequences of getting married, and this is why you should not get married when you are young. She told me to hold Maria's arm. So I was sitting next to her, and my mother wished her luck, and Maria screamed "Ayauuu . . . !"

My mother wished her luck so she wouldn't die. She said she was not going to die and that she was in so much pain because it was a boy. I was wondering what he looked like.

Since then Maria has helped other women, but we have not talked about it. I was not curious and didn't want to bring it up because she would think about the pain.

My mother told me that Maria would be in pain, but then she would eat and be well and was not going to die. My father had concentrated and said that another *uwíshin* was coming—Mánkash, Luis Mánkash, from Corazon de Jesus, from Kumpas—and he too said that he was sure Maria was not going to die. My father brought him so he could help my father to concentrate better. My father, until his death, was concerned about Maria.

She finally gave birth around two or three in the morning; Maria said she was fine, but her body was exhausted. Her strength won me over! I thought "Gosh—what's going to happen?" but she gave me my first son, and I was proud of her. I kissed and hugged her. We killed a chicken, and I cooked it and gave her some.

What Did You Do?

I loved Maria when she gave me money to buy medicine for my mother. She told me she had 5,000 *sucres* that she was giving to me. She had earned it selling birds and picking fiber (from the palm tree, for making brooms). Some of the women have this business: they buy chicks and raise them, or they get shares. That is, if you have many chickens that are going to last longer and have chicks of their own, then you share the costs and divide the chickens later. One person gets the hens, and the other gets the chickens. Well, she gave me the money when my mother had pneumonia. I loved her for that because she gave me her money.

My mother, Teresa, punished me when I said something bad to Maria. I was already old—I had three children, I was about twenty-five years old—but she punished me with a stick.

I was a little bit drunk one night when our son Gustavo fell on the floor. Maria hadn't meant to drop him on the floor, but rather on the bed. Well, I was angry. So I started yelling at her. She cries very easily—she was a coward for that—so she was crying. So I grabbed her by her hair, and I asked her why she didn't take care of the baby. "He fell? I will do the same to you!" Then after that she cried and screamed. Then she went to spend the night at Carmelina Antúnish's.

The next day my mother arrived, "What did you do?" she said.

"Nothing." I said, "Mommy, I didn't do nothing!"

"What did you do? Why was she crying last night?" she asked. And she had in her hand a stick of *guayaba*.

Then Carmelina arrived there, the wife of Antúnish. She lives next door to us and had heard everything, and she told my mom. Well, then my mom took me out by beating me with the stick.

I didn't say anything, I just bowed my head and told her that "I deserve it," thinking that she wasn't going to hit me, because she was never angry with me. But that day she was perhaps pretty angry; she wanted to protect Maria. She gave me about ten blows before the *guayaba* branch broke.

And after that I did nothing. The next day she made me fast, and then she took me up to the hill, to her little house, and then she made me take maikiúa, the maikiúa of arútam. Then she threw me outside, in a camp. If you are a man that has hit a woman, then you sleep by yourself, that's the punishment.

Thoughtful

The story of my marriage to Josefina is pretty complicated, but it was my lucky pleasure to take as my wife this woman from such a far-off place, from the forest, a three-day journey. She was having many problems, grave problems. She was accused of things by various enemies, relatives of her late husband. So I promised that I wouldn't leave her, and she too said that she wouldn't leave me.

I had some doubts when I thought of getting married to Josefina—I thought it was impossible, but I just asked her. Before we got married, I was thinking, "Why do I have to marry her, to have kids, to have to work to support my family and raise my kids?"

But things worked out well with this woman; she is very happy. And she is a powerful woman, in the sense of her work and her obedience. She is very understanding and respectful of the home and her husband, and more thoughtful than Maria.

Thoughtful? I mean, she thinks about me. She listens when I speak, when I say "All right, Josefina, you have to do this, and you have to look after that, and you have to work and take care of our children," and she replies, "All right, very well, I have to do this. Unfortunately, I don't have the ability—but in any event I will do it, my husband."

By way of comparison, Maria says, "All right, don't you tell me what to do, because I know. I am an old woman, and you don't have to give me any advice." So you see, she isn't as thoughtful as Josefina.

Josefina is everything! If we are out of something, if I say, "Maria, you haven't made *chicha* or something to eat," she says, "No, I haven't." But Josefina never does that; she pays attention to me. She is one good wife, and I am very pleased to have this woman.

But I suffered long and hard, struggling for her. Maria didn't like it when I married her—this was in 1973 (or was it 1972? I think it was fourteen or fifteen years ago). And then Josefina was summoned to court! They wanted to take away her children and her cattle! She was a widow, and the brothers and classificatory brothers of her late husband wanted to marry her. But she didn't want to marry any of them. So I helped her at court, I helped her with all the paperwork. And then we got married. I wanted to be with her, but she lived far away, in Waríns, so my father said to bring her here.

In 1976, when I was president of the Association of Sucúa, I had a permit to visit Josefina in Waríns for thirty days. She told me that because I was there I needed to hunt an animal for her family. Well, I am not good at hunting peccary. I had never hunted for peccary before, but I went hunting just to make her happy. My brother told me that there were some peccary around—I was wondering how he knew they were there—and I finally killed one, and she was very happy.

Josefina made me happy when she had her first son, Etsa. So I also named him Baudillo, and I was happy with my little son.

What Would You Think?

I met my third wife Marta in 1980 or 1981 (because our daughter Reina, Tsunkínua, is seven or eight years old). Pedro Kayáp brought me to Najempaim to treat his wife. Well, when people learned that a shaman had arrived, other sick people came to see me.

Marta was sick, and I treated her and her stepfather and mother as well. Well, she got better after a long course of treatment, about two or three months, and then she was in totally good health, much better. This was after much suffering; she suffered for years—since she was eight years old she was sick. She had been harmed by a *pasuk*, but I got rid of all her sicknesses with medication and shamanic concentrations.

Then, thankfully, she grabbed my attention and talked to me. "What would you think," she said, "when I am in love with you? And how can you protect your wives? Someone could do evil to you. Are you afraid?"

I said, "Nothing, I can't tell you anything. I need to think about this; I don't go into anything blindly. What kind of woman are you? What are you like? Are you already engaged?" I won't have a woman who is engaged, because you know that for our race, a woman engaged to another creates problems. Our custom is to have a woman who is not engaged, in order to live well and have a better life in the home. "So if you aren't engaged, well, maybe, but we have to think about it. What if your family, if your stepfather, doesn't accept this?"

But we continued talking, each time that I went to treat her. Finally she said, "All right, this is embarrassing."

But, well, I was in love with her, too, because she was a girl with a very humble, very happy, very open character. So I said, "All right, let's see what kind of luck I have with her."

So I went to her once, twice, three times, and then I said, "All right, I am not going to see her again because I can get in trouble and have to marry her." So I didn't go back; I stayed with Pedro Kayáp.

But then she called for me, "Come visit me, come tend to me because I have an unknown sickness. Maybe someone has made me cold or has poisoned me!"

Her in-laws came, her sister, her niece, and they said, "Uncle Alejandro, you know that you are interested! Your friend is sick. She just came back from Chankaza, near Logroño, and isn't well. Maybe someone poisoned her. She wants you to check her out, to go see her."

Well, that day was my downfall! I could no longer deny her. I went to her, and she didn't let me leave. We stayed together, and she said, "You know what? I love you. And I got better because of you. So let us live as we want to. I can give something to your life."

So I said, "All right," because there is nothing else a man can say. "All right, but don't abandon me when there's some problem in my home, with my other wives. Don't you run away. I know how to protect myself against all the legal consequences, and I know how to master my wives, not in bad ways but in good ways."

Well, that day she didn't want to send me away, and we spent the night together. The next day the stepfather and mother came. I asked for her hand. I said that I was having sex with my wife and wasn't tricking her, that I wanted to live with her.[6] So I took her home with me.

Marta loved me when I gave her a cow. I told her it was for her needs: "You can kill it or raise it or you can milk it." She also loved me for healing her, because she was always sick. She is okay now, so she is very happy.

But Marta often wanted to boss me around. She was a girl, and I needed to do everything for her, otherwise she wouldn't love me. "I want Alejandro to work for me because I am young; I can't do much work so he has to clear the garden and plant it," she said. So there were problems. She wanted me to clear the garden, to take care of the garden and keep it clear, and every time she wanted more gardens! So I said, "How can you want more gardens? You know it's expensive to take care of them."

She did not clear her own gardens the way Maria did. She did not take care of the gardens. For example, when you harvest the manioc and just throw the plant to the side, and don't plant it again, then the seed loses value. And if you don't clear the weeds, they overrun the garden. But Marta does not clear the weeds. She just harvests the "Chinese potatoes" [taro] and leaves the garden in a mess! She never had time to clear it; she would just go off to her mother's for months, and I had to do what she said. This is how she wants to manipulate me; she wants to have me under her command.

In Maria's system, the garden lasts six years, but in Marta's system it lasts like two years or a year, and then it is all destroyed; sometimes all the food is lost in the woods. I have told Marta that if she wants to stay in her mother's house, I can take the kids; but I don't want my wife to be stubborn like her sisters. It's okay one time, but not every time. I've done everything, but not any more! It's onerous; I give her birds, and she sells my things. "I feel sorry for you and especially for my kids. I don't want them to go like that. Now, I'm a man. I'm going to have a good job, a little house, and you can live like a queen and study and cook for your brothers; otherwise I'm going to get a wife, another wife," I told her.

I Know You Are Lying

Lorenzo was full of lies when he was a child! Okay, Nankichi, when Lorenzo was very little, four or five years old, I sent him to school in Huambinimi. He would come home and say, "Daddy, I fought with a kid that was bothering me, but I won." Well, he never fought; he was lying. I told him I was going to ask the teacher if it was true, or who the kid

Esteban Tsakimp carrying one of his children

Carmela Tsakimp and Umberto Shunta

was. "Who is bothering you?" I asked, and he said that he didn't want to go to school again because he didn't like it and they always teased him.

"Okay, go to school and tell your teacher when he teases you, but

Alejandro's daughter Bethy

don't fight. I don't send you to school to fight but to study, and if they bother you tell the teacher so he can reprimand them," I said.

Lorenzo lied to me once when he was in the military service, in 1985–86—or maybe 1983–84. He said, "Father, my colonel sent me here because I'm sick, and the medicine they gave me didn't work. I'm feeling bad here in my back, in the kidneys, and the penis, and neither the doctors nor the medicine could help me," he said.

But it wasn't true—it was just an excuse to come to see his woman. They sent him to the medical service in Quito for some exams, but he didn't want to go there. He didn't want to go back to the service in Montalvo, so he said that the colonel had sent him here because they were friends, and he loved him very much. So I took *natém* and "concentrated" my powers, and I asked him, "Okay, I'm going to take care of you, but why do you lie so much?"

I knew it was a lie in my concentration! I said, "Okay, don't lie to me. So as not to be embarrassed, you don't have to say anything. But I know you are lying. You were sent to Quito, but for some reason you don't like how they treat you in the service. So you've come to see your woman. Well, you're going to lose the military service, and we're going to lose the money. I already took out a 50,000-*sucre* loan to help you. Now you're

Alejandro's son Efren, carrying Alejandro's grandson

lying! It's this woman you found that has infected you, not a *tsentsak*! You're restless. Now you want to go to your wife, but you're going to have problems! You'd better live better. Go to the service and come back to your wife when you're okay."

Then Lorenzo said that they'd sent him over to see his father and that he'd left a paper for the doctors in his room.

So I said, "Okay, but don't lie again."

"I came to see my daughter Jeanette; my wife is already here," he said. I said that I didn't know where his wife was, and that he was lying.

Then he said that he was lying, that they didn't send him. I was mad. I told him that lies were a low thing in a person and he shouldn't do that; he was old enough to know better. "You should be open and not hiding things. Hiding things leads to trouble." That's the truth, Nankichi.

Once I was angry with Lorenzo. One day he asked me, "Hey, Dad, how is the project going?" This was a cattle project, in 1983 I think, and Lorenzo had already sold eight head of cattle.

I said, "What are you doing with the rest of the cattle? You sold one of my cows, so why don't you give me one bull? I could feed it and sell it." But he didn't listen to me that day, and he sold everything. I was mad inside me.

So when he asked me how the project was going, I said, "It's fine, everything is okay. The president is going to order an assembly for this year, and he said that I could work there. I have been there, and everything is fine." Now I was lying! I hadn't been to the Federation yet. Why should I if I don't agree with their ideas? I was mad that he wasn't following my ideas.

He Had Not Known

But with Lorenzo we had some good memories, too. He was twenty-two years old then—now he is twenty-eight or twenty-nine. He told me that he hadn't known how much I worried about him until I visited him and gave him money to take his family out of the Achuar Association. Then he realized that nobody else would do something like that for him. He was very proud and happy.

No Other Father

When we visited Esteban,[7] Nanki, he told me, in our own language, he told me that I had brought a new English family to his house and we were brought from heaven. Then he said, "I think that no other father visits his son with such a good family," and he was happy for that.

I hugged him and told him that I was going to be there for him always, no matter what, and if my life didn't turn out well, that Nanki [the author] would always be there.

The Best Thing

When Gustavo finished his military service, he told me that it was the best thing I had done for him. He was happy because he liked the military, and now he had a military certificate and didn't have any problems buying things.

Just Like Me

Gustavo once told me, just recently when he returned from the army, that he wanted to be like me. He told me he wanted me to give him the power of shamanism like his grandfather did with me so he could be an *uwíshin*. He said he was sure, and he wanted me to be sure, too. I told him to think about it carefully: he has to work, he has to be humble. So he said he would become a shaman when I died, a replacement. I will never forget how he said that.

It's not that he wants me to die, but he's thinking about how his grandfather died. Many people die, and this culture of shamans — doctors and so on — loses people. Like before, there is always somebody that comes next. That is what Gustavo thought.

Nobody from Our Race

When we were in Quito, my son Nantu said that he was thankful that I had taken him there, because nobody from our race had been there. Now he knows various officers and important people and is very happy. Now he's staying with Shíram [Gunda Wierhake], my German wife who has moved to Ecuador.

Like a Soap Opera

I never liked drinking *chicha* when I woke up. You know, I just wasn't used to it — I never drank Maria's. But I had a girlfriend once, and I drank everything! Her name was Juana, and she lived in Utunkus. This was in 1963, sometime after Lorenzo was born (that was in 1960). Maria knew about it. I was very roguish; I wanted my life to be like a soap opera. One day, a Sunday, I told Maria I was going to visit this family; she said, "Okay," and I changed my clothes.

Juana asked me if I wanted some *chicha*, and I said, "Just a little bit," because I get drunk very easily and didn't want to drink too much. Well, I went to bed with her, and around two in the morning the cock crowed. I said, "Damn! People are going to see me here," but she wouldn't let me be . . . she gave me more *chicha*, and I wanted to make her happy. So I finished drinking around five or six A.M., and I was drunk. But I drank it all so she was happy.

In 1968 I was working as an announcer for the radio, when I was president of the association. There was a girl named Cristina, who was working as a secretary for Father Juan Shutka and who was also cooking for the people in the health promoter course. I was taking the course, and she was there next to me all the time. I said, "Hi!"—I liked her.

"Hi, Alejandro, how are you? You're always here!" she said.

So one day I told her, "Let's go, I want you, let's leave—I will sell some cattle to pay for a vacation." I told Maria I needed some money for the course. . . . It was 2,888 *sucres*, but I took 20,000 or 30,000.

Father Juan was very protective of Cristina and watched me when I was talking to her. But every time he wasn't around I touched her breast and kissed her in his office. So I told her, "Let's get married; let's go to Cuenca and have the ecclesiastic marriage. I am married already, but by the civil authority, so I can get married again."

"You appear married in your ID," she said, and I told her I was widow (a lie). Then she said, "Let's live together."

One day Father Juan went to Kenkuim, so I was in charge of the course—the sixty-five students elected me as president. Then when the course was over I told her we were leaving, that we would fly to Cuenca. This was before they built the road; there was just a bridle path to Cuenca. But there was an airline, too, for flights.

So the sunshine was coming, and Father Juan was leaving in his Jeep, and then he saw me at the airline office buying the tickets.

"Hello, Alejandro, how are you doing? Have you seen this lady?" he said.

I said, "No, Father, I haven't seen her. Maybe she went to Macas." While I was talking to the Father, Cristina was in the woods hiding like an agouti behind a plantain leaf!

But Shutka kept asking if she had gone to Macas, and I was scared. This was a mistake. I didn't do this in my youth, but I was doing it now.

Well, now we couldn't go together because Father Juan was there. I thought, if I bought the tickets there, the travel agent would know. So I told Cristina to leave first and that I would leave the next day. I sent her to Cuenca and told her to send me a telegram when she got to Quito; then I would go by land through Pastaza to meet her in Quito. Everything was set. She left, and I had my things, so I went back to the Federation to work as an announcer. Then I got her telegram: "When are you leaving? I am waiting for you, because here I am without money. I was at the Salesian convent, then I went to wait for you at a hotel, but you didn't come!"

Later my friends said, "Alejandro, you have a woman in Cuenca!" But

I said, "No, no, no, I can't abandon my kids! People would laugh at me." Later she got married, but her husband left her. That's all I can tell you, Nankichi.

I once maneuvered a lover silently. It was in the year 1967, let's say between 1968 and 1970 or 1972. A man and a woman came to live with us. The husband (he's dead now) owed a lot of money, say like 90,000 *sucres*, to an *apache* in Macas. But he was always drunk, and his wife had to do some work. I felt so sorry for her and told her that she could live with me and I could look after her; I told her that we could live together. "Sure: I suffer all the time! It has been two years, and my husband is over there spending money. He never brings anything home for his kids," she said, and then she agreed to live with me. "After all, I can take care of you. I want to live with you," I told her, and she agreed. So I maneuvered that man, and after that I lived two years with her.

But one day she was subpoenaed because they had been married ecclesiastically and weren't divorced. So she went back with her husband. But we had two children together because I lived with her. One of them knows me, and the other knew me when she was very little, and I met her again when she was getting married. I wanted to meet her before she married, to give them a little help, like a piece of land. The girls are now with their husbands and have their own land, and I haven't bothered them since then. They always send me messages that they are okay, but they told me that Ruth was suffering. I was thinking of bringing her back someday, but I haven't had the time yet.

During the *fiesta* of San José in 1978 a lady told my wife I had married someone in Limón. I had gone to Ambato, but this lady called Maria and told her that I wasn't in Ambato. "Alejandro is in Limón," she said. "Alejandro is married to two women, and he was having dinner with both of them. I think they were *colonas*; I don't know if they are students," she said.

It was a lie. I was in Ambato, but when I got home Maria told me that I hadn't been in Ambato. But I told her that I had brought her fruits, that nobody had given them to me.

The lady wanted my wife to be mad at me and for us to have problems at home, because you know I love Maria, and she is in a good mood every time. Maria has a good heart.

I told her I was in Ambato at the chief's house, Marcelo and Gladicita, I was with them there at Glady's house with Clarita. Maria said, "Okay,

I'm not investigating this," and I told her that I was going to look for the lady there. I was going to find her to ask her if she had seen a *pasuk* or *supai* [spirit], if she was dreaming or what. One day I found her and asked her if she had seen me with that couple, if she had come to Limón to see me.

She said that she didn't see anything, and it was another man in Sucúa who told her. I told her we were going to the *síndicos* and were going to punish her because she was a liar, that she would have to clear the woods or pay a fine because she had made me look bad, and it was dangerous for my home.

She said, "Sorry, it was just a joke. Your wife didn't believe it."

I argued with her! I was mad, and I said, "Look lady, this is the second time you have said that! Last time you said I had an affair here in Huambinimi with a woman, and I had problems then with Maria, too. And now you do it again! If she were Josefina, she would have left me with the kids, and you would be guilty! Now you have to pay because you've lied twice."

The woman's husband asked her why she was lying. He was mad and didn't support her; instead, he was furious.

Then I said, "You were joking, but this is some serious joke."

But it doesn't matter. That's what I've learned in my maturity.

Another time Maria told me that this man was saying that Maria was saying that I was going to throw out all my wives and was going to leave her and go somewhere, anywhere, like to Miazal[8] to marry my uncle Jorge Péas's girls. That was what my brother-in-law was saying—that I was going to Miazal!

Josefina asked me if I had already sent the women a gift of cloth, and I told her, "Are you crazy? What's wrong with you? Did you sleep well or not? Why do you believe that liar man?"

Marta was mad too! She was mad and told me that if I was going to leave her, I should let her know because somebody must take care of the kids. She said, "If you are a man and love your wife, you have to say the truth: what you want and how you want it. Because you can't just leave, because I have rights because of the kids. Who's going to look after them? Who's going to take care of me? I can do something because I'm old, but the kids?" she said.

So we had these problems. . . . So when we were at the assembly I go to this man and I told him—in the middle of an open discussion—that he needs to talk to me. When the meeting ended, I told the *síndico* to get him, and I stayed with Josefina and Marta (Maria wasn't there, she was in Taisha because of our son Esteban's wedding). Then I asked him why he was talking bad about me.

I said, "Okay, mister, why do you go around saying things about me behind my back? What do you want to do? My wife is content; she is poor and has nothing, but my wives are content. And they don't bother you; they don't go asking for charity. Maybe they ask my friends for a favor, but they aren't stealing from you. So what happened?"

"Alejandro, I didn't say these things. People say that so you'll get mad at me."

I said, "But you're saying that I am going to get married, when I don't even know my uncle's daughter!"

"Me neither!" he said.

I told him, you are a representative at the family reunion and can't lie like that.

He said, "No, that's what people told me!"

Then Marta asked him to tell the truth if he was a man and to say "yes" right now, but he didn't say that. So the problem wasn't solved.

Then I said, "What if you are interested in my wife, is that why you're lying?"

And he said, "No, no, no, how can you think that? Don't think that, I would never think that," he said, but I really thought it!

He said, "If I've said that, please forgive me, but if I haven't, just God knows."

And I told him that I wasn't talking to God, but to him.

How to Make Money

Once I said to myself that I needed to contact the *Iwianch*. This was in 1962, 1962 or 1963 or 1964. I was twenty-three—already married to Maria—and was head of the Parents' Association in Utunkus. I decided to get in touch with *Iwianch* because I knew many *apache* friends had asked him how to make money, and he made them money. It was an *apache* from Guayaquil—Angel was his name. (I shared many bad things with him; we had a woman in one apartment, and he did things that I didn't like.)

Well, he told me there was a guy with the Devil inside, and when he's going to pay his employees, he goes to the woods and talks to the Devil, and the Devil gives him the money.

He was my partner when I was working for the laboratory. So he told me to buy a book about black magic and go to the cemetery at midnight to ask the dead souls for the Devil, and then the Devil would come. *Iwianch* takes your blood, he told me, and you have to sign and give him your blood. *Iwianch* in our language means richness, the gold's owner.

I don't like to talk about this. I went to my brother-in-law, Pedro Tunki, and told him that we were ready to contact the Devil because we didn't have any money. I wasn't sure, but my brother told me that he was sure it was going to work and that he was going first, so one night we were drinking and then we went to the cemetery. We did this for months.

Then, after a year, Maria saw a shadow, and later the shadow started coming more often. It was making messes, and Maria told me not to do that anymore because it was an evil pact, this bargain with *Iwianch*, and it wasn't worth the risk. Maria saw a man riding a horse who had made a pact with the Devil, and she said, "That's what Alejandro is doing, and I'm not going to let him do that." She was scared. One day she asked me if I was having an affair, because I was gone every night. I told her I was just walking through the woods to see how we could make more money, because I wanted to find the buried treasure of the dead, I wanted to be with the Devil. Maria cried and told me that if I kept doing that she was going to leave me. So I quit that. I never made any money, anyway.

A Country to Fight For

Today we eat cattle and drink their milk. It was different in the past. Before I didn't drink much milk. Also, my mother didn't cook with it because they said that cows were ghosts and couldn't be eaten. Then later with the meat scarcity we tried it, and nothing happened. Now we can eat venison even though our grandfathers said we shouldn't.

I'm anxious to have many head of cattle, to save money. This is something new to the Shuar, but I taught myself this desire; it was my own decision. I know that cattle are more profitable than any other agricultural product; that is why we have cattle now. I made this decision because I want money. I can sell a cow and buy something bigger, more exchangeable.

I long to have more kids and to keep having them for the future of my mother country, to enlarge my town, so there are more people in my Shuar town. We have the right to defend ourselves just as Ecuadorians do. The settlers have marginalized us. They look on us as inferiors and a minority, and that is why the government doesn't care about the Indigenous. But we are part of this country, the Amazonian Indigenous; we have a country to fight for, yes or no?

9

Shaman

The Dead and the Blind

Who was the first shaman? My mother and father told me that centuries ago two brothers sat together drinking chicha. They were not witches or shamans, although perhaps they felt they were shamans, but they were drunk, and one said, "Fine, my brother: If you blow on this chicha I will lose my vision. My vision will grow dark. And I, too, will blow, if you want, on your chicha. Yes, I, too, will blow on your chicha to make a curing potion."

"Yes, blow on it to make me skinny, skinny, skinny. I want to be skinny, and if it is to the point of death, I will die."

So they both decided. First one and then the other blew. Those two knew how to drink without being anything, without even being shamans. (In this time there was no one who did shamanism. They simply drank ayahuasca, or natém [a plant infusion], for digestion.)

Perhaps this is when and how they became shamans—to take ayahuasca, samiruk, and napuyasku, and to get tsentsak [a shaman's weapon]. Perhaps this is also how they came to know the powerful spirits. They advanced and were like shamans.

So after about a month one of the brothers began to lose his vision, and the other began to become skinny. He was no longer hungry and ate very little, so he got skinnier and skinnier until, they say, he died. The other was left without vision. It is believed that at that point this uwíshin [shaman], taking ayahuasca, was born.

And I Watched

I first knew that I wanted to be an uwíshin when I was little—four or five years old. I was always saying I would become an uwíshin. But I didn't actually cure someone until 1962.

The first time I observed someone cure, I was around four or five years old. I always stayed around when my father drank *ayahuasca*, but I don't remember everything.

One time, though, my uncle Miguel came and brought my aunt, Atsásu, who was sick. Sometimes she suffered from malaria. When this was the case and my father drank *ayahuasca*, he determined that it wasn't *tsentsak*, it wasn't witchcraft.

But other times he determined that it was witchcraft. One time, when my aunt was going to a work meeting in Asunción, she fell very ill with severe pain in her spine, like something was there that was witchcraft. Then, the day after seeing my father, she was better!

My father drank *ayahuasca* first while she stayed in the bed. He played the *tumank*, announcing [that is, calling] and imitating Tsunki [a mythic character], and I asked my father why he played this *tumank*, and my father said, "I am announcing, and be still, because I am calling the spirits so that they will give me the power to cure." So he said, "You will be still." He then said, "I am announcing via these myths, and the *tumank*, what happened to *supai* [spirit of a dead person]; what occurred that gave him power to cure."

He then smoked some tobacco from a gourd. He then brought my aunt to the bed and made her lie down. My aunt cried and shouted with pain as I watched. He sang and called out, and then he took the tobacco smoke and began to suck the *tsentsak* out of her body. He sucked three times and then stopped and rested. There was not so much pain now, and after a time he sucked a fourth and fifth time and said that he'd taken some kind of microbe. I wanted to see, but he said no. I was prohibited from seeing because the microbe could suddenly make me ill, and because it is illegal to show such things to outside individuals. So that is to say that outsiders cannot be involved in these occult doings.

My uncle caught the microbe under a lid and said he was going to see another shaman to see where the evil had come from, and also to make that other one—the shaman who had sent this sickness—sick himself. He was angry that someone had done this and wanted to know who this other shaman was! But my father advised him not to do it. Andrés said it wasn't worth the effort, and that in any case the other would die one day.

Another time I observed when Emilio brought his woman, who was sick, and my father cured her also. This was maybe a month or two later in that same year. Emilio is the son of my own aunt, Andrés's sister, Luz

Pakésh. So he is my *saich* [affine; one who is or may be related through marriage, e.g., a brother-in-law or cross cousin]. He arrived with his wife, who was suffering from much hemorrhaging and a powerful pain in her vagina. My uncle said, at that point, that he had gone to see the medic Ventimilla and had not seen any improvement, so he wanted my father to have a look. In payment for curing his wife, he gave my father a shotgun. The next day when I saw him, my father said the fact was that this was not a sickness. What had happened was that some other shaman had bewitched them, but that she wouldn't die. He would remove the ailment.

So he began to drink *ayahuasca*, and later he took tobacco smoke and prepared *piripiri* [a medicinal plant] to make himself vomit while leaving a little something in his stomach. I saw all this happen! Then he got a tube, from the papaya tree, and placed it in her vagina five times and then removed something like a worm and showed it to Emilio. After a little while she got better; she sat up and said she was hungry and thirsty.

She didn't speak for an entire day. It was very difficult for her to speak, but when I saw her she could eat and drink. She could open her mouth. The next day she was a little better and again the third time I saw that she could get up. I said to myself that I would do what my father had done. I made the decision that when I was grown up I would be a shaman.

From a Pinch of a Cure

And now my father says that I am "of *umpum*" [food that casts a spell]. "You are born," he told me. He said that my mother might have miscarried had he not been lucky enough to find a more powerful shaman, who was the shaman before my father. (This was before my father became a shaman and cured others). Say your wife, after having three children, miscarries because something is wrong. The pregnancy ends when the fetus is big, say three or four months: she hemorrhages a lot, and the fetus comes out. That's how it was with my mother.

At that time, when someone killed a person, people gathered. So when my great-grandfather himself, Tsakimp, then in Patuca, made the fiesta of *tsantsa*, our relatives gathered. Classificatory brothers of my father, Tséremp and Kasent—and in-laws, Ampush and Piruch—and my parents. My father told me that my mother was good at singing for the fiesta of *tsantsa*. I wasn't born yet; I was in my mother's belly. My great-grandfather gave my mother something to keep the child; he gave her a pinch of *pirípiri*. A pinch, a cure, a liquid, a mixture—for example, what I give you to cure a cold—is called *umpum*. That's why I'm "*umpum*." From a pinch of a cure from our great-grandfather—that's why I always feel like drinking *ayahuasca*, yes.

So they gave it to me when I was a little boy. I waited until they were drinking, and then I, too, drank a little of *natém*; my father allowed me to take just a little bit. I became "drunken" and saw some things, but it didn't last, and my body quickly fell asleep. I saw many things: how the people came, some beautiful colors, a temple, my mother and sister conversing. I saw that they were sleeping and that they were saying something about me and that they woke with the conversation—so they had given me these visions.

I was afraid, but then my father got this plant, this *shinshínk*. And so at that point I said, "Yes, when I am big this is what I, too, will do," and then I passed out, out, out.

When I said to my father that I would like to become a shaman like him, he said that when I am big I could become one, but not then because I was very little.

My mother said, "You poor child; when you take that you could suddenly die, or a *tsentsak* could kill you."

I said that I, too, could study and become strong like my father, and when he dies I can stay and become a healer and defend others and earn money. This is what I said to my mother. And she said that it was okay, but that I must always be a good healer and never a sorcerer.

Valentín said, "Fine," because it was already decided. I am "*umpum*."

Valentín didn't become a shaman. "I can't drink because I'm not up to it. When one is a shaman, one can't work." That's what my father said, because he didn't work much. When he worked, chopping down trees, he got a fever and suffered. This isn't worth the trouble.

But I am tough, because I'm *umpum*. But at times, Nanki, it makes me ill with a fever. But even with this, one has to do what has to be done. My father began to become ill and went to other shamans to fight the sorcery, and he suffered. In the end I told myself that, hidden from my father, I would study with the Alama [Quichua] shaman. This was in 1962, after my marriage.

Before then I was involved in my studies, in school. There was no way for me to do both. I didn't talk about this with my teachers at school, but

I did talk to Mike [Harner]. He was very happy that I, too, was learning to take medicine. He knew how to take *natém.*

After I Finish My Job

One day in 1961 my father fell ill. A man named Tunki, from Kusuim, Corazon de Jesus, near Tesoro, made him ill with witchcraft—a man who is now deceased. We had gone to work on a community project [*minga*] in Huambi, and afterward, when we were returning, this guy who is now dead followed us, arguing with my father over a girl that I liked. He said to my father that I had deceived them because I was married to another woman, and that now his sister couldn't marry.

Before I married Maria, my father had asked a man, Mukuímp, from Cuisime, if I could marry this senorita. He said that after I finished my job I could then marry this girl. But in the meantime, I found Maria. This is why this shaman was so angry that he marked us and followed us, smoking tobacco and blowing it.

My father said, "Fine, he sought her love so they should get married, but we shouldn't argue about it. Anyhow, why are you arguing with me? Your sister is free to look for another man." This other shaman was angry. He said that we had deceived him—that I hadn't married his sister.

Well, we got back to the house and started drinking chicha—we got fairly drunk—and I started dancing with my stepmother. Papa went to bed around midnight and awoke with a great deal of pain, shooting pains. I said maybe this is an illness, or maybe he's been made ill through shamanism or witchcraft, the argument of the day before. He said it could be, so I went to look for my aunt Maria Chúmpi, the mother of Rafael. She was a shaman.

She was my "Political Aunt"—her parents were classificatory brothers [parallel cousins] of my grandfather. (She lived in San José, but she's dead now.) She studied shamanism in Namakim, in Napo with a shaman named Juan Achayat' and with Katan'. Why aren't there many women shamans? You know, Nanki, it involves a lot of sacrifice. Fasting and more fasting. When one is a shaman, or studies shamanism, one is completely restricted. One must go for a year with fasting, and those fasts are without eating. The first few days are the hardest. One cannot eat manioc, bananas, or plantains—neither hard nor soft and sweet.

One also eats those little toads—just the little leg that I will show you. Then there are little fish from which one has to eat just the tail part, because it is forbidden to eat the whole fish.

But I once asked Maria Chúmpi why she became a shaman. I asked her when I myself was studying with her, when she gave me some power. She said, "My son, it's like this . . . when I was a little girl, sleeping on the beach, Tsunki gave me this *chuntak*, the special phlegm. From that point, I dreamed that I was immersed in romantic songs, and I awoke feeling somewhat drunk. But Tsunki told me in the dream that when I return to the house I must drink *ayahuasca* and fast. If I didn't fast, I would become ill. He told me all of this in my dream. I went to the house and drank *ayahuasca* and fasted; I then set out to find a shaman. So my first friend was Mánkash, who lives in Kumpas."

The Rest All Died

This is the story of Tsunki. They live in our rivers, like the Utunkus River and the Upano River. Sometimes at 5:30 or 6:00 they start coming out of where they live, but sometimes there are empty lakes and there aren't any Tsunki.

There once was a Shuar who ate all of these fishes, what the *colonos* call *caracha* and we call *nayump'*, that live at the bottom of the lake. For the Tsunki, who live at the bottom, these fishes are like cockroaches! They don't eat them, but this Shuar ate them.

"You are beautiful," the Tsunki said to him, "you will protect us from those cockroaches. Now we are going to give this woman to you."

Then the Shuar left the lake. He was already married, and he went to the home of his woman and her relatives. So, one Tsunki sent his daughter, Tsunkínua, with the Shuar. But the wife of the Shuar could get jealous of Tsunkínua, so the father hid her in a little bag. "You will save her in this little bag and take good care of her; whenever you take her out, she will turn into a woman. Take my daughter, but she's not going to turn into a woman just yet, so you can carry her in this bag. At night she will become a woman, and at dawn, she will become a snake. Protect this pretty little snake in your pouch. Keep it up high so that no one touches it, so no little children mess with it."

The Shuar put it on a high shelf and went to hunt. When he came back at night, the Tsunkínua had transformed itself into a woman!

When people saw her they said that she was very shiny, covered with preciousness, like the color of a boa, like a rainbow. And she was very big.

The wife of the Shuar said, "What is going on? Why don't you come sleep with me?" and she asked her husband who he was sleeping with.

"No one," he said, "you don't have to know anything; it's a secret, it's very holy."

"Oh," she says, "okay."

Later, his sons came, and the oldest one found the pouch. The Shuar had told them not to touch it, that if they touched it there would be a great flood. "We'll all die," he said, but they didn't listen. So when he went to hunt they took the pouch down. In it they found a snake, a very beautiful one, that was moving, with lots of colors, like a coral snake. Beautiful. It was in there, moving about, and they said, "Here is the snake that father has been sleeping with," and one of them grabbed it, and as he was grabbing it, it fell to the ground. They grabbed an ember because they wanted to burn it and cut it and hurt it.

At that moment it made itself into water. Just water came out of the snake—it was a miracle! And from there it entered into the river, and then there was a great storm with much rain, enough to fill the house with water. And those who were disobedient swallowed the water.

Then a little guy went running after the Shuar man and told him what had happened. "They touched it," he said, "they touched it, Papa, and they took it out."

And then the storm began, a flood, and the rest all died. This is the power of Tsunki, this is why all the uwíshinios and shamans use the power of Tsunki.

One Must Cure to Earn

Maria Chúmpi stayed in Kumpas with Mánkash, who gave her power and gave her tsentsak for a few months. Her husband Mashiant went with her and supported and helped her to become a shaman. Then she went to Achayat', in Santa Rosa, where my father first went. (Achayat' is dead now; he died in a fight with another shaman. He let his guard down and was stricken; he didn't get better.) She then went to Chiguaza,[1] to see Katan', where you and I were going to visit—Esteban is the old shaman now. My aunt's husband went with her and paid for all of it. And they didn't have sexual relations at that time because it was forbidden. But her husband went along to care for her and to pay for the studies. He would return home once in a while to check on the kids and get chickens for my aunt to eat and to give to the other shaman. That's how my aunt studied. When she went with her friend Katan' to Napo, it must have been around 1930, I think.

My aunt Maria Chúmpi told me this story: There once was a woman shaman named Waník. She was quite strong when she was a girl, before she married. But she was killed with a bullet because she started to do bad witchcraft. So my aunt said that when one is a witch, one mustn't do bad things to people. One must cure to earn, and to defend the health of your fellow man. This is what this woman shaman advised me.

There are differences between men and women shamans. There is more danger, more arrows,[2] with a woman than with a man. The *tsentsak* can't be removed if they are from a woman's witchcraft. That's the way history goes. It has been proven and tested. When one is struck by the witchcraft of a woman, one can't be cured. It has been shown; tests and analysis have been done that show that this is so. This is the history of the woman shaman. And if you haven't studied under a woman shaman, you can't cure a person. Maria Chúmpi was strong and capable. She learned all the methods until she was ready. Later she drowned in the river when she took a canoe for Sevilla. From that point people wanted stronger shamans, like myself.

I brought my father to Maria Chúmpi and told her the situation. She said that this was done by a shaman with whom he'd argued, and that he wouldn't improve quickly because the *tsentsak* would be very difficult to remove. The illness would continue because he hadn't kept a promise that he'd made about a woman. But in any case she cured him in one day and removed the pain and showed me what to do.

My aunt Maria Chúmpi took *ayahuasca* in my father's house and began to cure my father. My father also drank it. Both of them took it to see and also to protect my father. So then she began to cure him, singing and imitating *pasuk* [shaman's familiar] and powerful spirits. She then began to suck. She sucked two times and removed that bug. She removed the arrow, like an insect that is very difficult to find, and in this form she showed it to me. An hour or two later, my father could move the back of his neck and said he felt somewhat better. So we thanked her and paid her with a little piglet. We went home and returned a couple of days later for another treatment, and he felt better again.

I Went to Look

A week later my aunt went to another place by Méndez, but by the time she returned my father had lost strength again. He was stung in the vaginal area, or where it would be in my father—the urethra. He couldn't do anything. I went to look for other shamans, but I couldn't find any good ones. We looked over near the Río Negro, by Shimpis, and then for another near Cambanaca. But those shamans didn't succeed in curing him. Maybe it was because the illness was more concentrated. That is, it wasn't treated adequately; they didn't do it as they should have. He would get a little better, but then would have to go back. This was why I went to look for medicines in the hospital. The doctors gave me some medicines, but they made it worse and worse. We knew there were a lot of *curanderos* in Napo, Canelos, Puyo, and Sarayacu. When I was a boy, an uncle of mine, Vicente Kuja (he lives in Santa Rosa), told me there were some good ones around Napo.

He became more ill so I brought him to Puyo and then to the Vozandes Hospital. The doctors said that there was no possibility of a cure; he had a tumor, an abscess. The doctors said that he needed operations in different places that were swollen. My father said that he didn't need that operation because it wasn't a sickness. He knew because it was sorcery that he was suffering from. Later we went down to Puyo to the Red Cross, where he had a friend who once worked there—a Doctor Vicente. Now, by this time months had passed, and my father was very thin, like a skeleton. So we carried him to the Red Cross. When we left the Red Cross we had no place to go in Puyo so we just sat there on the corner, near the Shell station. And there we were; my father was like a cadaver, fainting, and my sister Imelda was crying (she was also sick with a toothache).

At the time she still lived with her third husband, Felipe, and Felipe also came with us on the first trip. He still hadn't gone to the barracks. This was back in 1967 when my brother-in-law still lived with my brother. So anyhow, a police sergeant came along and said, "What's the matter?"

I explained that we were from the east, from the province of Morona Santiago, from canton Sucúa, and that my father had been sick for some eight months. We told him what the doctors had said, and the policeman said that it wasn't a sickness.

This policeman, a colonist, said that in back of the cemetery lived a shaman, an Alama [Quichua] named Segundo Yasakam'. He said that this shaman had cured many people. He'd been curing for a long time; he was a friend and had even cured the police officer. He said that he knew the shaman well, that he was a good man, and that he could cure all kinds of ailments. He said he would take us in his pickup truck.

I asked how much Segundo would charge, and he said not too much—15,000 or 10,000 sucres. So I decided to do it because I had over 40,000 at that time. I had sold cattle, because at that time I had cattle, and I made about 800–900 sucres. Sometimes 1,600 to 2,800 for the larger ones, or 800 for the small ones. (In 1962 a machete cost 65 or 75 sucres; today one costs 2,000 sucres!)

So we loaded my dad in the truck, and we went there. The cop said, "He's my friend. If there are a lot of people, I'll ask him to see you quickly. Now think well so that he will get well."

When we got there I saw that there were many people waiting to see this shaman—a whole lot of people. Our police officer told him that he'd brought someone from the east, very ill, to see him. Segundo then asked the others to leave, and he was soon attending to my father. My father had fainted and could barely eat or urinate. I think he was just living from a little water now and then.

Segundo took his pulse and said that it was very weak and that he might not live. Then he was quiet for a long time. He continued to take the pulse and then he told us to think good thoughts and not to be sad. He said not to worry, to take good care of my father, and he would get better. Later he sucked at the spot that was swollen. He said that it wasn't your everyday *tsentsak*; this was a dangerous "chonta" *tsentsak*, like a spine from the chonta palm, or the peach palm, he said. There are different kinds of arrows; for example, chonta *tsentsak*, the snake *tsentsak*. . . . Some shamans have more *tsentsak*, some have fewer—it depends on how long they've been practicing shamanism. Well, believe me, it was incredible!

At that point he continued to suck and removed a *tsentsak*. He also removed one from the other side, because he said it had struck the heart. He then "died"; he was far away because he was protecting my father's arrows of power. He gave my father *ayahuasca* and protected him with *ayahuasca*. He then said, "So, it is removed," and he showed it to me. It was a spine of chonta—and he also removed another from there, like a stinger from an insect called a *sapi*. And Papa—boom—died! That is, he fainted; no, his heart just palpitated, and he stopped breathing. I said, "He's dead."

But then Segundo said, "No, there is still strength. He is only fainted. I removed what had struck his head." He then blew and blew and blew and called out. He breathed for maybe a quarter of an hour, then asked my father how he felt.

My father said, "Like I almost died. What happened? What did you do to me?"

"I am attending to you." Then he gave my father a pill, and he was tired, tired then.

I asked what pill it was, and he said a shaman's pill. My father was tired, so Segundo gave him a little drink, but he said it was bitter. He told me it was really bitter. He then began to tire here in the stomach. And after a little while Segundo gave him a good puff of *natém*—and he reacted.

The following day Segundo did another treatment, and my father reacted the same. We slept and the following day had to go back to the house. So I stayed there.

Segundo said, "Let's go fishing to get something for your father to eat." So we went, and when we got back Papa was a little better. He could sit up by himself.

I said, "Papa, how do you feel?"

He said he was a little better from what had been done.

It was at that point that I said to myself, "I'm not going to go back home without asking if I can study under this shaman. I must ask for some arrows from him." The arrows of the Quichua are different from the arrows of the Shuar. The arrows used in the shamanism of Morona Santiago have phlegm so they can enter and do more damage to a person. But the arrows of the Quichua are without phlegm; they aren't *tsentsak kukach*, and for this reason can return in an instant. For example, if you are seated here, and you make an arrow and send it, within a couple of hours things have turned, and the arrow has returned. You might suffer violently within twenty-four hours and die, or even in an hour the arrow could enter and hit you like a bullet.

At this time I hadn't studied, but I had thought about it. I had thought about doing it for two reasons: I thought about becoming a shaman to do harm to those who had hurt my father; and I thought it is better to become a shaman to protect the health of my family. Then I thought it is much better to protect my family and cure my fellow man.

So my father continued to get better, and in the month of May—on May 12 there is a celebration, the fiesta of Puyo—and he was better. We went to the party, and Papa went, too. It had been October, November, December, January, February, March, April, May, and then he was finally better. So he said, "Let's go, friends, let's go to the party. And we all went, the whole family, to Yasakam' in Puyo. And later they gave Papa some beef stew, saying it wouldn't cause any problems. He blew and blew and concentrated hard. Then he ate the stew, but he didn't drink any liquor. Well, we went back to the house and continued to drink, celebrating, and there was another shaman there, Lorenzo from Napo, a Quichua.

I Don't Know What I Can Do!

He was called Lorenzo Vargas. He called me "brother-in-law," and I called him the same. I said, "You are a shaman. Do me the favor of allowing me to study. I want to." He was my first teacher. I studied with my aunt and with Segundo Yasakam' later.

Lorenzo said . . . well, we spoke secretly because my father did not want me to study. My father said, "Hey, how are you going to work?" He had always thought that being a shaman is very tiresome, and you can't get work done.

Lorenzo had some doubts that maybe I wouldn't be able to handle the fasting and all that would be done to me. He said that it was very complicated, that you have to fast a lot and that maybe I would advance if I would make a good shaman. And if I didn't advance, maybe it's because I wouldn't.

"Good," he told me. "You are a man," he said, "so carry yourself like one. Only men can do it. When we are cowards and are afraid, we don't study. That's why no one studies. You have to fast, you have to take very good care of yourself," he told me.

But I was going to do it to help myself.

You see, my father, because he'd been sick, wanted me to care for him. I told Lorenzo about my sacrifices and my sufferings that I had gone through to cure my father, searching for those who were as good with medicine as the shamans. "Some shamans wanted to kill him; they keep trying to hurt him," people told me. "As I am not a shaman, I don't know what I can do! I want you to give me strength, to see if I can do it, to see if I can take the fasting and all that. With time, I'll be able to work," I told Lorenzo.

He said that when my father was better, maybe then I could study.

I said, "Okay, I'll think it over."

Paradise

Well, I saw brother-in-law Lorenzo, and he said, "Look, I know that when I took *ayahuasca* I could see that you want strongly to be a shaman. Well, we'll do it, happily."

Lorenzo first told me that I shouldn't get together with my wife, that we should separate for a time, eight months. Sex would be very dangerous, because the power of the *tsentsak* he would give me would leave me if I had sex with a woman, he told me. If I could take that, then I could take a year, he told me, and that would be very good. I told him that I'd see. It all depended on me; if I couldn't, I couldn't do this.

The other thing he told me was not to eat pork—it could cause bumps to appear on your skin and they won't heal, and your nose could rot from leprosy, he told me—and not much food because it wasn't good, don't even eat *ají* [chili pepper], he told me. "Just a little bit of salt and no meat from the tapir or armadillo. Just a little chicken, nothing big, no large hen, no rooster," he told me. "No guinea pigs, no fish—just little fish, but only a half and not the head. Frogs and snails, yes, you'll eat them in the meantime," he said.

So he gave me *ayahuasca*. He blew on me and concentrated hard, Lorenzo did, and he gave me the drink. When he blew on me he asked for powers of analysis of arrows. Then he said to drink it, but to fast. And I said, "Okay, I am strong."

So I had already taken *ayahuasca*, and in a little while it hit me fairly strong. Hell, I was in paradise. It made me see some people differently. I saw some people with a full band of music. Just black people who brought me to a temple. Then I was seeing strong, and I said to myself, "Help me, *kare, kare, kare*"—*kare* means strong in Quichua.

"Good, then. You'll be a man," Lorenzo said. And he blew on my head, and it seems to me that he poked me with a thorn on the crown of my head. After that, I felt pain here, and it bothered me. Those were the arrows that he blew into my head. They cost 100 *sucres* each, which was at that time a lot. He gave me let's say five the first time and five the second, so ten arrows total.

In between the first and second times, I stayed there in Pastaza, in the house of Segundo Yasakam'. He said, "Yes, you're going to take it." Later my father also said, "Right, I see that you are studying."

And I said, "Yes, Father, I am. Look at how many shamans we visited. We asked for strength; we asked for help. And we paid money to all of them, but none could help you. None could cure you. So now I must study, so that I can protect us in our place."

The second time Lorenzo did quite a bit. I felt that my body was stinging, and those were the arrows that he'd given me. Then he gave me *ayahuasca* again and said, "You are going to see some flying snakes." And I saw exactly that. I saw how the snakes flew.

Nanki, I'm going to tell you what Lorenzo, my first friend in shamanism, told me when I asked him what powers I needed to become a shaman. Well, he said that I would need powers for protection, so that my fellow shaman friends do not do me harm. So I said, "Yes—how can I protect myself?"

He said, "It is like a curtain, when you take *ayahuasca*, *natém*, and concentrate very hard. You see something like many huge machines; those are what protect you. Also the spirits, like an army, but very different. Those will protect you from these enemies of mine, these other shamans."

Then I asked what one can do to defend against the witchcraft of those fellow shamans, and he said that one can make an announcement to the spirits to let them know that we, too, have this witchcraft. He said to call the soul in a very different way, and he taught me some very traditional chants and some very different chants calling a "temple of Sangay"[3] and a "temple of the deceased," so they are called. And then you remove the "arrow"—it seems to be the soul of the other person, the other shaman. Then you blow three times, and that's it.

Then you go back a week later and do the same thing again. Shortly, the other shaman, or whatever person you'd like to harm, will fall victim. This is the study of sorcery, he told me, here in this area.

And to cure, I also asked him, "How do you cure here?" He told me that it was the same way that Segundo had cured my father. "You drink *ayahuasca*, you concentrate, in a very quiet serenity. No one makes a racket. Only the shaman should make his noise—nothing else should interrupt. Not even the children can be present, just those who are helping (it can be the wife or someone)."

I then asked how frequently one must drink *ayahuasca*. He said to drink it every eight days and then quit at least three times for one month, because the *ayahuasca* will ruin you and you'll go beyond the point with the drug—*natém*. So I did what he said for my studies.

Later, I said, "How do you do 'the blow,' to harm others?"

"You do 'the blow' this way: it can be in liquor, in cola, or in *chicha* where we drink in secret. Also, we do this without singing, without speaking, only thinking. And we blow—giving force by wind. This is our part.

Well, this is what I asked. And I also asked about this power to drown in the river that you have—that we have; the power of *Tsunki*, as we say, the power of the spirits of *Tsunki*, of lake and river. This is the power to transform into a boa, *panki* [anaconda]. And to go by canoe or to bring the animal—the boa specifically—to the enemy of your choice. I have never done this, but that other shaman, Mánkash, did.

Mánkash gave me a blow of *natém*, nothing more. No, I didn't want his arrow, it was one of the bad arrows. Nor did he teach me how to do that transformation. I don't like it because my father and mother told me that if you use sorcery to kill people, you can't live for long. You'll encounter many problems, and they can kill you.

Lorenzo told me about the transformation, too. Well, I said, "Fine, friend, but I do not want to learn that. I want to learn how to be a good shaman, to cure, because in my land, the *Oriente*,[4] there is much sickness. My people pay quite well in order to get better. But sometimes we don't get well—my family at my *centro* are very ill because of sorcery that has been sent against them." So then I asked that he cure me well, that he send me away with good concentrations. I would be thankful and would pay him well. I paid 10,000 for that, and he was so happy.

I never returned to visit Lorenzo, because I never had the opportunity. I returned to Puyo, but he wasn't there. He'd gone to Napo to

Canelos. So that is when I studied with the shaman Yasakam', Segundo Yasakam', the one who cured my father. I had returned to Puyo to make a payment for the treatment of my father, and I met up with Segundo Yasakam'.

I said, "Now friend, teach me something better of the ways of concentration."

He said, "Fine, because I see that you want to become a shaman—that you would be a good healer, a good shaman. So I'll give you what you ask."

In this way I asked him. Then we drank *ayahuasca*. "I know that my nephew, Lorenzo Vargas, has given you the first concentrations."

So then I said, "Yes."

"Very good, sir," he said. "You will reach manhood. You won't look for your woman's knee. You have to be a very good man for some months. If you want to be a good shaman, you have to be here for a year."

"Right," I said.

I went a year without a woman, and without eating pork, because he said it was very harmful, and I know, too, that it's very harmful when one is concentrating. Pork is the only animal that makes the arrows worse—it causes a reaction that causes new arrows. Now I can eat pork; nothing happens now. It's in that period when you are concentrating with *tsentsak* that you must abstain.

I studied with Segundo twice, for two concentrations. The first day he blew everything away—he cured me well. He blew on the hands, on the body. He disinfected my body with liquor and gave me blows. He gave me strength, and later he blew on my head. He blew on my forehead, well, for my science, for my training, for my intelligence, my human wisdom. He blew three times at my forehead.

It seems like one time this gave me a tremendous chill that lasted some three minutes. Then it passed, and he gave me *ayahuasca*, good and strong—a thing that was in the air, flying. I wanted to sing, but I couldn't; all of the romantic songs of the *uwishin* appeared before me, and I could see them clearly. This was the first time that I learned the songs. Segundo Yasakam' taught me how to say everything. (Later my father also taught me.)

After I had taken *ayahuasca*, he said, "How are you feeling my friend?"

I said, "Completely fine. I see it all."

"Shush. Don't say anything. Keep studying, concentrating."

Then I returned to see a great temple. Many friends from faraway lands. Marvelous people, unknown people from other countries and other nations. But everything, everything, everything happened—just like on television. Then I returned to think of my house—how is my woman, my son? And I knew that my babies were sleeping and that my Maria was sleeping.

So from that point on, I had his approval. I learned a lot. I enjoyed more and had more energy—more strength to continue studying.

I said, "Tomorrow night give me more concentrations, okay?"

The second day he said to me, "You have to suck my tongue." Then he says, "If you want to be a good shaman, a good healer, you're going to suck my tongue." From that point on, I was able to remove *tsentsak* quite well by way of my tongue.

He gave it to me while blowing a little *natém*, and he gave me this drink; and he gave me a good amount of tobacco smoke. First he made an *ayampaco*, it's called—you wrap something in leaves and then you roast it, and we call it *ayampaco*. After twenty minutes you take this *ayampaco*, and you put a little water on it. Here we use water, but in Napo people use liquor. At that point you light the tobacco, and the smoke comes out, and you inhale it.

He was in the dark—there was no light. And I was concentrating, and I sucked his tongue. And when I sucked it was like, Nanki, like when you suck a sliver. He was hurting my tongue, like when you suck a thorn. My tongue felt like that, only very different. I sucked, sucked, sucked—three times, then it felt dead. My tongue was mortified. So I felt dead for a day. I was hypnotized—like my mouth was hypnotized, and I wasn't hungry. The next day he removed the arrow from me, and he made me concentrate on the same.

"Now," he said, "we're going to give you an arrow. This is the arrow of arrows—you'll know how to fly. It is the talisman that you will ride. This is the talisman of attraction."

Then he gave me a little piece of the magnetic material. But I later lost it; I drowned it.[5]

Later he said that "Tomorrow is the last day. For the fourth time we are going to give you food, a dinner." They made a little food of each part, a little chicken, a little guinea pig, a little salt, peppers, soup, and that's it—and *chicha*.

So he gave me all this, blowing well on it, so that I wouldn't be harmed—so that the *tsentsak* he gave me wouldn't return to him. Then I finished the curing.

Then every fifteen days I continued to take *ayahuasca*, and he continued to give me more protections and virtuous things for defense. And today they give me a way of assuming the form of the tiger,[6] the cat, and the little monkey. From this I can transform, he told me. The tiger, he explained to me, will proceed you invisibly when you go out. The monkey will make you wake up when there is some danger seeking you. It will tell you who has been speaking badly of you. He did this to protect me against enemies, against other shamans that might want to do me harm. (Recently—in 1988 or 1989—I did a test to see how well I could do it. I believe it worked. I'm certain it worked because my pal saw it, my pal from Natemtsa. He said that he saw that when I was going to arrive, a little tiger arrived ahead of me. And then when I arrived, the tiger was gone!)

So I said, "This is my passage." Very well, so my curing was done. I had gone to Puyo and stayed for a year. He told me I could cure a child who had not yet been dirtied by sexual union with a woman. I paid Segundo 15,000.

In Case of an Emergency

So when I was finished, after eleven or twelve months, I went to Warínts on a trip, accompanied by my mother-in-law. That's Josefina's mother, but this was before I married Josefina. Her mother is also the aunt of Maria Kintanúa. So my aunt and my brother-in-law invited me to come visit them and to get to know the land there. That is, on my way back to Utunkus I traveled by way of Limón, so I could accompany them to Warínts. Then I went back to Sucúa and about seven months later studied with my aunt Maria Chúmpi. I was about twenty-one.

I asked Maria Chúmpi for a concentration, to study how it is to be a shaman of the woman's way. So she gave me this protection; she gave me *mikiut*. Mikiut looks like *maikiúa*, but it's another plant—another preparation—and it's for the *uwíshin*. She gave me *pirípiri* of *Tsunki*, *chucchu* (that's the Shuar name for *pirípiri*) of *uwíshin*. So she gave me this to take each time when I was concentrating.

So that night when I was concentrating, she gave me *natém*, and again she removed this woman's arrow *tsentsak*. It was like a little piece of rubber or plastic, but shaped like a figure; and she said it was woman's tsentsak.

When I saw that, I became nervous. I didn't want to be scared, but my whole body was shaking. Later when I concentrated with the ayahuasca I felt better.

A precious little woman, just lovely, kept appearing before me. Even now the woman is in the habit of appearing to me—very lovely and wearing different robes. She was like Tsunkínua from the lake.

When I drank pirípiri and other things with my aunt, I felt stronger, more alive. I came across many enemies, animals that were ghosts. I had visions, it was like I was in a plane, above everything, above the earth. I saw many people from where I am from. Figures passed back and forth: clowns, monkeys, a beautiful woman, and several other women. Thousands of beautiful women and a temple, a big structure, passed by, but it was very different and marvelous. That's what I saw that night as I was concentrating on pirípiri.

I conversed with my aunt. I asked, "These concentrations are coming out of me—What is this? What is that?"

She told me that it was going to last, but that I had to be careful—one can die instantly when the arrows come back at you.

"So," I said, "I can stand it." I requested that she accept me, this tsentsak. I asked the tsentsak to accept me . . . and it happened. I was thankful. I told my aunt, and she was happy. I told her that I would help her in whatever way possible through shamanism. "If you are dying, I can help you; if you suffer from an illness or a spell or an illness from the wind, I can help you, or your grandchildren, or your relatives." She was thankful. Then I paid her 5,000.

The shamanism of my aunt Maria was different from that of Segundo and Lorenzo because they blew on the crown of my head, and they gave me the ayahuasca to concentrate. But my aunt gave me phlegm, like this, taking out her chuntak. She made me put it in my mouth and swallow it, but when I swallowed it, it didn't . . . I wasn't getting it in. It made me nervous when I swallowed that phlegm because they say it is like the spirit of a woman.

One of the tsentsak I bought from Maria Chúmpi was the cheas tsentsak. It's like poison. Yes, it's for killing. One doesn't use it. I still haven't shot one of these arrows at a person or any animal with blood. No, nothing with blood, not to be a witch. One uses these arrows every four or six months, to shoot them at a tree that doesn't have blood. One doesn't want to develop the vice of doing harm unto others!

For such secret work, I take *natém* at night and then look for a serviceable tree nearby. Then I shoot my arrow into it, and it will die. If it doesn't die, I have to repeat everything until it dies; this means my treatments work.

Now, if I wanted to hurt people, to ensorcel someone, I wouldn't practice on a tree. I would use an animal that has blood, like a bird, or a pig. That is how someone would practice, before actually ensorcelling someone.

My intention is to heal people. I haven't studied in this manner, killing animals with blood. My father and my mother prohibited me: "That's no good." I purchased this *tsentsak* only to protect myself, or in case of an emergency. . . .

Now That We Are Both Shamans

I didn't have the opportunity to study with Maria again. I was busy with the Federation, so I didn't have time to fast. But I studied twice with my father. I wanted to receive the powers that he had. Later, I handed myself over to *namur*—what they call a "talisman." It was so I could learn to cure like he does. He gave me some talismans of his so that I would begin to cure as well. He gave me protection so that other shamans couldn't hurt me, so they couldn't do anything bad to me.

When I was training with my father, I saw the spiritual powers of *pasuk*. I also saw powerful arrows and learned how to make the arrows fly and how they sound. I saw how my father sang, and I learned the songs of my father, the songs to call forth *pasuk*. My father taught me all this, how to chant to attract them. He taught me how to call the monkey *pasuk*, and others, like *uwíshin* and *amaru* and the jaguar of the lake and the *kaniakts* [alligator] and *apup* [freshwater dolphin]. My father gave me powers from *Tsunki* and from the woman from the lake, who is called Wanani.

I took *ayahuasca* with my father and saw everything that he had taught me about. "I see all of it," I told him. Except I didn't see what he'd told me about Wanani. So, he gave me more *ayahuasca*; I concentrated hard and then I saw it.

I said, "Now that we are both shamans, how would we defend ourselves when other shamans attack us?"

He said that nothing would happen to us, no one could do us harm because of our arrows. But he did say, "We should maybe take care, because they could get to us through other means—such as *umpum*. If they can blow on us, there is no way to escape, so we should take good care." This is what my dad said. "You should also take care, as you've been concentrating and seeing things each time." So this is what we talked about, and about how we can do harm to someone who might be against us.

Then my dad explained to me how his late brother-in-law was a witch—Tséremp, the one that died. He said that his brother-in-law could blow *anakma*, he could blow in the form of a scorpion or a snake. The *anakma* would wait on the path, but invisibly. It would bite a person and then disappear, and you wouldn't be able to find it. It could also take the form of a tree. The tree can let a branch fall off and kill someone. This is what my father explained to me. In the future, when my father has died, I want to practice all these things with other powerful shamans from far away. I didn't pay my father with money; I paid him with clothes and with a machete; later on I gave him a shotgun.

But I Didn't Have the Money. . . .

I also studied with Luis Mánkash for a little while; just to blow *natém*. My father got sick again, another sickness. He was ensorcelled; his feet hurt him and were swollen. We didn't go to a doctor because my father said it wasn't an illness; it was something he stepped on, like a nettle. He saw it in his dreams, it was an *anakma*. What I mean is this: let's say I blow on this paper, and then you step on this paper—it will hurt you. So this is a secret way to make someone sick. You blow on something, like a nettle. Then the person steps on it and gets sick. "Was it the nettle?" But it was not. His spirits told him what it was, and he knew there was nothing he could do about it because it was in his foot.

I could not treat him because I was not practicing; I was not in my healing period yet. My teachers prohibited me from healing for two years, to give me time to improve. And we didn't have the money to go back to Puyo to see Lorenzo Vargas (there was no road back then; we would have had to charter a flight). So I went to look for Luis Mánkash; he lived in the *centro* of Corazon de Jesus. Yes, he is my father's classificatory brother and an intimate friend of my father's. He had been a shaman for a very long time and was very advanced.

I went to his house and asked him to heal my father because he was dying. So he went with me to my house. My father had already drunk the *ayahuasca* he had cooked earlier, but he needed his friend. He was in a lot of pain; he had fever so he drank the *ayahuasca*. We got there around 7:00 P.M., and Luis said he was going to do the concentration to see if it was a sorcery, so he drank the *ayahuasca* and saw everything. Then Luis sucked three times and took the microbe out, this *napi* [snake] *tsentsak*: there was like a sharp eyetooth, and half of it was blood and the other half a bone, like a snake eyetooth. He was smoking his cigar and told my father he was going to get better, because he had taken out the *tsentsak*. And the next day my father was better. He gave my father the *mikiut* drink to keep him warm at night, and he blew on him some.

I told him to give me some also so I, too, could get his knowledge. So Luis made me drink some so I could study with him. He gave me the *natém* to blow, and I learned about the spirits, too. I saw the spirits very clearly, without shadows or lights; it was very clear (otherwise you see darkness, and you don't see anything). He gave me *tsentsak* (those cost about 600 *sucres*, or a shotgun), but I didn't have the money to buy any *pasuk*.

Something Could Happen. . . .

The first person I treated as an *uwíshin* was Shimpiúkat, Tsamaraint's son, from Warínts. I went there because I was looking for land, and my brother-in-law, Miguel Tiwi, told me I could find it there. Tiwi was visiting us and told me I could get land for my kids over there.

I got there and stayed with my brother-in-law. And Shimpiúkat's father, Tsamaraint, said, "Won't you cure someone? My brother-in-law told me that you are a witch, an *uwíshin*. My son is very sick and dying. So won't you help us? We don't have anyone here who can cure. And he is gravely, gravely, gravely, gravely ill. I don't know if he will live, but do me this favor."

"I don't know how to cure," I said. I wanted to conceal it from this man. "I don't know how to heal, I don't know how to take *ayahuasca*," I told him, because I was very apprehensive. I didn't know what reaction the people were going to have, or what they would say, and I was so far from home, far from Sucúa. Then I thought, "Something could happen with these Shuar."

But then his mother came begging; his family came to me, crying. "My son is going to die! Can't you please do us this favor? God will help you."

So I said, "All right, I'll go see him. But . . . I haven't cured anybody yet. But my training period is over, so let's see what I can do. If he's young, I'll treat him, but not if he's old." My teachers, the *uwíshins*, shamans, had told me, "You should never treat a man who has had sexual relations with a woman because you won't do a good job; you're still a low-grade shaman. So it would be better to limit yourself to youngsters."

So I asked how old the boy was, and they told me he was twelve years old; he had just finished the sixth grade. So I said, "All right," and I went there. They prepared the *ayahuasca* so I started at night. But I was apprehensive—what if something happened to me?

But when I took the *ayahuasca* it had quite an effect on me—it was good, good, good, everything opened up, perfectly, very nice, and I saw it immediately: he had a microbe, that is, a *tsentsak*, in his stomach. I recognized it—it was the *wánip'* [snake] *tsentsak*. It looked like a worm that you find in dirty water.

When I drink the *ayahuasca* to examine an ensorcelled person, I see everything, as if the person is naked. I see the form of the skeleton, and I can see if the person will live or die. So I examined him, and there was also a different smell, like when someone is not very clean, as if the person had not bathed. And he had diarrhea, too; he was not eating much, just water. I saw him carefully, and I thought: "This is the *tsentsak* that wants to kill him. This isn't an illness; he got it from *chicha* and through a concentration."

"Yes," he said, "when I drank *chicha* at an uncle's house four months ago, my stomach started to hurt. The doctors have given me shots and pills, but they did not work." In Waríts there was a health center, and the health promoters had given him medicines.

I thought to myself, "I can't do this, this is too much for me, I don't have the courage. Damn, I'm really going beyond my limits." I called on my spirits and began to work. I put my *namur* [talisman] on top of the boy's body. I took tobacco and *pирípiri* and was floating. After a few moments I gave him some pirípiri and said, "Drink this pirípiri; it will protect you, it will chill your body because you have a fever."

So I sucked on his body; I treated him and sucked out the worm. When I sucked out an arrow, it got stuck in my throat. But when I took pirípiri, it got better. So I took them out, and after twenty or thirty minutes I had relieved the boy of his pain. He calmed down and stopped screaming, and he said, "Thank God, I hope I am getting better now." After two hours he could get up, he could urinate by himself.

His family said to me, "Before it had appeared that the boy had cramps, wringing him out, and now he is better. 'All right, Mom, give me something to eat because I am hungry,' he said around midnight!" And they paid me with three birds and gave me 3,000 *sucres*.

So this was my first healing. I wanted my concentrations to pass, but they continued until two in the morning. Then I went to bed—I was done in, but nothing bad happened to me. My spirits brought me good things, music and songs, in my sleep.

I Was Not Guilty

My friendship with José Chau broke up in 1963 or 1964 when I was studying shamanism. He, too, wanted to be a healer. He was studying shamanism because his father was a shaman, and he wanted to be a shaman, too. He said he wanted to be a healer like his father and that when he became a father he was going to learn to cure new diseases so when his father died there was somebody there. He said he was drinking natém and mikiut; he said that Antonio Tsamaraint, from Yavintza, made him study that. Just like other friends had done, I told him it was good that he was studying. That's how we talked before our falling out.

But he started slandering me, and I didn't like it. He used to tell people that I was a liar and a bad shaman. I asked him if he really thought I was like that. I asked him when I wasn't being fair. I told him that I was his loyal friend. And I told him that I, too, was a shaman. I told him he had to work without doing something wrong to other persons, because if he was making up stories he could get somebody killed, and it wasn't worth it. I said that if he had something against me, someday it would be obvious, but he would regret it. I wasn't guilty, and I told him he could finish our relationship. This conversation was in 1979, late 1979 in December, because we had a meeting here at the Federation. I have not talked to him since then. It's just a matter of shamanism. He changed because of all that ambition he had. He wanted to be the most powerful doctor and have all the patients. I wish he didn't have this job. We had been friends. Good is the saying that goes "A loyal friend is a friend of himself."

I'm not sad that our friendship ended, because I was not guilty of anything. He knows that now, so we say, "Hi, friend," when we see each other, but nothing else. It's better to avoid the problems. When this relationship ended, I told my father what had happened, and he said it was better to leave things like that.

10

The Shuar Federation

Help Us

The Association of Sucúa started in the year 1958 or 1959. The first *centros* were Utunkus, Asunción, Yampas, Shimpis, Saip, Yukutais, Tuntaim, and then Santa Teresita. There were eight groups with their *síndicos* [trustees], and we selected a president for the association, Miguel Minki. The first *síndico* of Utunkus was my father, and he was reelected in 1961. Miguel Tankámash Chiríap was *vice-síndico*, I was secretary, the treasurer was Juan Jorge Kajékai, and the representative of the heads of households was Rafael Mashiant. Rafael Mashiant and I also ran for *síndico*, but my father won because an older person motivates people more than a young one, and my father was experienced. My father had already made some improvements to the paths, both the one that runs from here to Asunción and also the one you came in on.[1] We made a big and clean path to Asunción, and when they were doing something they invited us. My father was *síndico* until 1963.

But the Shuar Federation was the idea of Father Juan Shutka, of the Salesian mission. At the Evangelical mission they didn't think about credit and the progress of the community—all they were concerned with was preaching the gospel. They offered only ideas and suggestions by telling us we had to work, but they did nothing to get us credit or to help us get the cattle raising going. This was back when Miguel Ficke was the head of the Evangelical mission.

I first met Father Juan Shutka in Utunkus when he arrived to replace Father Albino in 1959. I was married but didn't have children yet. Father Juan said that now we're going to work, that he was going to be the adviser of the Shuar and that we were going to work like we did with Father Albino. I stayed out of it and didn't speak with him; Miguel Tankámash Chiríap represented us—he was the catechist [lay Catholic leader]; he acted like he was religious and said, "Here we are, Father, help us to be very happy."

After I graduated from school, my parents and the missionary—that would be Father Luis Carollo, who has since died—gave me permission to teach literacy. Father Juan Shutka came to visit me in the school and told me that I worked very well. He said that I was a patriot, that I was working without pay, and that I was a good person. He said that they were going to help me receive some more education and that my wife was going to get a three-month course from the German doctors so that she could learn first aid. He said that I was a good guy to be working like this and asked me where I studied, and I told him that I studied in those schools. "Very good, Alejandro," he said. I told him that I had studied in the Evangelical mission and that "I was there until eight or nine years ago," and he said, "That's fine with us; we've never been against their mission."

It's Our Law

I never talked to him about religion back then. I did later, though. That was in 1963, when Mercedes Kapain was hit. She is my wife's sister-in-law from the commune of the Evangelicals on the other side of the Upano. She'd been hit because her husband had found her with another man, Juan Santiago, a professor who was in love with her. The husband attacked him with a machete and badly cut his head. He hurt him to get out the bad blood; that is our custom.

Well, Father Juan Shutka was making his visits to *centro* Shimpis around Chiguaza, and they told him what had happened. He called me and asked what I thought about what had happened to my sister-in-law, and he asked me if I could do the same thing. Then he told me it was wrong. He told me that this type of thing cannot happen, that we should give up old ways like that. "You can punish someone, maybe with a belt, but there are some things, like cutting a person, that are unacceptable." He said that I should never do something like that.

I said that I didn't have that kind of anger, but that maybe if it happened to me—I don't know, I mean it's our law! Don't tell us otherwise—it's stated that the bad blood must come out.

Anyway, the lover took off. He fled before they could get him; he abandoned his lover. The Father then told me that what we had here was a lesson not to do this sort of thing.

Then we became buddies. My son Chínki was very ill with bronchial asthma as a child. He was in agony so we went to see Mother Maria Troncatti so he could be baptized because maybe the baptism would help him. Father Juan baptized him "Esteban" and was also the godfather. Since then we are buddies, and we've been working together. I like the Father.

A Good Tourist

I met Father Germani, Father "Aíjiu" in Shuar, when they had sent Father Juan to Méndez. The director in Sucúa made Father Aíjiu the adviser to the Shuar, so he started to work with us. He's been here for several years. He spoke with me about religion and told me that since I was "married," I had to make it a legitimate marriage by doing it in the Church. He also said that Maria and I had to get baptized, but I told him that we were of another religion and didn't want to. He said that it didn't matter.

For me it's impossible to go about imitating a religion from elsewhere. I am Shuar; I have my religion, how can I change? For me it was hard because I had to maintain my faith while I was given so many ideas and thoughts regarding another religion.

Father Aíjiu said, "Fine; they don't believe in the Virgin." He said, "So your religion doesn't believe in the Virgin, but why won't you believe when we have preached to you that Jesus Christ was the son of the Virgin Mary?" The missionaries told me about Saint Joseph taking care of the baby Jesus and also of the Virgin, his wife. The missionaries talked about this in their preaching. Well, I can decide if they're going to baptize me. My children, who are being raised in the faith, they can be baptized if they want; I won't prohibit it. If they should take up that life, well . . . I have read the Bible, and if they want to follow that life, they should plan well. If I am going to make an agreement, I should stick to it; if I am going to be a tourist, I should be a good tourist. That is to say, they should familiarize themselves well.

So That We Wouldn't Be Slaves

I liked both of these priests; I never had problems with them, and they were good advisers. They thought like you, Nanki! I thought we were going to plan works like we're doing now, but much earlier. When I was young I wanted a town and a school in each community and to put a health center in my town. I would always talk about it, and I wrote letters to Europe. I thought that Father Juan understood my ideas and was working on them; for example, forming schools in the communities so that we wouldn't be slaves and servants to the *apaches* [non-Shuar].

The *apaches* used to mete out punishment by tying up your hands; then they kicked you, beat you, and abused you with their rifles. This happened from 1941 to 1943. If a crime was committed, they would nab you and do cruel things. My mother and father told me of how the *apaches* would form commissions; they would appoint a Shuar, saying, "You know these people; come with us and show us who did it. We're going to get them and punish them." My father had been on many commissions with them and knew a lot. They told him a lot—how they treated the Shuar, how they tied them up, how they put the gun to them and then left them with the women and other Shuar watching. Everybody was badly abused in those days. Damn, everybody was repressed. But with strength, the Shuar were never dominated.

Ownership

The Shuar Federation was an idea of Father Juan Shutka's, when the Shuar's problems began with the *apaches* over land. Father Juan said that we had to form the Federation and build a headquarters. While we were installing the Federation there were problems. "The Salesian Fathers are going to be the owners of the Shuar communities," the settlers said. Filimon Lopez, and others, said that the gringos had to be owners of the communities. It was a crazy idea. He said that someday the Shuar communities weren't going to belong to them and that the gringos, the Italians, were going to be the owners. But Father Juan always told us not to believe that nonsense, that they didn't understand the organization. He said the we should go on working for the community.

That first time that I talked about the idea of a Federation with Father Juan, we were at a meeting of the Association in the headquarters (there was a house, yes, inside of the mission, where the school is now). The committee that formed the Federation was Father Juan Shutka, Father Añiju (Alfredo Germani), me (I was secretary of the *centro* Utunkus), Ernesto Tséremp (the *síndico* of Saip), Miguel Minki Tankámash (*síndico* of Asunción), Julio Saant (the *teniente político* of Sevilla don Bosco), Rafael Mashiant (the *vice-síndico* of Utunkus), Miguel Chiríap, that's

Miguel Tankámash Chiríap (the *síndico* of Utunkus), Bosco Chuínt (the *vice-síndico* of Saip), Jorge Kuja (the *vocal* of the Saip, the first *vocal*—a councilor, that is, he represents the community), Utitiáj (*síndico* of Shimpis), and Eugenio Samik (the secretary of Asunción). All of them had studied in the Salesian mission school.

Ernesto Tséremp worked on things for the community of Saip; he also worked for the development of cattle raising. And he attended to the people's health by making first-aid kits for all eight communities. He also fought for the well-being of the community and its lands. He's my *saich*, because he's the son of my uncle Yankúr, the classificatory brother of my mother.

Miguel Minki Tankámash is from Asunción. When he was young, he was already worrying about his people and the communities in the province of Morona Santiago. He went about with the Salesian advisers, telling people that they had to have more communities and more *centros*. He helped people plan to work in cattle raising and to get credit. He helped with everything—like how to plan some community centers—and for that he was well regarded and well received by the people. His mother and my mother are classificatory sisters, so he and I are classificatory brothers.

Miguel Chiríap is from Utunkus. He is a nephew of Andrés, the son of Benjamin Chiríap, my father's brother. Benjamin Chiríap's sons are José Chiríap, Miguel Tankámash (not Miguel Minki Tankámash from Asunción), Vicente Naichap; there are more sons in Asunción and also Miguel Chiríap. Miguel Tankámash Chiríap also worked collaborating as a representative of Utunkus after my father, in 1962 or 1963. Then he worked as a replacement representative after the term of my father ended, and from there he also collaborated on behalf of the needs of the Utunkus community.

Rafael Mashiant was *vice-síndico* of Utunkus. He is married to Nohemi Chiríap, the daughter of Benjamin, the sister of Vicente. So when Vicente Naichap left for Taisha, he sold his land to his brother-in-law. This is how Rafael ended up in Utunkus. He's a good one. He gets along well and doesn't fight with anyone. He helps a lot with our projects and lends a hand. He's been a good guy.

First, Father Juan Shutka made a plan regarding how we're going to plan our work; the Shuar *centros* of Sucúa approved a statute. Then, after the plan was made, we talked about how we would form the Federation, link the various *centros* within the Federation, and continue forming more *centros* and making the necessary agreements. From there, once we were installed, we would get some loans and assistance from the Europeans or another foreign source, which is easy to do. With this money we could do good works in the communities and not be so manipulated by the *apaches*.

All the authorities who were there said it was a good plan. We were going to do all this because when the Shuar get assistance they can dedicate themselves to good works (like we are doing right now with IEOS [Ecuadorian Institute for Sanitary Works]). When someone planned well we worked quickly, so we agreed that the *centros* would work together to make the Federation. All the representatives cooperated; everyone was in complete agreement. "We're going to do this," we said.

So, after we agreed to it, a group of Italian and German volunteers arrived along with the Peace Corps. They came to help move stones and start with the *centros*. Everybody from the eight *centros* of Sucúa collaborated by providing food and drink—and that's how we built the Federation.

Afterward, Father Juan started planning the finances and credit. Father Juan said that the loan we received would be invested in cattle raising and health and education. We'd form a works commission and plan carefully and look for funding. We'd establish cooperatives to promote the raising of cattle and bring in agronomists. So we planned and looked for aid; I think it was the Germans that helped us out the most with the cattle raising.

The cooperatives were the idea of Father Juan Shutka. A cooperative consists of a group of six or more members who secure for the Federation a loan of 200,000 or 100,000 *sucres* from another country. For example, Italy gave a donation—not a loan, a donation. Such donations were invested in different parts of the Shuar community. So some people would work, and when they sold cattle they had to speak to the president, secretary, and treasurer, because the money had to be accounted for. A well-administered cooperative can achieve a lot. When a cooperative is run by agronomists that don't visit the *centros* and don't do anything to help with the cattle, it doesn't work. And if you don't concern yourself with running it well, involving skilled people, it won't work.

Credit

Later, in many cooperatives, like in Utunkus, the administration was done poorly as the members of the cooperative began to sell the cattle and spent the money poorly. Our cattle cooperative was formed a long time ago, during the second presidency of Miguel Tankámash, back when they had credit, back when Hans the German [a German volunteer technician] was here.

In 1986 or 1987, we had problems with the cattle cooperative. The Uwijintias group was a block in the cooperative and was administering the loans poorly. The bank liquidated the loan, but the debt remained. The Federation collected payments from cooperatives, but the cooperatives were always forgetting to make payments. This created problems for the people who were taking out loans as families and as individuals. So we called for an assembly in the centro to solve the problem. Members of the community and members of the cooperative met before the president of the Federation and had to come up with a solution. "All right, you have to account for your payments, because the statutes that we have approved say that when a centro has a debt, we can't continue giving credit or loans. So when you've paid off the debt, you will once again become eligible for more loans." This is what he explained to us.

Three years ago the members quit selling cattle, though. Things were badly run. An agronomist, or president of the cooperative, is—according to the statutes—responsible for monitoring all expenses. But the president of this cooperative didn't do anything. So the members divided up everything, and everybody took their cattle, and that was it. They lost money—even now we still owe. Working like that, you don't achieve anything.

I remember how everyone said, "Go, collaborate in collective works like the cooperative," and then, "This is how we're going to work, and it'll pay off; everything will pay off if you work this way. You have to be a man; you have to be obedient; you have to be the kind of man we can direct, in this cattle project. Then everyone in this community will obey you; we'll obey you." But this was not certain. I worked with this feeling, this happiness, for twenty-five years, but it turned out that it was far from certain that it would work out well. Well, I'm not going to obey their rules my entire life. So it fell apart, and there are still problems between me and them, and I don't like these problems. Now I bear a grudge; these feelings have remained. I have these profound feelings because I lost many benefits, and moreover, I lost the opportunity to pursue other projects during that time.

He Made Agreements

We voted for the president of the association. Miguel Minki was elected president. I voted for Julio Saant, but more voted for Miguel Minki. Miguel Minki was the first president in 1961–62, until around 1965. He was a good president. He did many things; he made agreements with the Ministry of Health and had meetings with the government. He made an agreement regarding agrarian reform with the executive director in Quito. He was welcomed; he was received by the minister of relations and of agriculture regarding cattle raising. He also got assistance from the Ministry of Education. He was well received in the ministries, and even today he has friends there.

The leaders of the Federation had a meeting every two weeks. The representatives would go back to their communities after the meetings and would bring everyone in their respective *centros* together to ask what the people thought about this and that. They would tell us the plans being made with Miguel.

"These plans and projects from the Father are good," Miguel said. "What do you think?" I told him I was as happy as the rest and that we wanted our comrades to continue coming. Miguel told me that I had to be a leader because we were going to have many problems, economic problems. Where are we going to get money from? Where are we going to meet? In order to start the association everybody had to ante up 10 *sucres*. Miguel was going to lead us, and Father Juan said he would help us find funds from foreign sources. He was sure we could do it, and we were all going to work equally hard.

Nothing Would Change

All this was planned especially for the progress of our people, and by the Federation. Nothing would change—the Father told us our religion would be as it always had been, and our language would be used, and the projects would be planned for our benefit. So there wasn't a problem with the elders because they, too, knew how to organize and to work. They were well suited to work and could be useful for the well-being of the community.

Things Have Changed a Lot

I spoke with Father Juan in 1981 when he talked about politics. He felt that the Shuar should not involve themselves in political matters. Politics are only for the *apaches*. But nowadays things have changed a lot; now we're involved in political matters. I don't know what happened. It's in our statutes that we shouldn't get involved in politics because it isn't good for us, maybe because we aren't cut out for political matters. But at the national level, we have a democracy, and everybody participates. There are people well suited to work on behalf of their province.

You'll Have Your Community, and We'll Have Ours

I have spoken to settlers about the Federation. I was telling the *colono* Don Reinoso about all this. I talked with him about what we'd done and asked what he thought. I told him we'd have our own communities and that we'd go to Huambi to work, not Sucúa. I told him we wouldn't be ordered about by the *colonos* anymore, and that we wouldn't work with them. "You'll have your community, and we'll have ours." It was like this that we went on talking.

"That's fine, my son," he said, "do that."

I told him that we were working together with eight other *centros* and that Father Juan Shutka was helping us to plan things. "Oh, good," he said. "We, too, were aided by the Salesians; we have our parishes, and we've advanced. Very good! These Fathers are helpful up in the mountains, doing good things. All over the world they are bringing people together to work and are doing many good things."

My Father Won

Later I spoke with Filimon Lopez and told him about what Reinoso said. Lopez said it was worthless. He was arguing with me a bit. He didn't want to hear any of it because his land had been taken, and he had been harassed for a while by us in Utunkus. He took land from my father! In 1962 we had to go to the authorities, to Mr. Alfonso Barzallo, the *teniente político* of Huambi, and Mr. Hernandez, the *jefe político* of Sucúa. The two authorities came but couldn't resolve the problem, and the argument ended in a stalemate. Mr. Filimon didn't pay attention to the authorities, neither to the *teniente* from the parish nor to the *jefe* from the county. So the *jefe* said, "Okay, if you don't want to sort it out right now, you can do it later with the IERAC [Ecuadorian Institute for Agrarian Reform and Colonization]." And that's how we ended up going to the IERAC. I went with this president of the association, Miguel Tankámash, and he and the IERAC reached an agreement to send the engineer and the topographers (Mr. Mata and Italo Moreno) to fix the boundaries. So my father won! We took back some pastures and did some work for Mr. Filimon in compensation. But Lopez said that this wasn't right, that his land had been taken and that this priest was bad, that he was a communist. I said I didn't know. Father Juan didn't pay any attention to this kind of gossip; he said it was a lie.

It Was Like That

Well, at the next meeting our president, Miguel Tankámash, had to speak. He said that we'd begun to work and that the headquarters of the Federation was coming along. He said all the communities were going to help. He said the *síndicos* would come together to help. People would have to help with the labor, and that's how the Federation office was built.

Later, after we'd installed the Federation, after it was done, the third floor of the mission, where we used to meet, burned. We realized that it was a jealous colonist who had done it, but there was no proof because it happened late at night.

There's No Way to Go Back

Everything changed completely around 1965. We received a loan of 100,000 *sucres*, and money was circulating in the communities. We had work to do for the community to prepare the schools. Moreover, the

Agrarian Reform Law and the colonization in our province of Morona Santiago completely changed everything. The Agrarian Reform Law was good in a way as everybody got title, and their rights had to be respected. Communal reserves were established, and that was good. The only problem is, you couldn't sell just a portion of your land even if you had a lot.

At first, the engineers explained that everybody had to have title so that they would be treated fairly. Everyone was to get title so that you could sell the land when you wanted. You could do what you wanted with it; nobody, not even the state, could do anything because it was to be private land, and everybody had their rights. But the Shuar said that we didn't need them. The communities, like Utunkus and Shimpis and others, said that they didn't need the engineers to come and measure so that the government could give them land. The engineers were going to give out 50 hectares to everyone, but the Shuar already have their 80, 60, 70 hectares and didn't want anyone messing with their land. Some had 200, 300 hectares! For example, in Yunkuankas the Shimpis had around 1,000 hectares each, and they didn't want to be left with less land.

So the government started to mark off plots of land for Shuar communally. Some people—*colonos,* Shuar—didn't want to do it like that; they wanted to get individual title. In fact, my land is mine, because we were one of the *centros* in the Asunción parish that took out individual titles. Utunkus won't make their land communal now because the Agrarian Reform Law doesn't permit it. Once communal land has been given individual title, there's no way to go back.

The Federation rejected individual title as a rule, though, because they knew that the Shuar would eventually lose the land if that was done. Communal land was Miguel Minki's idea, because when we realized that all the Shuar were going to start selling their land—where we lived—to settlers, we saw it would be bad. We'd be left with no land, and our children would be left aside. They thought it was better to do it communally as a Shuar reserve. That way there would be only one title for all 1,800 hectares, and within that everybody would get their own piece.

First, IERAC measured the lands of Asunción and San José. But there were title problems in San José. The Chúmpis sold their land. In the north, Masurash sold land to *apaches,* and there were lots of problems. The *apache* didn't want to leave after they sold it to him, and there were

177

Girl in *centro* at Utunkus

lots of problems between the settlers and the Shuar. Julio Zuniga and Cesar Cambisaca bought the land. They still live by the river, where you crossed in the tarabita [gondola].

Building Bridges

Miguel Tankámash was president when they built the highway. I remember because that cable for the suspension bridge into Utunkus was donated by the Italians. It was left over from the bridge that crosses the Paute River, which CREA [Economic Reconversion Center for the Austro] built when they were making the highway to Cuenca. More colonists began to arrive after the Agrarian Reform Law. Some who lived inside of the reserve were good people. But there were others who caused trouble; they looked for problems with the Shuar. Like in Saip right now—they had some problems because some settlers entered the Shuar reserve. This type of problem is going on right now in San José de Morona, Santiago, Zamora, and in the province of Morona Santiago.

Then Julio Saant was president, but he lacked a real desire to work and to undertake his assignment. He was in it for the money. After Julio Saant, Domingo Antún' from Taisha was president. At the assembly it was decided that someone from the other side of the Cutucú should be elected, to learn to work in the offices of the Federation, so that it would be easier to have agreements with the Achuar. Shuar and Achuar had been enemies for a long time, so there were problems. Some of the indigenous people here didn't want to see the Achuar. They thought that the Achuar should form their own organization over there: "We don't want to mix with them, in case we might kill one of them or something like that."

But the Achuar said: "Let's forget about that. That's past; our fights are history. We can get along like brothers."

We answered that it's better if we don't start a war. We were going to respect them and work together for the progress of everyone. So Antún' made an agreement with the Achuaras and also worked closely with them.

I Don't Know Where It Went

Then Tankámash was president again, because Domingo Antún' did a lot of things, made lots of agreements, that we didn't like. He did some things well, but in his second term he made an agreement with CREA. CREA was supposed to build some classrooms and to make some paths in the forest. But it didn't happen—the money disappeared. I don't know where it went—it was lost. I think he put it in his pocket or split it with the others. All 45,000 members of the Federation were unhappy because the institution was going poorly. The economy, too—we lost credit for cattle, the cooperatives were poorly run . . . so nothing was good. But Miguel knew how to run things and would look for new projects.

He Always Had a Project

Miguel Minki Tankámash was the most beloved of the graduates from the Salesian mission. When I was around twenty-six, already a father, this made me envious. I thought: "He's always there. People love him. Why is he helping them all the time? Maybe they give him money?" He was always the president, and I thought he should let somebody else to do what he does. This was an envy that I never talked about; it was all in my mind. I realized that he was popular because he always had a project and an open mind. He knew about planning and projects. I didn't know anything about it. He has worked hard; his life was dedicated to the work and the association. He got the money to buy a Jeep for himself by working. When he wanted to buy cattle, he got a loan from the bank in Macas in the province, and he also got some help from friends and some donations. He doesn't spend frivolously; he knows how to save.

I Tried to Consider Their Feelings

When I was president of the Association of Sucúa I worked with Miguel Tankámash. Carlos Kunamp had been president of the association, and when he left office, I replaced him. I formed more *centros* and divided those that were spread apart into separate ones. Santa Teresa has a *centro* called Sunkants, and children there had to walk two hours to get to the school in Santa Teresa, and that was tough. So, I divided the centers into northern and southern districts so that each one would have its own school but at the same time maintain the same center. I did that with Sunkants and later with Uwe because it too was far from Santa Teresa. One of the members over there complained because I had decreed this when they weren't present. So there was an argument, but in the end the people and the *síndico* of Sunkants and Uwe were thankful. But there were always fights. I had tried to consider the feelings of all the parents, but I regretted the way it started. After all the insults to me, however, in the end people were happy. I didn't divide Utunkus into northern and southern districts because back then you couldn't; a colonist still occupied that land, so it had to be done later (but now the northern district has its own school). I also wanted Miguel to get money from the Ministry of Education, like the colonists were able to do. He told me that my ideas were good and that he would implement them.

I Thought I Was Going to Help the Community

Another project that has been very important to me is the planning of a dispensary, a health center, for my own *centro*. First, people said to me "All right, Alejandro, you need to take a course, a course in nursing, a health promoter course, if you want to open a dispensary."

So I said, "And you, why don't you take the course, too?"

And they said, "No, you have more interest, more knowledge," so we went ahead, developing our community. We got a donation for the benefit of the community. I thought I was going to help the community with this dispensary, so in 1973 I installed it. It was good; there were some profits. But later people didn't pay, and they complained that I wasn't there to check people and that I didn't visit the ill, so I regretted it; I learned that it was not a positive thing.

He Didn't Work

After Tankámash, Julio Saant was president in 1976 and 1978, but he didn't work. He was always at home, managing his farm. He was from Sevilla, and the majority of the votes for him were from Chiguaza and from Sevilla. It's not that the Shuar from Sucúa and the Shuar from Chiguaza are so different. But the people from Chiguaza voted for Julio Saant because he lived near them, and they would have more access to him.

Vicente Jíntiach' was next, but he didn't last more than three months. He didn't like to fight; he didn't like to manage; he didn't like to be troubled by problems. There was an assembly, but he didn't make a presentation, he didn't say anything. He just quit and walked out. He has an academic degree, and the people wanted him to do something more for the Federation. But he didn't like it, and he wasn't up for it, so he quit.

Miguel Wouldn't Accept That from CREA

So the assembly elected Miguel Tankámash again, from 1978 to 1980—yes, his third time as elected president. Miguel worked well in his third term and motivated the Shuar. They organized a group of women that is still working now and is able to get credit and to make money. Before, the women were ignored, but now this committee looks for donations so that it can do an adequate job. The Federation supported the formation of the committee. Miguel also did other projects, one was against CREA, which wanted to establish cooperatives within the zones of the Federation, in Achuar and Chiguaza and Sucúa. Abad [the director of CREA] and Bolivar Lituma were pushing this, but Miguel wouldn't accept that from CREA.

Abad wanted to destroy the indigenous community! He was trying to take away the land by invading it and bringing people in from the highlands and forming colonies in the form of cooperatives. He thought that the jungles that are Tras-Cutucú were free for the taking, that the Shuar weren't the owners. He thought that only the state had rights, not the Shuar. "The Shuar should only get a little bit of land"—that's what Abad would say.

Ricardo Tankámash, the brother of Miguel, was going to become a lawyer, but someone killed him. They didn't find out who did it, but people suspected that it had to do with the conflict between the colonists and the Shuar, that the *colonos* were jealous of him. He only needed one more year to graduate, and they didn't want it, so they killed him.

Anyway, there were some consequences and some problems between CREA and the Federation. So Abad left CREA and was replaced by the guy who's there now, Dr. Mancheno. He's been a better coordinator and has worked in terms of the agreements between the Federation and the government. He respects our rights and helps the communities. In some parts of Chiguaza he's helped to form some cooperatives for aquaculture. He's worked with volunteers from the Peace Corps. He's also built some schools and made some basketball and volleyball courts. This has all been done during Dr. Mancheno's tenure.

After Tankámash, Pedro Kúnkumas from Yukutais[2] was president from 1980 to 1982. People viewed him favorably, but he made some mistakes. He gave land from Kimi[3] to the municipality. I don't know how they worked it out because people weren't in agreement. But all of that hill behind Kimi now belongs to the municipality. He just said that he was president and that he was in charge, so he had to do his job. But maybe the buyers would have given a little more money or something. But it wasn't made clear to the assembly, so there was a problem.

Another thing was the agreement with CREA, to get 300,000 *sucres* for the Federation. But that credit disappeared! Those in Yukutais know about what he did. The house he has came from money that should have gone to the coffers of the Federation! He got the 300,000 and used it for himself. So this created problems between him and the members, and he wouldn't do the things he was supposed to do, like solve the problem between San José and the *colono* Julio Zuniga. He didn't want to help us as the director of the Federation, because he was friendly with the colonists and still is.

They Think That the Federation President Is Going to Help

We had some problems. Julio Zuniga was injured, shot by the members of the San José cooperative. It was a fight over land. Zuniga came looking for trouble with a gun, and with this same gun they shot him. So, on the radio, Kunkúmas said, "They think that the Federation president is going to help? No sir! The members of the Federation should think! The Federation isn't going to help Shuar who, instead of working peacefully, assault the settlers." This is what he said over the radio.

But Ernesto Tséremp, who was *vice-síndico*, backed up San José Utunkus. I sent word to Ernesto that he needed to help, to get us a lawyer in Cuenca, to help us find a solution. He said, "No problem, Alejandro." He went to Cuenca and got a lawyer. The lawyer helped us through a lot of problems in Utunkus. He didn't let the police enter the *centro* to make an arrest. So there was a fight among the lawyers. Later, Zuniga ended up with only part of the land he had. He'd lived in Utunkus ten years, and, according to the law, he who has already lived more than ten years in a place has the right to own part. So now he lives in his house and keeps his plot of land. But right now there's another problem that's going to cause another revolution to get him out. He isn't accepted by the Shuar community. There's a colonist living there! That's still a problem.

We Do What We Can

Kunkúmas wasn't known as the president in the *centros* of Sucúa. He only went to visit Achuar; I think maybe to inspect their cooperatives. He didn't do anything big. He did make problems for the Salesian advisers, though—for Father Juan and Father Aíjiu. Father Aíjiu worked for SERBISH [Shuar Radiophonic Bicultural Educational System]. Father Juan helped our planning by looking for credit in his country and in other countries. He built that big building for our Assemblies and also made that rest house for those who come to take courses in Kimi. But Kunkúmas said the priests shouldn't be in the offices, that only Shuar should. So he changed this. He said that it's no good that the priests are advising us, because Shuar should be doing everything. "A priest shouldn't be doing it—a Shuar should." He and Juan Tiwi spoke at the extraordinary assembly for presidents of the association. They felt that the Fathers shouldn't have leadership positions over the Indians since there was a sufficient number of people qualified to do that sort of work.

Miguel Tankámash, however, said, "The Salesian advisers have their work, and we do what we can. But to do all these things, like coordinating, and so on, one has to be a professional. How are we going to get by without a legal adviser? Where are we going to get financial help? If you think you can do what Father Juan and Aíjiu do and get money for us like they do, then fine, we'll accept that. But we don't have anything! We have no credit, no contacts, no one from whom we can get help."

Kunkúmas didn't say anything. He couldn't say how he would do those things. All he said was that we should elect an adviser and that the Fathers should go back to their missions.

Miguel Minki then asked: "Did you study? We were educated by the Salesians. You think that you can go against the priests and the missions?"

"I was educated," Kunkúmas replied. "We shouldn't be led by the Salesians if we want to maintain our culture and tradition; we should be pure Shuar and not have Salesian legal advisers."

But Miguel Tankámash answered, "You don't understand! The statute was approved; the majority agreed that the coordinator has to be a Salesian. It was decided that he would work with us, and we accepted that when we started the organization."

"Fine," said Kunkúmas, "we'll go on being ordered around by the Salesians."

Miguel then said, "This will never happen because they don't order us around. We have to respect and reclaim our rights. We have to be positive, not negative. But these ideas that you want to reject . . . it isn't useful to reject the Salesians. You can't do this. You aren't the people; you aren't the organization. You are just a president that we elected. You can't do as you please."

Well, we talked about this until the secretary said, "No more. I say that you should ask for an audience with the missionaries. I was not educated or raised in the missions, but I thank them because they helped start this Federation. We take courses with them on cooperatives and health. They are preparing us.

"I could go against the missionaries—people always have a complaint. If one doesn't complain about their religion, one complains about the credit.

"But if Father Juan and Aíjiu aren't doing a good job, tell them to their faces and discuss it. You can go over their plans with them and tell them what's wrong. Tell them to leave. The priests don't have to advise us, but we are still tender, my brothers.

"You all are still educated by the Salesians. Although I was educated in different schools, you were helped by them, you received scholarships from them. Today you are a teacher because of the help they gave you to go study in Quito or in Macas."

The vote was in favor of the Fathers continuing as our advisers, so that was it. Father Juan and Aíjiu didn't say anything because it wasn't worth it.

He Did His Job

After Pedro Kunkúmas, Bartolome Máshumar of Sevilla was president in 1982–84. This was when I was secretary of Utunkus. He did his job. He did a lot of projects in Mutints and Chiguaza and formed some parishes. He did a good job and got along well with the advisers and whomever else he dealt with.

By this time, the majority of the colonists were getting along better with the Shuar because they had reached an understanding that we had rights as landowners. Some even helped us, like Roberto Calle. These are men who have lived here for a long time; their sons are already fathers. And many of them have helped and worked with us. For example, Laura Villa works as our treasurer, and other colonists, like brother Freddy, work with us, too. Other people, however, were bothered over issues of land and boundaries, and there have been invasions of our land. These were the ones that went against us and the organization.

But there were mistakes during the term of Bartolome Máshumar. On the other side of the Cutuku, by San José de Morona, people from the highlands took over our land. They grabbed unused land that exists in San José de Morona, but then they discovered that the indigenous people were still owners of the land. But the government gave credit to those people who could work more than the Shuar, and they made themselves owners of the land. Then Bartolome Máshumar and the executive director of CREA made an agreement regarding unused lands that would respect Shuar ownership. So, CREA stopped, and the projected colonization was suspended. The settlers abandoned the land—there wasn't transportation, and sometimes the plane didn't arrive, and lots of people had problems with all the flies and lack of food.

Worse Than a Disgrace

After Bartolome Máshumar, Bartolome Juep was president from 1984 to 1986; this was when I was *síndico* of San José. Miguel Tankámash also ran for president at that time, but the assembly didn't accept him. People were always talking about him, saying that "Miguel is always president"; "What's going to happen when Miguel dies?" or, "We want other people to work and know how the Federation functions." He was the only one that was advising us, so it was very difficult for anyone else to do anything. Pedro Kunkúmas also ran again, but we didn't want him back. So Juep won, but he was worse than a disgrace, Nanki.

Juep was a teacher from Bomboiza. At first, he made an agreement with IERAC that more colonists couldn't enter the Cordillera del Condor. Then he and the directors started to make deals with unused lands on the other side of the Cutuku so that Ecuadorians could plant African palms; this was under the government of Leon Febres Cordero. The representative of the Federation in Quito back then was Enrique Nurínkias. He accepted an agreement saying that in the Amazon, across the Cutucú, there is a lot of land. The government wanted small industries to be able to plant African palms for their oil and other products. Enrique Nurínkias made an agreement, but meanwhile, other leaders, like Miguel Tankámash and Ernesto Tséremp, investigated the whole thing. After they saw that it was a shady deal, that it wasn't good, they took measures against Juep and his directors.

Then Juep and his cronies said that they were going to form another group, another organization. He said that we Shuar couldn't accomplish anything because the organization is advised by the Salesians and is controlled by foreigners. He said that we should separate ourselves and work as a new organization and make a new deal with the government. But they were pushing this just to make more money for themselves. Enrique Nurínkias told the government, "If I'm elected the next president, I'll give over to you all the land for the mines that exist in our eastern lands."

We closed the door on Juep when he was in his house, and we didn't let him back in the Federation again. Then the teachers of the Federation came before the assembly to explain what was going on, how Nurínkias wanted to be president of the Federation, how he wanted us to sell our land, how resolute he was that we make a deal to sell the land to the colonists.

So Enrique Nurínkias got heated up and said, "Fine. Now we'll leave this meeting room, abandon this assembly."

And right then fifty people left with Enrique and Bartolome Juep. They took the Federation's car and damaged it, and they formed a new Ecuadorian organization that now has its headquarters in Macas. The new organization was going to get credit and make cooperatives and raise cattle, they said, but it was all a lie. They couldn't do anything; the old Federation won.

We won the fight.

After that, all the teachers who work in SERBISH told Tarcicio Kuja that he would be the president. And from there the teachers took all the posts and continued fighting with all those little cumpachumas as we call these sectarians, these groups that formed the new organization, Bartolome and the rest of them.

Then the assembly met again and elected a new president, Angel Tsamaraint. He was president from 1986 to 1988 and was very good. He continued working through these problems that were created by the agreement with the government. He ended up investigating everything—the losses of credit that had been made. There was a lot lost. But the new leadership faced the problems and solved them to the point of leaving us free of them. Tsamaraint addressed some serious problems facing our organization, and he made an agreement with the government that it wouldn't be allowed to enter into the Shuar zone in the Amazon to pursue projects like mining and petroleum.

What Does the Community Need?

From my observations of the Federation, I think that it's weak because of its leaders. The directors need to do a lot more. They have to undertake more works for the Shuar communities in the associations. Speaking over the radio and giving presentations is not enough. We are a marginalized people. What does the community need? If I'm giving chats over the radio, sitting comfortably, I think that my brothers are in the same situation as me. No. I've got to go out and see, to observe my community.

Second, there are some that make deals with the *apaches*, regarding land, for example. IERAC gets involved in a dispute and tells us what to do. But the Shuar don't have to accept. The majority of the Shuar don't accept it. The president should say, "I don't accept it; I won't sign it. I won't sell my people out."

Another thing that I've noticed is that the agronomists don't administer things well with the cattle. There aren't medicines or druggists for the animals in the associations. But now, I hear there are. Miguel Puwáinchir has gotten medical kits for the agronomists, they have them for the associations and for the Achuar, too. This is the work of Miguel. He's done a good job. Tsamaraint would have worked on these problems, too, if he had the time. But he always had to be fighting against the new Shuar Organization of Ecuador, the rival federation, and solving that mess.

Puwáinchir is also doing well in his work of getting title for land. Some of the members don't always comply with the laws, so sometimes they get into conflicts over land. It's also good that more people are getting educated. The level of education is higher now than it was in the time of Kunkumas and Bartolome Juep. There are more classrooms, for example. To me, this is good.

But Nanki, you have seen that there isn't a lot of financing and credit available. Just now FODERUMA [Fund for the Development of Marginal Rural Areas] loaned 95 million *sucres*—you didn't know that! But I think, if I'm not mistaken, that FODERUMA has loaned 95 million; including 20 million for classrooms and 5 million for the committee of women. I also think that they are making loans so that people can raise poultry or pigs. In San José the cooperative got 200,000 to buy pigs, and it's still functioning. I've also heard that they have a project, in which Julio Tiwíram and Miguel Mashu are involved, to make loans to people to raise poultry and fish and guinea pigs. I think all these projects are good.

What Have I Gained?

But when I ask for money for something, the Federation tells me there is no credit. They tell me that everything was lost, that it was all a disaster in the time of Bartolome Juep and Representative Enrique Nurínkias.

The Federation was left with nothing, and all those millions for the institution were lost. This is what Miguel Puwáinchir told me. I went to make an application for some help to educate my son, and they told me, "We can help, brother, but we don't have funds." The little we get is for the cooperatives and is on credit—they have to pay it back.

Once I even wanted to forget about being a member of the Federation. Around 1986–87, the Federation took some land above my brother's farm. I had paid for this land but had used it as collateral for a loan from the association. They didn't want to understand me! I said the land was mine, I had the title, but I needed the money because I have kids, many kids. But that Dionicio Atamaint, the president of the Association of Sucúa, didn't want to understand me. So I got mad. I said, "Well, you don't want to help me. As a member I demand my rights! You help people, but you are questioning me, and you are saying I have other means. But I don't have them! The Federation should give me the facilities of a member; I have the right," I said. I thought of quitting because they weren't taking me seriously as a member. So I'm going to get a lawyer and go to IERAC to solve this. If they go any farther, I'll hire a lawyer to save my land. So I'm going to put my foot down. I'm not going to be a member; well, if they want me to be a member, I will be, but we'll see how it turns out. I should just work and tend to my own chores and forget about the Federation. I wanted to forget the law and statutes and the organizations, I was so upset.

Then, in 1989, the vice president, my nephew Bosco Chiríap, didn't take care of my papers. I wanted a loan from the bank for 500,000 to do my work. He said he was going to give it to me through the cooperative. But when I wanted the certificate, he played dirty with me; it looked like he was playing with me.

When I was drunk I always wanted to get him, to hit him. And I spoke to him, gravely, about death. I asked him why he hadn't done my papers yet if I'd paid. The bank wasn't going to give me money. I told him that if my father were there, it wouldn't have been that way . . . he was guilty of my father's death, I said—but I was drunk.

And then he said to me, "All right," and then he cited me to the magistrate. I went there, but he didn't show up. Well, we couldn't solve the major problem about the payments. But I'm not going to touch that again, because I was also guilty because I was drunk. That is how we solve problems.

So in 1990 I told Maria I didn't want to be in the Federation. "What have I gained from all my life working in the Federation? What help have I gotten? I haven't gotten any benefit for my sacrifice. I requested a loan of 300,000, and I have submitted all the papers, but they don't listen to me." So I thought of quitting, to piss them off.

I want to get more credit, more work, and more for my own *centro*. I would like to have a better community, good electric lights, potable water, and more classrooms. I wish to have my house finished and well painted. I want to have a big house and better gardens. One day I was very anxious thinking about all this, and I wanted so badly to go to another country. I was so anxious because I thought I could get a donation or a credit for the community or I could work for myself and have more money if I went abroad—because other Ecuadorians tell stories about the good salaries, and now there are some people of our race, like Juan Tiwi (he was working for CREA), who have gone abroad. Also Vicente Jíntiach'(who is a college graduate) is working and studying outside, I think in the United States or Germany.

This is what I've seen; this is my judgment of the Federation, Nanki. I've seen it all.

II

Friend and Enemy

Just Like Me!

All the Shuar have the same wishes. I mean, I have looked into this because I like to see how people think; I wonder what a person is thinking for the future. For example, I once talked about this with Antún, my late uncle. It was April 21, 1981—I remember the date because I wrote it down. I know it like I know my own ID! It matters to me, and I always talk about these conversations with my family, so we don't forget anything.

I asked him if, like me, he enjoys working, hunting, panning for gold. He told me he enjoys hunting with a rifle.

"Just like me!" I said, "Antonio, I too enjoy hunting with a rifle and with a dog."

But he enjoys hunting with a blowgun more. He likes gardening and helping others when they have difficulties, whether they were in a fight over some unfairness, or because of love or women problems, or because of family. He asked me if I enjoy all that, and I said, "Yes, I help people when somebody makes them feel inferior, or makes fun of them."

"You are like me, Nephew," he said. "I help people who can't defend their rights with a lawyer; I've solved many problems. And I also would like to build a big house, so you can come visit, and I can have my wives, kids, grandsons."

So I told him that we had the same ideas, the same wishes. But he has fulfilled them already, and I haven't.

I had a conversation with Segundo Tsakimp in Tuntaim. He said that he also enjoys having gardens and planting crops like manioc for making *chicha*—not for drinking it himself, but for guests, or for *mingas* [work parties]. Just like me! I don't like *chicha*, but I like preparing it. But I guess I drink more than he does.

I'm Not Thinking about Myself

My uncle Nejempaim would sit all night until sunrise before going to work. I asked him what he was wondering about, what he was looking for. So he told me he was worried about his family, and he was looking for food for them, some meat, fish. "I'm not thinking about myself," he said.

Custom

In 1990 I spoke with my friend Carlos. He told me how nice it was that I had my profession of shamanism, and he said that he wanted it too, but that it wasn't his custom.[1]

He said that his custom was to work and plant manioc and plantains. A house, birds, pigs, and his work were all he had.

I told him that his custom was good, but I was working my medicinal plants because there were people begging for cures and families asking for treatment.

He told me that another custom he had was to raise lots of pigs and chickens and to give some of them to his kids so they can have this custom, too. He told me that it was okay that each of us has our own custom.

I told him, "Yes, Carlitos, my custom is to have kids—sons and daughters. I marry a woman when I love her and she loves me too."

He said, "Damn, no way! I don't have that custom; none of my women have loved me. I've loved them, but I haven't been so fortunate. How do you do that?"

"I don't like to cheat on my women. Yes, if I'm involved with a woman, then I take care of her for always," I said.

I told him that my custom was for my kids to go to school so they don't suffer later. "Carlitos, why don't you look for education for them? I know you worry about your kids."

He said that God gives us our kids to feed and dress them, but that he does not care for studying. He cares about agriculture and his wife but not education.

I told him that education was very important to me. I could be without pants but not without education for my kids so they know how to read and write—because it's good for them, at least to sixth grade. That's what I talked about with Carlitos.

My Best Friend!

Pichík' is from Wichim'. He is an Achuar, and I met him in 1984; he was thirty-eight years old then. He knows my classificatory brother Alberto Mejéant, who lives in Sintuch [by the Peruvian border]. When Mejéant was visiting my father, I treated him. So when Mejéant returned home he told Pichík' that his brother is a shaman. Pichík' said, "That's good to know, because I have family, a brother-in-law, who is very, very sick."

So he came to see me and said that he knew my brother, who had married a relative of his. He brought his brother-in-law, Wíakach', who had been taking medicines but wasn't getting any better. I treated him, and he got better.

Then Pichík' said to me, "So as to remain on good terms, so that you will serve us as our doctor-shaman, let us do this custom of the Achuar, the custom of swearing friendship, so that we never think poorly of each other."

So we became friends: we grabbed each other and hugged, and we swore a promise to each other never to get angry, never, until death. And since then we have given each other presents as friends should—a headdress, itíp', blowguns, and other little Shuar crafts. He was my first friend.

Pichík' is my best friend! We shook hands, we hugged each other, and we swore to each other. Pichík' left in April. The three of us made a little going-away party. He went to buy chickens in Sucúa to thank and congratulate me, and Maria made chicha, and he said, "Friends, I appreciate all"—we danced and stayed up until 3:00 in the morning! He left the next day, on the fifth of April, for Wichim'. Since then we are tight.

Later Nukuim, his saich [affine; one who is or can be related through marriage] and the uncle of Wíakach' came to stay with me. Since Pichík' is my friend and Nukuim is the saich of Pichík', I can treat him as my own saich. Besides, he really is a relative. Wíakach was reared by my uncle Shiki. Shiki was married to my own aunt, Luz Pakésh, but then he married Wíakach's mother.

But a friend isn't like a relative. When we say "friend," it is because we are exchanging, because of business. For example, I give Pichík' something that he does not have anything like right now. I give him something, a crown or a blowgun. He asks, "How much is it?" I say,

"Nothing." So you think to yourself, this is a friend. When he takes a shirt, a chicken, a machete, a knife that you give him, those are then gifts to a friend. Or another example: we are friends, and I have to give you something for free, without any price; or if I put a price on it, you can pay me back whenever you want. So here we are, intermediaries exchanging in business, and it makes us close friends, because you support me and I support you. And if someone tries to kill me, tries to avenge themselves against me, you will support me, saying, "Here I am; I am his friend." Or I say, "Here my little friend, take this little rag, it is for my friend." But I would never do all this with *saich*—never!—because they are not my friends. I can sell them things that I have—a shotgun, for example—but since they are not my friends, they have to pay me now.

The next time Pichík' came to visit was in September of 1988, when his eleven-year-old son had died. The son was in primary school and was bewitched by a very fine Achuar shaman. I was in Gualaquiza by that time, working in Sacramento, so when Pichík' first came here, I couldn't meet him. He took the son to the doctor, and the boy got a little bit better, so they both went home. Soon afterward, the son died in his house. Pichík' then came and stayed with me for a month.

In August 1989 he came to visit me again and brought me baskets and beads and some cloth. And we talked about the feelings of my friend Pichík'. He spoke of the misfortune of losing a son who was studying and was soon going to the first grade. He said, "Unfortunately, my son died . . . and what can I do, my friend?"

"Well, you have to think of the good. Yes, all of us go through this. But we don't want to make trouble; we don't want to have more problems in this life. It's better to live in peace, to find happiness instead of trouble."

Then my friend Pichík' said, "Right . . . at this time I am a catechist, so I can forgive all for what has happened to me. It is better to bring happiness, and I thank you for your message, your counsel. Because you are my adviser, my friend who has helped me for the good. Some people could say go to war, defend yourself. But no—it is better . . . I am also a catechist. I am close to putting myself together and forgiving . . . because that kid got sick. . . .

"All because I got into an argument with a shaman during an assembly . . . he said that sooner or later I was going to cry and would regret my having threatened him. 'You had better not do the things you're saying; sooner or later you'll regret it,' the shaman said.

"I am afflicted. But through your advice, through this good word, I know better. You are my friend. I will go on. . . ." and then we dropped the conversation about the feelings. He cried, and so did I because of my friend's son. My wife cried, and my cousin, too.

We also talked about the politics of the period between 1988 and 1989. For example, we talked about aviation and all the flights. Pichík' asked me how much the tickets were here. He told me it costs 50,000 *sucres* to send a planeload from Wichim' to Sucúa. And sometimes when we want to send something to a friend, the captain does not want to, because the plane is reserved for someone else. We talked about all this in the assembly: how to get lower rates or a mixed flight according to the economic situation of the passenger. (Now the planes are no longer in hands of the Salesian mission; they are finally in the Federation's hands. This way the situation will improve.)

We talked with Esteban about our organization, too. There was a disagreement about what the Achuaras wanted, and about what we wanted—a community, a good school, a good health center. About why couldn't we have good doctors that could help us in the *centro*? Why couldn't we have good education and a center for Shuar-Achuar history? We need all these things, but the directors of the Federation aren't worried about them. They're thinking about other issues and about the money. They don't visit the community and don't know our necessities. So we aren't doing well politically. Pichík' used to say that if we are all agreed, then why aren't we doing well politically? "We're fooling ourselves," he says. "We Achuar know how to think, and we'll demand more."

He said we were going to cover all those issues in the assembly, including how the planes should be in the hanger of the Federation. Everybody spoke out that we should have the planes in the Federation, and not in the mission. The delegations of Achuar confronted the presidents of the associations on the issue of financing, as did the pilots. "So the mission made us an offer, but then they give us materials only on credit. The Ministry of Education is going to give the Achuar money, but you of the Federation give us only material? Why do they do this? You buy something on credit and then use the money that the Ministry of Education has budgeted for our classrooms and educational expenses," said Pichík'.

So President Miguel Puwáinchir said that there was no deception. He explained that the *cumpachumas*, the sectarianists—Enrique Nurínkias, Enrique Chiríap, and Pedro Natale from Sevilla—made the mistakes; they spent all the money. They did this when they left the Federation in 1986 or 1987 to make that new "Ecuadorian organization."

Pichík' told me all about this when he came to my house. "I waited at the assembly to dance, to drink, and to sing with you, but unfortunately you weren't there!" (I was in Quito.) But he had waited for me to come back and had brought a dried fish, peccary and tapir meat, and a bird—actually, two birds. He brought them to me as a gift, and I felt happy because he really loved me after all he had suffered. We talked about politics with Pichík'; and he said that he was waiting for my return; and we danced and sang with the kids to welcome him. That is how I spent my happy day.

Concerning Envy

Concerning envy, well, I'll tell you. There's this man who's always bothering me. He has his work, he has his great loans from the bank, and still, my dear friend, he continues bothering me, and this to me is wrong. My cattle die, and it's a disgrace, but he keeps at it. This happened in 1983 and 1984. My friend Pepe, in the *apache centro* of San Luis, said to me, "This man wants to eliminate Alejandro."

"What can I do? God willing, I'll strike him, or use some dynamite."

Pepe said, "No, let these things be. I can help you; don't do this. He has business, but why are you envious? He has his business, and everyone has the right to their own possibilities. Consider this well, think well. It isn't worth living with envy." So my friend Pepe gave me these counsels, this help.

In 1986, or 1987, or maybe 1988, I was talking to my son [classificatory son] José Nantip of *centro* Natemtsa. He said, "I have problems with my uncle. I have envy because this elder always lives like so, he has his farm, he has his work, he lives happily, while my family and I always live in sickness. I can't live or have a life in peace. Why does this man have it all? I don't know why I have this envy to the point of killing him."

So I helped him by means of this advice: "If you kill a person out of envy, afterward you won't be happy, because it isn't enough to kill a person. So it's better for you to change, to live thinking, that is, thinking about something else, some other way of life, so your children won't suffer."

He answered, "Yes, but I always have this desire, that one day this old man will be done with—even though he's my uncle."

But I tell him, "Don't say that, Son, this isn't right. Let it be, because everyone of us has a judge that makes this decision, so we shouldn't judge one another."

So he said, "All right, I'll comply."

"Because this is what I've always told you," I said. "Look, I don't envy anyone, even though I don't have anything. It's different when one dreams and talks this way, but when people should wake up they shouldn't think of envying and shouldn't make accusations against someone. It's better to keep going; it's going to help you, Son."

Justice

Sometimes the *colonos* say the Shuar kill each other, that we are wild and ignorant. But I'm not like that. Recently you and I talked about our myths and our customs concerning wars and death. But the war that used to exist between Shuar and Achuar was not because of ignorance or savagery, like the *colonos* say. It was to defend our land, to defend and respect the boundaries of our tribe. That's why the chiefs killed each other. If you're an Achuar chief and I'm a Shuar chief, I could say, "We've killed five of you and you've killed two of us, so who is stronger here? Who is losing his people? Is it you or I? We're going to kill more of you the next time! So let's solve our problems by talking." In this way the war ends, and there is justice between warriors.

Forgiveness

There are different ways that you can forget a problem and keep peace. For example, say somebody killed one of my brothers. Once I'm in a dispute, I'm in it for good. A Shuar never forgets, never. Either you kill him, or he kills you, do you understand? This is like legal justice, we call it.

Or you can pay for it, so I say, "Hey, you have to pay me so I can forgive them." But it has to be a woman or a gun or a dog, something really big, really valuable, to be forgiven. So let's say I insult you, I ruin you, Nanki. I say, "Nanki is evil, he's a sorcerer, he's violent, he's evil, evil." Well, according to our justice, if I am to be forgiven I have to pay. I would have to go to you and say, "Sorry brother, take this gun." That is, the two parties can send intermediaries to negotiate. I could send my wife, who would tell you that "Alejandro needs you to forgive him."

They Agreed to Have Peace

For example, when I was around twenty-five, my father had a dispute with a relative named Jiúkam (the father of Pedro Tunki and Antonio Nekta, my mother's cousin), over the death of my father's brother Antonio Akachu. Jiúkam had betrayed Antonio Akachu: he poisoned Akachu, and Akachu died. So my father, Andrés, had the right to revenge.

First he said, "Let's have justice," and he tried to go to the magistrate. But he didn't get anything; he had no money to make a case, so he couldn't get the government to punish the people that had poisoned my uncle Antonio Akachu.

Then my father sent messages with Jiúkam's wife. "If you want me to forgive you, you have to pay. Jiúkam has to pay me. If he doesn't, I won't forgive him until his whole family is dead."

Then Jiúkam said that it wasn't him but the Kankuas family, other people, who killed Akachu to avenge Maria's father's death. Jiúkam said through the messages that he hadn't killed Andrés's brother. He said that when he went to Akachu's house Akachu was already sick.

One day my father and Jiúkam met in Yaap', and Jiúkam asked Andrés to forgive him because somebody else had killed Antonio Akachu, and the real killer had since died. Jiúkam said that he was going to die too, but he hadn't done anything wrong. So, okay, they agreed to have peace between them.

These Things Get Solved

Another example was an argument between me and my brother Valentín. Around 1989 or 1990 we had an argument because he wanted me to give him the indenture of the land. He had married a younger girl in Santa Teresa and then had problems with some of the people there. So I said, "Brother, come live here. I'll give you a little piece of land to live on. And if you leave it, I'll pay you for whatever work you did—just don't sell me out! Because I'm saving that land for my son; it's my son's land. But I'll let you live on it now, because I feel bad for you."

So my brother said, "All right, but I'm going to give you a head of cattle to let me live there." And he gave me one head of cattle.

But then we had problems! He said the land was his and he could sell it. But I had the title to the property, and I summoned him before the president of the association.

"I'll pay you for what you've planted," I said. "I don't need the house—you can take it apart and take it away. But I'll pay you for what you planted."

Then his son Rafael, who is single, said, "All right, you're right, Uncle. Please pay us for the crops, the seeds . . . we don't have anything! All we have is our house. If you want the house, you can pay for the house, too."

So we settled this, only recently, when he repented for what he had said, when he admitted it wasn't right. But I was hard on him—I said that I couldn't take it, me being his brother. I even threatened that I was going to do something bad to him. I can't forget it, but now my heart is in peace. These things get solved.

She Is Unhappy That He Loved me

Right now, in this year—the year of my father's death—I'm having this problem over land that I have right now, that I want. I don't want my siblings to sell it to someone else. I always say, "You don't want to sell it; it will stay here. Nobody wants it, but if somebody wants it, we can give them money." Because everybody has the right to their share of my father's estate, but . . . how could we break it up? How could we destroy my father's land?

So I ask, "Who wants to sell the land? Who wants to cultivate it?" We'll give it to them. I don't want anyone from another family, like Tséremp or Uwijint, to come into possession of it; only those of the family Tsakimp, the grandchildren or sons.

But this uneasiness came upon me. I don't want to make Imelda, my oldest sister, happy. I'm mad at her! She started this problem—and she is accused of my father's death! It'll take a long time to investigate this, although I think her partner was involved. But I know, Nanki, that my sister doesn't have anything to do with our father's death. So I say that Imelda should be happy with her lot.

I don't say anything to her, and she doesn't have to see me. But she's unhappy about this. I know how she feels; I've had these feelings myself. When I was twenty-two years old, I wanted my father to tell me that I helped him a lot, but not that Francisco did, too. "I help more, don't I, Daddy?" I would say. And he would say, "Yes, Son, you help me a lot, but Valentín doesn't." And now Imelda is unhappy that he loved me more.

I Am Only for Life—but This Man Made Life Impossible

I am only for life, for health, for society, for loving people, for the progress of the *centro*, for the power to live, to struggle, to defend our rights, so that our children will live better in the future, so that our Shuar nation will be more advanced, so that we'll be happier in our work, and so that I'll leave a memory as an elder. All this I've planned during my life. Had I been for fighting and killing people, arguing with people, then I wouldn't have been capable of this. I can act violently—but no. My divine love of the divine force of nature, the *arútam*, has brought me to this point. For my future rights, I'll fight with paper and pen, not with bullets. With this paper, this approved proposal, this agreement from which comes something for the community. For example, now we have water, as planned by Maria Ornes, comrade of the Peace Corps.[2] I said, "Let's request this for the community. Let's work in this manner." Now they recognize who has made the project: "Baudillo has done it; Alejandro has done it; this is his doing."

And now this embarrassment, this guy, this Shuar who is sleeping with my sister—he doesn't even say "Good afternoon, how are you, what's up?" to me! If I didn't respond to him, then it would be something else. But it's he who has never had this custom. Calisto was never, never, friends with me.

After Imelda separated from her third husband, Felipe Abarca (his father was a *colono* and his mother was Shuar), she and Calisto made for themselves a ranch in the forest, in order to hide from Felipe.[3] My father said, "Right, I can't give you land, but here is this little lot that you can have. Take it, my son, so that you live here with my daughter until these problems pass." My father loved this man! He was a friend to him!

But from then on Calisto wanted to make himself owner of everything. He is very shrewd, as they say. So I confronted him: "All right, here you stay; keep what you have. But you don't deserve anything on the other side of this road, that is, the path of the *centro*. You aren't even properly married! When you are properly married, ecclesiastically and civilly, then we can give you the land."

Before my father died, he said to me, "Son, he's taking wood without permission; I haven't given him title to the land, so what's he doing here? Why is he against you? This man has to go—you have to send him away."

And I told my father, "You didn't say this before; you ought to have said it! I told you before: throw him out, send him away, because we can't have such a screwed-up guy in the *centro*. We have to send him packing."

So my father said, "Let's send him packing. I've been a little ill, but when I get better we'll settle these problems."

So this is a problem between Calisto and my father over land. He wanted to become the owner of our piece of land, but I protested: "All Right," I said, "how ought we to do this? The inheritance ought to be equal."

But this man, he came making life impossible. For this reason, frankly, I hate this man.

Unforgiven

SR: Is there any example of when it's possible to make peace, when there's no need to kill someone, and you can just give a gift?

AT: Yes. But I'm going to tell you a secret; this is very secret. For example, with this guy right now . . . I'm not going to forgive him ever. He dies there; this is in my heart.

SR: But because of a crime?

AT: For my father's death. I won't forgive him; my sister also isn't in my heart—she's out! I wish she'd die of illness, although I'm not going to do anything.

SR: You're not going to give gifts anymore?

AT: No, nothing, nothing, nothing. As it was in the time of my grandfather, this is my decision. And it's fair; Shuar don't forgive each other in those strong cases. For example, you're my dear friend, and they kill you. You tell me, "Alejandro, I'm strong, but he's killing me," or "I'm good, but he's killing me." You're strong, you aren't sick; the doctors examine you and find nothing, but then you, Esteban, die. And I'm left here, and it hurts me.

This is intolerable. This is for always; I'll no longer have peace. Even if he gives me ten women, I won't forgive that man until I see him die, too. One day, if I'm dying, I'll leave testimony about these people. That's how it is. This is our custom when one is sick, when one is dying. This is it, Nanki.

12

Orphan

How We Have Suffered

The saddest day of my life was July 8, 1989—the day my mother died. So, well, this day was the saddest . . . it was very, very, very, very sad, because my mother just left me . . . she died.

She gave me her final counsels, final encouragements, and final sentiments. She said, "Right now, I'm withdrawing from you and your protection. And my protection of you won't be alive; rather, my protection will only be of death. It'll be an invisible protection. Right now, I can still see you perfectly, and I have cared for you . . . but from now on you won't see your mother. But invisibly, I'll indeed give you my protection."

In her final moments, my mother said to me, "Come, this is your bosom with which I nursed you, with this bosom; and you, Son . . . I'm resting, I'm not dying, but I'm resting. . . .

"Don't be angry with your father, because your father isn't killing me . . . but my grandchildren have done something to me, some injury. I'm not a sickly person, but I caught this malady one moment when you were in Yaup'. You were taking out cattle, and I met a shaman who tricked me, but maybe this person. . . ." So this was my torment, my sadness.

When my mother died, I said I wanted to forget my mother. "I don't want to suffer. Tell me friend, what am I to think?" I asked one of my friends.

She said, "Alejandro, it isn't worth it."

"I want to do something because of my mother's death. I really could, sometimes. I'm mad!" I told her.

She said, "Don't do anything rash! Calm down, because there's a better life."

Besides, I have my North American families. So I'd better memories about my mother in peace now that I have many friends. Thanks to my very loving friends I can continue.

But no . . . how we have suffered, how we have suffered. . . . Yes, I'm sad; yes, I wander here and there. My life and home are a mess. One wife is here, one wife is there; my children are here, my friends are there, and then I just don't have the strength to go on.

Well, it's better now. I feel better, I'm going to work, I'm going to live in peace. Like my father said, "Don't get angry at anyone. Work well. Here is your friend Nankichi, and there are others who have come. So you'll work and live. Do it for this land. You know I won't be taking it with me when I die."

Papa, Look, Didn't I Tell You?

My father was sick in May or June. My father wasn't a sickly man—this was the first time he was gravely ill. When I left for Warínts [where Alejandro's wife Josefina owns property], in July or August, my father was healthy and didn't have any problems. Then when I came back they had already done him in! It was the enemies of my father. They had come from Santiago and from Huambi.

Before I left, when Apup¹ was here, I treated my father for the first time. I took *natém* and I saw his enemies.

I said, "Papa, look, didn't I tell you? Please, you have to get rid of this guy. Send him away, please! I'm not trying to anger you, but I tell you, look at what he's doing now, look at what will happen!"

My father said, "All right, as soon as I get better I'll take care of this task; but now this is impossible."

First they made him weak, to demoralize him. They made *tsentsak*, but I cured him, I acted against them. Then I went to Warínts.

When we returned, Nankichi, he said, "My head hurts."

He got up and greeted us, and he said that, so I cured him again, removing more *tsentsak*. But he didn't improve; he had already eaten the *umpum* [food upon which a shaman has cast a spell].

He said, "I can't get better." He said, "I feel that I'm not going to be better." He said, "I feel like my stomach is burned." This is because of an *umpum*.

Umpum is blown into food or drink. Let's suppose I take this liquor or soda, but then it produces a sickness in me. You can feel good and healthy, and then die!

So after this, my father got worse, but all the medical tests were negative. In September I went to matriculate the kids in school but delayed two months. I came around January—the assembly had already met. Then, on the 18th of February, my sister Teresa told me "Hurry, my brother! Come, because my father is dying, our father is fainting. Hurry, he isn't well!"

I came as soon as possible. But I didn't meet him.

Five Shamans

Five shamans killed my father. Let's see . . . here, that is, in San José, there are two shamans, but there are three more: this Tupikiá (Yuma is his proper name); Kapitián, Daniel Kapitián (of Santiago); and Antonio Tsawant, or just Tsawant (he lives over there; he married a woman of Yunkumas); and also this other, this [long hesitation] Lorenzo, and he lives here.

Calisto is the author of the deed. Calisto has said to me, "You deny me land; you don't want to give me land." Calisto knew that I was angry with him, and he killed my father because he feared that we would kill him. Calisto said, "I have to get back at this shaman, this witch, this senior mage."

So they just made a plan, uniting with other people with different motives. Daniel Kapitián Antún'and Yuma Tupitiá are the brothers [parallel cousins] of Jorge Tiwi of San José. They joined for Tiwi's sake. My younger brother, Miguel Tsakimp, stole Jorge Tiwi's wife Teresa Uwijint—now they have two children. Jorge and my brother have fought many times.

After they made their plan, they began to take *ayahuasca* in the house of Antún' Unup'. His house is in San José in the northern neighborhood. He abandoned the house when he heard that I, my brother Lucho, and my sons Gustavo and Lorenzo were going to kill him. He fled to Santiago.

They killed my father with witchcraft and not with a bullet, because they didn't have the right. For example, the woman that my brother Miguel took advantage of wasn't Antonio's wife, the woman was Antonio's brother's wife. Besides, they were also afraid of the law, the civil, penal law. With killings like this, through witchcraft, there aren't any witnesses. I can talk about all this, I can go to lawyers, but nobody will believe me.

One night, at eleven, I returned home, and I said, "Gosh." I was concentrating with Papa.

Papa, *Wuaandres* ["my little papa"], said, "Gosh, something is going to happen to us; you see, these guys are talking about us."

I said, "They're talking."

"Yes."

"Look, I'm going to find out what's going on."

So he also called the *pasuk*, and the *pasuk* advised him.

So I said, "Now look, this is no lie, what they are planning."

"Well, they aren't going to do anything to us. They are some pricks; they are willful; they drink too much booze and then say that they are shamans, that they are mages."

Yes, I was with my father Tsakimpio that night when we concentrated at Josefina's. But he told me, "These guys are garbage; they aren't worth anything, *yajauch uwíshin ahh, nukurwishinayajatma*.[2] What's this? What class of witch is he? He is nothing; nobody can do anything to Andrés."

I Want Proof

On the one hand I learned all of this from the mouths of other people. And to see if it was the truth I then began to take the concentrations [of *natém*]. All right, some things people said were mistaken, but in the concentrations it came out perfectly how it was: how they had prepared, who was there that night. So I knew.

When my father was dying, I went to Cuenca, where there's a woman spiritist. I've known her for a long time. She told me that it was "a bald man, in front, and this man is very strange. He's never known to people; he's never friendly with people; he's had problems with your sisters, your own sisters; he's had sexual contact with your own sister . . . he's a very bad man; he's very dangerous. He prepares poisons, and thus this family has died long ago; he has this custom, this man.

"Your father had been alive for many years, and he hadn't been sick. If he'd been sick the doctors could cure him. Because you have dealt with doctors."

"Yes," I said, "I dealt with doctors. He had an examination with the doctors, and nothing came out, and he died in the hands of the doctor at the clinic. That doctor didn't know anything; he only said, 'Don't drink any intoxicating syrup. His intestines, his kidneys are all messed up, as is the stomach, and he doesn't have anything else.' "

Then I said, "I'd like to know if my father will continue to suffer."

"Yes," she said, "That man isn't afraid, he isn't afraid. He's going to begin doing these things, this dangerous man. He's eager."

"Yes," I said, "yes, he's eager."

The woman told me all this. "They've made a plan. There are five persons, two authors, and one woman who participated."

What else are you going to say? So it is one woman who participated; so it is my sister.

"If you want to send them to the cemetery, I can help you."

I felt deeply, damn, if it's my own sister I cannot kill; if it's my sister, I can't kill her; you can't kill a human being.

I know that there are those who kill, who talk this way, but this is the way morlucos [slang for mestizos from Cuenca] think.

But my mother and my brothers—we can't kill. It's better to live, to await the death. Damn, it makes me cry; I cried.

I said, "All right, my sister be damned." What did my father do to them? Nothing. He was always very generous; my father was very generous, super-generous. And for this—what did he do? What demand had he made? Maybe my father said, "Get rid of your husband, get rid of your sons." Is this what my sister thinks?

Even now she doesn't come to the grave of my father. "I'm going to go visit his grave. Up to now, I've only visited his old house. I think perhaps that he could be coming back, thinking something," she says. But he is dead.

So this is what I am thinking, right, just wait for her bad luck. She did it; she gave him this umpum. And our father will come then, will come for her; this is her end.

I can live; I'm a man; well, when I'm drunk or something, some disgrace happens to me, but I'm a man who cares too much for my life, for my future, and for him. I have to eat; I have a hand; I have strength to work gardens, to eat. She, the poor woman, she can't make gardens; she can't do anything; she just lives thus, defeated, waiting for her husband. I, no, I have people; I have memories of you, of Shíram, of everything, of my idea, my project. I reach this point and would do it, do that thing, but I can't.

The woman continued: "Thus is death. First he took sick, and you, sir, cured him. And then you went away, no?"

"Yes," I said, "ma'am, miss, yes, I left before this sickness began. I don't want to know about this . . . I, I am nothing. Where I live there are no spiritists whom one may consult. This is why I have come to you."

"No," she said, "you, friend, you are also a shaman, you are," she told me. "You are a shaman, a witch from the east; you are one of the good ones, they say."

But I didn't say anything.

"No, no, no, don't tell me no. As a friend, don't deny it!"

"Yes, ma'am," I say, "It's the truth. Why did I lie? I want proof."

She says, "His own daughter, his daughter did it. The daughter began first; she made him sick first, before the other man." And thus she divined.

So I said, "All right, okay. I troubled you just to find this out. But to kill someone, to hurt a person, how much would you charge me?"

So the woman told me: "To kill a person costs 290,000."

I Wanted to Do Many Things

Nanki, I wanted to do many things; I had a very dangerous idea; I grabbed my weapon. As I say, one hundred for one hundred. I say thank you, Nanki, thanks, Nunkui, thanks. *Petsani Arutmaru, inkis kuptur kamamje yuminksajmei arutmaru, ti penker pusisjamte* ["I want to live well, to be well, and if this man is taken out, it will be well"]. If he's not taken out, I'll go looking for him.

I have friends. I'm not bad, Nankichi, but I'll look for him, and you'll say, "This is how Shuar are." I'll pay a shaman in Otavalo [in the northern highlands]; I'll pay a shaman in Misahualli [in the northern Amazon]; I'll pay the mages that kill.

[*I asked Alejandro, "What difference would it make to kill Calisto with witchcraft? Why wouldn't you kill him with a bullet?"*]

Well, I would destroy my home, leaving behind a mess, abandoning my children to hide myself from the police. This is why—it isn't for cowardice, or for fear of the police, but so they don't put me in prison, leaving my children and my wives. Marta, Josefina, and Maria have to be well protected.

I spoke about this with Maria. She said to me, "Defend yourself in life. But it's wrong to kill him, because now you aren't a man like any other man. You're with us, you're with our *inkizas* [non-Ecuadorian people], and, moreover, you're educating your son in Quito. Now you ought to think about our son. If you leave us you'll see—he isn't made of steel or iron or stone; he's not going to live for centuries. Your poor sons, your friends, all are going to be very sad when you kill this prick and then run away. I don't know where you'll go, but the authorities will call on us many times; they'll bother us, so don't do it!"

I told her, "I won't kill a brother of some authority; I won't kill a brother of a police officer. I will kill someone who deserves it! This guy has been bothering us already for many years, and I'm going to shoot him. Don't say 'this is wrong, these things are wrong Alejandro.' "

"I know what you can do because you talk," she replied. "You talk when you are sober, and when you are drunk you talk more, I know. But no: it's better to live! You have much better plans than we do, we women; you've made plans—about your people, about medicines, about your community, in general; you have planned. So how are you going to leave all this? So some prick can say, 'Aha, now see how Baudillo, Alejandro, is screwed, because he doesn't think? He used to think about many things, but he couldn't control himself, and so he committed this crime.' And then others would come for revenge, and our children would continue fighting with others, at least Gustavo, at least Esteban, Lorenzo. It's not worth it."

Okay, I think these things, too, but these things don't upset me. I wish that the law could help, that I could go, let's suppose, to the president, and say, "Please throw him out, send him away, let him live in Yaup'—he has his own land, he has sufficient land there." But he is pushy, this man.

Calisto, he is pushy, pushy, pushy, pushy! In Saip he met up with a settler, and they went to a lawyer and turned against the Federation; this to what end? And he returned again to Yaup', had a fight with his brother, and put a judgement on the brother for cattle. He fought with his own brother!

Of my sons, I have not yet talked to Esteban. But with Lorenzo, with Gustavo, I have talked all about this.

I said to Gustavo, "Yes, son, I'm ready, but the money—where will it come from?"

He said to me "Papa, do as you think."

"I think," I said, "there are lands of my father, there are woods, there are pastures. I could sell some, sell some to the Federation. I could distribute all these lands to the heirs, and sell my inheritance, and spend the money on bullets instead of food, to avenge the death of my father. I'm not going to kill as a coward; I'm going to kill as a man, with bullets. And when I do it, you just stay in peace. You help your brother, help your mama; do you want to do me this favor?"

"Yes, Papa" he said.

"Okay, but now what I lack is money," I said, "so I'm going to part with my inheritance. I could get at least 600,000 or 800,000 to buy a good weapon and some good military supplies. I am going to speak to other friends in Chiguaza. We'll kill just like we used to, as was our custom before, our law."

So Gustavo said, "Right, then, it is decided. But I don't want you to suffer in prison alone. I'm going to go, too, Papa; I'm going to do this. You're an old man; you stay with Mama. I'll do it, and I'll go to prison. Yes, I won't hide. I'll present myself before the police. I'm going to do this, so do you give support? Do you want this?"

"Yes," I said, "yes."

But Maria said, "No, no, no, this is wrong!"

And Lorenzo also said, "I have decided, I'm going to kill him. "I'll kill him with a knife."

I don't want even to meet this guy! Since my father died, Calisto hasn't visited. Nothing, nothing, nothing. He didn't even ask, "How did he die?" He hasn't said anything. He hasn't come close. Only Imelda has been there at my papa's grave.

I haven't yet spoken to my uncle Manuel Tankámash because he's sick. I haven't spoken with Miguel, or with Teresa, because Teresa is supporting Imelda. I said, "No, no," but now Teresa is accusing my stepmother! Teresa said that she killed my father, that she is a killer of husbands (because her first husband, Antonio Akachu, also died). I don't believe Teresa; she says it as a favor to my sister and Calisto. They don't like me.

I've spoken with my brother Valentín, but he won't help. "Why not?"

"I don't want to say anything, Brother, because I'm married to Calisto's aunt," Valentín said. "I don't want problems with my wife and son, and with my brother [parallel cousin]."

Last night, Lucho and I spoke about everything. "I'm behind you," he told me. "Wherever you go, I'll follow you."

Now It Is Not as Before

I talked to Cristobal, I talked to my older uncle Tiwi, I spoke with Yankúr, I spoke with the Chuíntias family. I went to my grandfather Tiwi (he and Andrés were classificatory brothers, so I call him grandfather), and I said, "Grandfather, this happened to me, this happened, and I want you to support me in this. You see, they'll kill me, too; I too will become sick!"

"No," my grandfather answered, "nothing will happen to you. Now it is not as it was before. Let it be, my son. Don't do this thing, don't shoot him. If he'd killed you with a bullet, if he'd killed Andrés with bullet, if he'd killed Andrés with a knife, maybe. But Andrés died by malice, and you should get back at him the same way. In this way I'll give you support, I'll give my arútam so that you'll be strong. The same thing happened to my son the teacher—after this shaman killed my son the teacher, the shaman also died, but not by bullet, no, but by shamanism."

And Yankúr told me, "I too am here, just let it be." This elder, Yankúr, he is my in-law, saich, kana saich, kana saich [person related by marriage only], because he is the classificatory brother of my mother, of Teresa Suanúa. So this, too, he told me: "Nephew, don't think about doing this harm."

I said, "What am I going to do, damn it? I want to shoot him like a man. I want to see his blood spill. If I can't spill this guy's blood, then I can't be satisfied! I'm not a coward, afraid to kill. But I give thanks that I'm not the kind of witch who kills either. What I can do? Give me a reason."

And he said, "Let it be. Be calm. First, go . . . then when you're ready, call us. Then we'll come, then we'll come to you to console you, and we'll talk the truth."

So their counsels sustained me.

My nephews told me the same thing: "We await the punishment of arútam, and of Iwianch muisak arútam iwantri arutma andris arutmari iwantri andresa muskarini iiste, the damnations of the suffering that my father endured during his illness, our grandfather; we'll wait for this." They don't want to break the law.

So with this, too, I am sustained.

I Would Rather Die

When my father died, I was mad. I wanted people to ask me how I was, and I wanted to destroy people. I said that I decided to divide the land among my kids and leave for the city. And if Maria were to say something, I would hit her. That was my idea.

Lorenzo was asking for his land. I said that I was going to mortgage the land and leave everything for the bank. I would take my father's money because my projects were no good.

One day I told my daughter Bethy to wash my clothes, and she got mad at me. I told Marta that I didn't want to go back home [to Maria's house] because there was nobody to wash my clothes. I told Maria that I was always going to Marta's house because she was always there and cooked for me, washed my clothes, served my friends.

Maria asked me why I was so mad at her, and at Bethy, since my father's death. She said, "You weren't like this before. You weren't like this. Your whole character has changed."

So I thought about it, and I realized, damn, that I was hitting my daughter because of the pain I have in my heart, because I have no one else to vent my anger against. So without reason I turn against my children. "I would rather die. I don't want to live," I thought. So this disquiet, these thoughts, came to me.

But this month I had a change of heart. I said, "All right, my Nanki is here; why can't I have my life back? Someone can ask you, 'What happened? Why are you like this? Your houses, your wives—where are they? Your girlfriends—where are they?' No, this isn't right. You're going to be civilized." This is what my conscience told me.

But I went to Quito before I cured myself of this rage. While I was in Quito, Miguel Tankámash hosted a party in Asunción. I was thinking: "Maria, return to your house back home, please; I don't want you to stay. If Nanki has come to attend the party, return home together, and quickly. But you have to go home. Nancy, my daughter, please go home. When I return, I don't want any problems. Because in the past people obeyed. They didn't attend parties. They would visit a family, have food, and return home. People used to be more respectful." But Maria and Nancy didn't obey me; they were just having fun, going to parties . . . Tuesday, Wednesday, and Thursday, and not doing what I wanted them to do.

You see, someone had filled my head with all these worries, someone was bothering me, making problems for me. But finally I went to Nancy's and asked what had happened, and she said, "Nothing, Daddy."

She said they had left the party at midnight, and I asked if their mother was dancing. She said that Maria was just watching the people dance. I told her that they should be quiet.

I went home and ate very little. I told Maria I had eaten somewhere else, but really I was still thinking about the party.

I asked Maria if she was partying, and she asked me why I was thinking that. She said that they went there just for the awards they were giving out. She said that she told them that we lived far away, and that I was not there to keep her company.

I told her that I wasn't jealous; it was just that I wanted my kids to learn how to behave when they get married.

She said that she just danced with uncle Miguel Minki and that after the awards she left.

So I regretted all my worrying, and I thought, "I need a job, like before; to be happy I need to work on my projects."

One Question

Thus was the death of my father. And thus I am planning, me too, Nankichi. When I too die, you will have in this book, in this recording, what is the Shuar law—how it ought to be, why one can't do it violently, because the law prohibits it. It's not out of cowardice, but because I respect my wives, because they're my second mothers, and I have my children, who don't want to live in chaos.

One question, Nanki: would you want me to live badly? No, no, certainly, not. When you are in the United States, never think that I could commit murder and be incarcerated for eighteen or twenty years. It's not worth it, no. I get these feelings. I want to reflect on my indecision. . . . I want to think of my wives, my children, my friends, my brother Esteban.

These are the things that have happened in my life during these months with my father, Nankichi, but by all means I'm going to continue to see how I can arrive at a better life in my community. Now we have water, now we have it all. Let's see if we can inaugurate the new water system, and we'll continue conversing more, and we'll do our work. So let's leave it at that, Nankichi.

Part 3: The Return

13

At a Loss

Vincent Crapanzano once observed that, for all its theoretical or ethnographic pretensions, "The life history is often a memorial to an informant-become-(distant) friend, a commemoration of a field experience, and an expiation for abstraction and depersonalization—for ruthless departure" (1984: 954). Indeed, I began working on this book as an attempt to better understand Alejandro. This has not been for me a purely academic exercise, because Alejandro is far more than a representative of a society I chose to study. In some ways I used him: he provided me not only with information critical to my research but also with access to other Shuar, and he guaranteed my physical safety. He also used me, at times getting money from me, and at times using his relationship with me to increase his prestige. We also depended on one another for companionship; we lived together, ate and drank together, and often traveled together. While in Ecuador I often wondered, with far greater anxiety and distress than curiosity, what sort of relationship we had. When I returned to New York, unsure how many years would pass before I would return, these feelings intensified.

It is a commonplace among anthropologists that the culture shock of returning home is worse than the culture shock of living abroad. I am not sure that it is worse, but it is quite different. Culture shock in Ecuador crept up on me very slowly. Oftentimes in Ecuador I waxed nostalgic for the United States—for pizza, rock and roll music, and good coffee; these things are easy to miss because they are easy to do without. It was not until my third year in the field that I was overcome by that profound uncertainty of who I was and what I valued. This seemed less a form of shock than a slow form of dissolution.

Back in New York it took only two months—long enough to realize that I was not taking a vacation from fieldwork but really was "home"—for culture shock to crash over me and knock me down. This time, however, I did not question my values or my identity. Instead, I had to confront the nature of my attachments. I was thirty years old and unmarried. When I was in graduate school, I would not allow any personal relationship to prevent me from going to Ecuador. I could not have stayed three years, though, had I not formed close friendships (with both Shuar and Euro-Ecuadorians, as well as other North Americans). Nevertheless, I never let a relationship develop that might make it difficult for me to return to New York. And once I started feeling truly at home in Morona Santiago, I left. Now I was haunted by my memories of those friends, guilt for having left them, and uncertainty as to what kind of personal commitment I was capable of making.

Crapanzano's *Tuhami: Portrait of a Moroccan* is a touching memorial to the anthropologist's dilemma, created by "participant observation." This approach to ethnography pioneered by Malinowski, less a method than a way of living, demands involvement and detachment simultaneously. Such a life inevitably affects our relationships with the people with whom we live. As we study their culture, they must become both our teachers and our friends. "I wanted to possess everything that Tuhami knew and could tell me—and even more," Crapanzano wrote; "I wanted to know him completely" (180: 134). Instead, he learned that we can never know another completely, and that the process of knowing, the ethnographic encounter, never ends (1980: 140). How, then, can one ever leave?

And yet (and this is the dilemma of life, Tuhami explains) everyone must take their leave some day. Crapanzano left Morocco in 1968 and was not able to return until 1973. It was only then that he learned that Tuhami had died a year before. The life history that he published seven years later is, among other things, a testimony to tormented attachments, a mediation on saying goodbye to a loved one.

This life history of Alejandro, though, is motivated by other feelings. I returned to Ecuador for summer research in 1998 and again in 2000; both times I was able to spend considerable time with Alejandro. If I am lucky, I will be able to go back again in a few years and see him again.

Nevertheless, I avoided going back for a long time. I had told Alejandro, Miguel Puwáinchir, and others that I planned to write a book about them, and I did not feel that I could go back until I had kept my word. More importantly, though, my ambivalent feelings about Ecuador, the Shuar, my fieldwork, and Alejandro himself lingered for years. Although I liked him and cared about him, it was often hard for me to take his ambitions seriously, and I resented his obsequious but persistent requests for money.[1] These conflicted feelings were compounded by the insecurity and vulnerability I felt as a graduate student with a huge debt and an uncertain future. This life history is more an attempted expiation for a rueful relationship, rather than a ruthless departure.

Indeed, I never doubted that I would have to go back. Many Shuar had told me of people who had passed through, taking photographs and "studying" them, but who had never returned. I felt an obligation to go back, to prove that I was different from those other visitors. Besides, I cared too much about the people I had met not to want to know what happened to them after I finished my dissertation research. I often fantasized about seeing my old friends again, giving them copies of the photographs I had taken of them and copies of the book I would write about them . . . some day.

"Some day" was not good enough. I was still writing my dissertation when Elke Mader, an Austrian anthropologist who has worked in Sucúa, called to tell me that Maria had died.

I had never imagined that I would never see her again.

I did not find out how she died until I met with Marta, Alejandro's third wife, in 1998.

SR: I want you to tell me how Maria died.

M: Maria?

SR: Yes, and I want to talk without Alejandro because it is very difficult for him. I think it is better not to upset him.

M: That is true, Nanki.

Maria said she was going to take some wood from this tree that had fallen. So she went over there, and I continued going along the road. As I was walking further back, I didn't see the snake bite her.

So she went to cut this tree, and I left her there cutting. She likes the little bananas, the *orito*, the *majech*. So she said, "I'm going to go cut this banana, but I'll be back very soon." She'd gone without boots, just wearing shoes like these. So when she went to cut the bananas, the snake bit her on the foot.

She said that an ant had bitten her. But you could see that something was moving. Then she said, "A snake bit me today." It bit her on Sunday, at nine in the morning.

So we went to the house, and Esteban got the horse [he had just come from Nayumpim, on the other side of the Cutucú, to visit], and he said he was going to take his mother to the hospital, Hospital Pio Doce. So they got everything ready and put her on the horse; they were ready for him to carry her to the hospital.

Mariana, Gustavo's mother-in-law, had just come from Sebastián's. Mariana the *colona* [she is a native of Cuenca], frankly, is partially to blame. She said, "Come, Esteban . . . take the seed of an avocado, and some booze." She said, "That hospital is no good!" She said, "Leave her here, we'll see what we can do . . . I can cure her."

So Esteban took Maria down from the horse and put her in the kitchen, and they gave her that remedy. We didn't want to leave her alone. All of the children were there, but as is Shuar custom, Nanki, you can't look at someone who has been bitten by a snake. Nobody can come in and look—just one person, the person that is treating her. (In old Shuar times they knew how to put leaves in water and to cover it, and administer it as a cure, using hot water, leaves that worked against the snake venom.) And, you can only give them water.

But I went off to Sucúa to go buy the remedy, anti-venom.

Alejandro was on the road coming from Sucúa. Lorenzo said that he was going to go tell him; he ran off on the horse. He told Alejandro what had happened to Mama, that she had been bitten by a snake. This is what Lorenzo told him. He said, "Look, Dad; Mom has been bitten by a snake. And now what are we going to do?"

Alejandro went to the house, only to blow (with booze and tobacco); that was a treatment. He had gone to give that treatment; it is his custom. As an *uwíshin*, he wouldn't give an injection; it was against his *uwíshin*-ness.

I had returned from Sucúa. I went to buy a remedy for Maria, but the doctor wanted to come. He told me it was cheap, 60,000 for everything, including the house visit; this is what they told me. But as I didn't have the money, I just bought the medicine—they didn't want to give it to me, Nanki—and then I left to go give it to Maria. I bought everything for her! An injection for the swelling and pills for the pain.

Esteban then took it. We gave it to him, so that he could give it to her. "You don't know how to give it to her," the doctor told me. That's why we wanted to send Esteban, so he'd get someone to do it, or he could administer it himself.

I don't remember the name, but it came in a little envelope; it was like a big pill. You have to put it in a liquid, in a juice drink. I gave her two pills, and she calmed down a bit.

"The force of the snake. . . ." she said, "it isn't going away." So Esteban wanted to cut her foot.

Just then, Gustavo came from the plaza. They had been having a bazaar, and he had been playing volleyball. He said, "Please don't give her that remedy! I don't want her to die; I don't want to have to bury my mother. Don't give her that remedy you bought from a pharmacy. My mother-in-law made this remedy from avocado; give her this remedy; it's very good!"

Esteban said, "Don't make trouble, Brother—we all want to give her this remedy." Lorenzo also wanted to give it to her. "Inject her!" Esteban picked up the ampule to prepare the injection.

"No, don't give it to her. It will interact with the remedy my mother-in-law gave her! And that remedy is enough. Save the injection for later; we'll see whether or not this passes."

But it was too late. She died four days later, at two in the morning . . . she said her head hurt. . . .

Alejandro has been many things to me, but Maria was much more like a second mother to me than anything else. Our relationship was often constrained by Shuar gender roles. As a man, I could not develop the casual relationship with Shuar women that I could develop with Shuar men. Moreover, although I interviewed her about her childhood at the Catholic mission and about certain issues in her family, she was relatively uninvolved in the matters central to my dissertation research, like shamanism or Federation politics. But I lived in her house and ate her food, and she never missed an opportunity to make fun of me. For Maria had a personality that transcended the limits of Shuar convention.

Shortly after meeting Alejandro he invited me to visit some friends of his in Natemtsa, a Shuar *centro* south of Utunkus. He met me in Sucúa and told me that we would try to find Maria, because she wanted to come. Alas, she was not in town.

At that time there was a regional strike cutting off transportation in and out of Morona Santiago, and the province had essentially run out of gas. We paid an exorbitant amount of money to a bus driver to give us a lift to a town half an hour south of Sucúa, and then we walked the remaining six hours to Natemtsa. The last two hours of the hike were on

Maria Tsamaraint holding her granddaughter

muddy trails through the forest, and at one point we had to walk through a river. Stupidly I was wearing cotton socks, and when they dried they stiffened and began irritating my feet. We reached another river, and I asked Alejandro if we could take a break.

We sat down on some rocks, and he began talking about his wives. "Marta, she is really hot," he told me, "and Josefina is a good wife, a traditional Shuar woman. But Maria, Maria is like my mother. She is a marvel." He was certain that she would find her own way and meet us in Natemza. Even as we arrived at the *centro*, as the sun was setting, he insisted that she would come later that night. Thinking back about the hike through the forest, I doubted it.

That evening Alejandro treated a sickly young man, and then we started walking to the common house where the members of the community were going to host a party. As we were walking up the hill, he paused and pointed to a figure coming out of the forest.

"Maria!"

I still miss Maria. But harder than learning about her death was having to bear it by myself. There was little that Elke could say to me on a long-distance phone call. A friend that I came to know when he worked for the Peace Corps in Morona Santiago was living in New York; he had met Maria and could understand my grief, but he could not share it. The hardest thing, though, was knowing how terrible this was for Alejandro and his children and not being there to offer him some sort of comfort.

I thought back to the day his father died. His stepmother and sister Teresa were sitting next to the deathbed, wailing. His brother Lucho turned to me, sobbing. When I hugged Alejandro, he shuddered. I felt uncomfortable. I desperately wanted to shed my role as anthropologist (despite the ethnographic importance of such a scene) but was unsure of how to be a friend. At least I was there.

Death, Somerset Maugham once remarked, makes for a proper ending to a story. For the widower and the orphans, however, it is not the end. Alejandro has had to face many tragedies in his life and will no doubt have to face more. And so I have realized that there is a far greater torment than having to say good-bye. It is the distressful knowledge that departure is not an ending, and the painful struggle to be a distant friend.

Perhaps the only relationships I have had that are as complex as the one I have with Alejandro have been with members of my own family. My experience is not unique; many anthropologists and informants come to refer to one another in the language of kinship. At the end of her life history of a !Kung woman, Marjorie Shostak remarked that "Almost every experience I have in life is colored and enriched by the !Kung world and the way Nisa looked at it. I will always think of her, and I hope she will think of me, as a distant sister" (1981: 371).

Ironically, Shostak was aware that Nisa did not think of her as a sister. Just before Shostak left, she explained to Nisa that she would write a book.

Delighted, she [Nisa] spun a fantasy of my work—a fantasy that has since proved true. "Yes, you will listen to me and when I say something that makes you laugh, you will laugh aloud and praise me, 'Eh-eh, my aunt! My aunt, I still have you with me, here in my home.' Yes, you will feel love for me, because I will be there with you." I agreed, "Yes, I will look at all our talks, from years ago and from today. Some day, we will see how it turns out." She said, "My niece . . . my niece . . . you are truly someone who thinks about me." (1981: 371)

Shostak understood Nisa's words as a prediction about the future, but Nisa was also describing their present relationship as that between an aunt and a niece. Why was Shostak unable either to understand or accept Nisa's view of their relationship? Kamal Visweswaran has suggested that Shostak might have been too invested in the Western feminist notion of sisterhood, or too uncomfortable with the "unequal child-teacher relationship" suggested by Nisa's language (Visweswaran 1994: 28). I suggest that Shostak's slip reveals more about a problem in ethnographic writing: while conducting fieldwork abroad anthropologists must surrender a good deal of power, but while writing back home it is very tempting to reclaim that power.

In my case, the difficulties in translating kinship terms across cultures are complicated by the fact that my relationship with Alejandro is not easily confined to any one kinship term. In fact, we often addressed each other as *yatsuru*, or "brother," although Alejandro often addressed me as *saich*, as "brother-in-law" or "affine," as well. I certainly was happy to use either of these terms, as they implied a sort of equality in our relationship. But I know, from how he talked to and acted toward me, that by the time I left Ecuador he thought of me as a son.

It has taken me a long time to appreciate how well our use of these terms expressed our complicated relationship. As comfortable as I was addressing him variously as *yatsuru* or *saich* while in Ecuador, these terms often struck me (in a way that, I think, was unfair to Alejandro) as conventionalized ways of classifying relationships, rather than as evocative and meaning-laden forms of address. Did he really think of me as a brother or brother-in-law? What do these words really mean? Once Juan Bosco Mashu took me to the offices of SERBISH, where he needed to pick up some papers. There he introduced almost everyone we met as either his brother- or sister-in-law. At first I thought I was lucky to have a friend so well connected. As I spent more time among Shuar, though, I realized that almost every male Shuar could be addressed as *yatsuru* or *saich*. These terms are used to represent the social order that connects almost all Shuar, and they do not necessarily involve any personal feelings or loyalties.

At one point I wondered if the social world of the Shuar consisted of nothing more than a flexible network of relationships, predetermined by rules of kinship, that could be relied upon in various ways at various times. Alejandro did not refer to his childhood companions or contemporary neighbors as "friends"; he referred to them only by either their proper names or the appropriate kin terms (or sometimes the Spanish fictive kin term *compadre*, the term used to address the godparent of one's child). Notions of friendship, like notions of family, are culturally and historically specific, and I came to doubt that there was any room in our relationship for the kind of friendship I had been brought up to desire.

I knew that Shuar do have a notion of "friend," which they call *amíkri*. But I also knew from Harner that this word comes from the Spanish *amigo*, and that this term refers to "trading partners [who] formalize their essentially contractual relationship with a ritual" (Harner 1984: 128). Indeed, Alejandro's *amíkri* are Achuar with whom he had established trading relations. These relations were established in adulthood between men who were otherwise strangers.

I spent some time with him going over these relationships, hoping to find some analogue to what I meant by "friend." Were all of his close relationships matters of convenience?

SR: There is another question. Pichík' is one of your best friends, isn't he? But you became friends only in 1984. When I was little I had several friends. When I was a teenager I had more, but I don't know where all of them are or where they live; nor do they know where I live. Nevertheless, I still know some of them, and we talk once in a while but not much. I have just one friend from my childhood and two from my youth. My question is, do you have any other close friends, like Pichík', but from your early years?

AT: Yes, I do.

SR: What is his name? Are they many or just one?

AT: For example, I have some friends from my childhood who are still in my Indian town. You know, it's a very small town, and we know each other—it's not like in your country.

SR: When I said "close," I didn't mean physical distance but. . . .

AT: Yes, not close in distance but in feeling from the heart. My friend when I was little is my teacher Gustavo Molina. I always remember him, and I'm always with him.

It is only now, with the detachment learned through the passing of the years, that I can fully appreciate this exchange—my own anxiety over the fact that I would soon leave, and my fear that Alejandro could not understand what I really meant. And I think it is only now that I can fully appreciate how much Alejandro really did understand what I meant. He was speaking of Molina, but he was also speaking to me.

In fact, I think the real issue was not the possibility that Alejandro could not understand me, but the fact that I could not understand Alejandro. I grew up in a largely Christian society that is uncomfortable with the blending of material self-interest and generosity, commerce and affection, law and love. I knew that Alejandro's relations with his siblings and in-laws often arouse great passions, but too often I accounted for these through purely material causes, such as the desire for land. But the kind of anger Alejandro has toward some settlers is quite different from the anger he reserves for some members of his family. Categories of kin are not merely locations in a web of social rights and obligations, nor loci for conflicting interests. They are magnets for emotional investments and conflicted feelings.

Similarly, although Alejandro's relationships with his amíkri revealed none of the torment of his relationships with his sister and brother-in-law, it would be a huge error to view them as merely commercial relations. The ritualization of the friendship testifies to its gravity, and Alejandro's joy as he recalled his time spent with Pichík' was heartfelt. I knew that Alejandro benefited materially from his relationship with me. It was not until he and I spoke of Pichík' that I realized how much of the pleasure he took in my gifts owed to his feelings toward me, rather than the feelings toward the objects. This pleasure was matched only by the delight he expressed when giving me gifts. I believe that the challenge in understanding our friendship lies in valuing equally its material and sentimental dimensions. A sociological analysis of such relations is incomplete unless it has psychological depth.

Drawing on the theories of Georg Simmel, George Herbert Mead, Jean-Paul Sartre, and Jacques Lacan, Crapanzano suggested that we know ourselves only by way of our experience with others. By "other," he meant not only other individuals but what they stand for as well, for example, the social roles and cultural styles they embody (Crapanzano 1980: 9). Thus, Alejandro understands himself as a son through his relationship with his parents; he understands himself as a healer through his relationship with his patients. And anthropologists understand themselves through their relationships with their informants. Crapanzano further suggested that this process involves far more than learning about social roles; it is the very process through which we come into existence, not as lumps of flesh but as minds and hearts and souls. Our psychic existence depends on our being recognized by others.[2]

Crapanzano identified this space in which individuals define themselves with the space in which cultures (through ethnography) define themselves. This is so for the informant, who responds to the anthropologist. For Crapanzano, then, life history occupies a space in between (and that thus blurs the distinction between) biography and autobiography:

> The case history, like the biography, presents a view of the subject from the perspective of an outsider; it bears the impress of a narrator who may even permit himself the luxury of "objectively" analyzing and evaluating his subject. The life history, like the autobiography, presents his subject from his own perspective. It differs from autobiography in that it is an immediate response to a demand posed by an Other and carries within it the expectations of that Other. (Crapanzano 1980: 8)

And it is equally so for the anthropologist, who leaves his or her own culture for an encounter with others in a setting that calls into question the conventions, the social masks and etiquette, that usually render such encounters safe and predictable (see Crapanzano 1980: 133–43). As a product of an encounter between two people, then, life history entails a variety of reciprocal desires: the desire to understand the other person; the "desire for recognition by this essentially complex other" (10); and the desire to understand one's self through the encounter with another (139; see Ricoeur 1974: 17; Rabinow 1977: 5).

There is, however, an unexpected lacuna in Crapanzano's work. Without making any claim that Tuhami is a typical or normal Moroccan (as if such a person could exist), Crapanzano wants to learn about him in order to learn more about Moroccan culture. That is, Crapanzano's encounter is simultaneously with another person and another culture. However, Crapanzano depicts Tuhami's encounter as being merely with another person. In Crapanzano's account, Tuhami encounters the anthropologist as a man, as a stranger, as a friend—but not as a representative of the West, of Christianity, of modernity, or of an imperialist state. And through this encounter, Crapanzano learns much about himself but little about his own culture. The portrait of this encounter is surprisingly asymmetrical, and the effect is to bound life history by the same myths that enclose and limit traditional ethnography.

Perhaps this asymmetry reflects the relative isolation of the anthropologist in the field and the fact that the anthropologist is in many ways more vulnerable than the informant. As Crapanzano observed, "[t]he savage is, so to speak, less cowed by the ethnographer than the ethnographer is by the savage" (1980: 138). Indeed, when I lived in Ecuador I was, for the most part, at Alejandro's mercy. He had knowledge that I needed if I were to have a professional future, and he dictated when we would work. It is true that he had a material incentive to work with me. Nevertheless, although the gifts and loans I offered him at times made his life a little more comfortable, they had no enduring impact on his lifestyle. He did not depend on me in the way I depended on him. For both of us, our encounter involved more than difference—it involved inequality.

Significantly, once I left the field, this personal inequality reversed— for I have benefited from my encounter with Alejandro far more than he has, at least financially.[3] Indeed, even in the field I had resources that Alejandro could barely dream of. Although I have not been able to provide him with all of the money he has asked me for, I continue to represent for him (and those around him) the wealth of the North. My friendship with Alejandro not only elicits his knowledge of himself and his culture; it reveals to him what he—and his people—are not and do not have.

Once Alejandro asked me for money to buy a chainsaw. What could I do? I did not want to contribute to the deforestation of the Amazon (even though I knew that if Alejandro did not own a chainsaw, someone else would still cut down the trees). Moreover, it has seemed that every attempt others have made to help Shuar achieve economic equality with settlers ends up creating greater inequalities among Shuar. Although Alejandro was disappointed that I did not give him the money, I think he was content that I still helped him buy clothing and medicine and gave him money when he needed help to travel. Still, the last time I was in Ecuador I met with the *síndico* and members of another *centro* in which I wanted to work. They asked me what I would do for them, and I offered to donate a blackboard to their school. One of the men stood up and said that what they really needed was a chainsaw.

There are those who believe that the only response to such a situation is withdrawal and separation. Such a gesture effectively reproduces the logic of apartheid, and it is important to recall that although the ideology of apartheid claimed to protect African culture, the practice of apartheid institutionalized the oppression and exploitation of Africans by White settlers in the service of the global economy. Similarly, the prohibition of contact between individual Shuar and non-Shuar would not stop the process of colonialism and its effects on Shuar society. It would merely hide from Euro-Americans the effects of colonialism or even create the illusion that Shuar are entirely responsible for these effects.

Although many of the first Shuar to encounter settlers in the early years of colonization responded by retreating into the forest, Shuar history over the past century has been dominated by a very different response: engagement. Andrés and his brothers, for example, actually moved closer to the colonial frontier in order to block Euro-American expansion. The Shuar of Andrés's generation had to rely on those few settlers and priests who had learned some Shuar as intermediaries in their dealings with Euro-Americans. However, they sent their children to mission schools to learn Spanish, so as adults they would be able to deal with Euro-Americans directly. When these children graduated and formed the Federation, they were institutionalizing the principle that Shuar autonomy is based not on isolation but on confrontation.

Similarly, I believe that the only response to the colonial situation is to become more involved, in the hopes of better understanding how it works, and more conscious of its effects. I began Alejandro's life history by subtracting myself from his tale, but I cannot end it without bringing myself back in. It is not enough, though, to bring one's self in merely as a Lacanian "Other." As Crapanzano's work illustrates, an exclusive focus on the local, interpersonal encounter can distract us from the real inequalities and asymmetries within which we operate. In my case, it is not enough for me to recognize without resentment my dependency on Alejandro in the field. I also have to recognize myself as do Alejandro and others: as a representative of a wealthy and powerful country (even if, as Alejandro and others also recognized, I am not a particularly wealthy or powerful American). It is the nature of participant-observation fieldwork to forge intimate and interdependent relationships at the intersection of these inequalities. I appealed to a romantic notion of friendship with Alejandro—a friendship that is disinterested and spontaneous, mutual and personal—as an escape from the risks and responsibilities inherent in our situation. Alejandro taught me that the only mutuality in a friendship must be based on a recognition of difference.

It is only when I pause from asking my own questions to try to answer his that I can begin to feel the complexity of our situation. Just as *tsentsak* connect Alejandro to shamans in Puyo, and cattle connect him to markets in Cuenca and Quito, my questions and notes connect him to the United States. These connections mark differences that simultaneously push people apart and bring them together—and it is for the people caught in the middle to try to negotiate, and in effect to deconstruct, the contradictions and asymmetries in these situations. A true friendship is a response to this situation, but cannot be an escape from it.

As I discussed in chapter 2, I have learned to doubt the view, common in Western discourse, that societies like mine not only have but also make history, while societies like Alejandro's live in history's shadow. As I described in chapter 1, it was not long after I arrived in Sucúa that I learned how hard it is to be a conservative in Alejandro's culture, where Shuar are actively making their own histories and counter-histories. Leaders of the Federation, and members like Alejandro, would use me to demonstrate or promote their own power, in ways that would bring them into conflict with one another or with somebody else.

What I could not—or did not want to—appreciate fully at the time was how my surrender to their politics would necessarily compromise my desire to be subversive at home. This compromise is rather indirect, so although the principle is obvious, I try not to blame myself for having been oblivious to it while in the field. All of Alejandro's answers to my questions about his life add up to a story in which Alejandro cannot be loyal to the values of his culture without somehow furthering some of the colonial project, and in which he cannot resist colonialism without betraying not just other individual Shuar but the Federation itself. These paradoxes are unavoidable when the individual represents both Shuar egalitarianism and capitalism, and the Federation represents both the Shuar people and the state.

These paradoxes necessarily define my situation as a member of a state and a capitalist society—and that of Euro-American readers of this book as well. Thus, I cannot help either Alejandro or the Federation without at the same time being an agent of the capitalist economy and American power abroad, and I cannot subvert the authority of the West, or resist its spread, without in some way betraying my Shuar friends. The facts of this story overwhelm any simple opposition between them and us, between conservatism and subversion. Of course, most Euro-Americans, who live far from the colonial frontier, can avoid this struggle, or at least avoid thinking about it. Anthropologists cannot. I did not have to confront this complexity in its entirety when I began fieldwork, when I was asking Miguel Puwáinchir and Alejandro Tsakimp to do something for me. I could not avoid responding to it, though, when they and other Shuar began asking me to do things for them.

The responsibility for how I respond to their requests, and for this situation as a whole, is mine. But this situation is not of my making, and when Shuar ask me for such things as chainsaws, they are not merely seeking something from me; they are seeking something from the society to which I belong and thus represent. By virtue of my citizenship, I was able to take out student loans to underwrite my education (I would bet that the money I borrowed to pay for my education would be enough to provide every Shuar child with a college education in Ecuador). Thanks to my education—both at university and in Utunkus—I now have a job and access to even more credit, as well as grants. Yet I still cannot bring myself to donate a chainsaw to the Federation or its members.

"But, Nanki," Alejandro points out, "you have seen that there isn't a lot of financing and credit available" for the Shuar. And Shuar desperately want such credit and the things it can buy—whatever the risks. As a shaman, Alejandro has the courage to put his own life and the lives of others on the line as he involves himself more and more deeply in these contradictions. I have spent years studying and thinking about colonialism and the Shuar, and I am still afraid of acting for fear of doing the wrong thing. For money is as powerful, and as dangerous, as tsentsak. Alejandro made this crystal clear to me when we met in the summer of 1998, and I asked him about what had happened in Utunkus after I left in 1992.

Bosco Chiríap, the son of José Chiríap, was the síndico of the centro. I was the vice-síndico. And we applied to the Dutch [Netherlands Development Organization, or SNV], who have helped underwrite health centers in Ecuador, and we received some credit. I made an agreement with the Dutch organization; they agreed to give me some assistance for a health center in Utunkus, a little house. So on the fifth of May, I deposited the 250,000. The money was in the bank del Austro in Macas; the deposit book had the name of the síndico, Bosco Chiríap, and the secretary, Luis Kajékai.

Gunda and I got the money, and we started to work, getting the materials ready. So, after we spent that money we had the framework of the center, and there was a little bit of money left to buy materials, etc. But it didn't work out.

This man came by, Luis Kajékai; he was then the secretary of the centro, but now he is a criminal. So he said, "The money isn't here to pay for the materials, for the cement." This is what he said. So, some síndicos arrived, they wanted the money returned. Luis had the money; he had gone to the bank and taken it out—two hundred and fifty thousand. He said he lost it on the road; it fell out. This was his story. He said that he lost it, but he was going to return it. But this was a lie. He spent it on something.

One Tuesday we had an assembly and elected a new directorate. Bosco had been síndico but was replaced by Eduardo Tunki, and Hilario Tunki was elected vice-síndico. I continued as coordinator of the project. Cesar Juan Panki Uwijint had been the treasurer, but they elected the sports captain, my son Lorenzo, as the new treasurer. And Kajékai was reelected secretary.

After the assembly, the others came to file a complaint about the money. "I lost the money, and I'm going to return it," Luis said. This was a problem for me, because I had deposited the money in the first place! But the assembly accepted his story. So then we waited and waited, but nothing happened.

Eduardo said to Luis, "I'm not demanding the money as the síndico, but Lorenzo is the treasurer, and he wants you to give him the money. He's going to punish you; he's going to ask for a warrant."

Then we celebrated Mother's Day. Since my wife had already died, we called on my sister; she was there by herself. So we came at night, drank chicha, and danced.

Then he came, Kajékai, protesting, demanding the money from my son. "How is it that you said you deposited the money on the fifth of May; what happened?"

Lorenzo replied, "If the money had come from the community, it wouldn't matter—but my dad got the money and will be held accountable; he made an agreement with the Dutch. The receipts have to be presented in August, showing that the work is finished, and the health center ready. If by the twenty-fifth of August the project isn't done, you'll be taken to jail. That's why we have to settle this now." Lorenzo said this to Luis, right in front of me. He said, "My father is the coordinator; Shíram, Gunda, is the intermediary, so please, Uncle, give it up."

Well, what we didn't know, Nanki, *uchiru*, was that Luis Kajékai had stolen two head of cattle from a *colono*, Raul Lopez. We didn't know anything about this until the police arrived with an arrest warrant. So he said, "I'm going to give the money for the cattle as soon as I can." This was his idea, what he did to save himself.

Eight months passed, and we continued working. I went to Cuenca; I came back. All this time the treasurer was complaining, and Kajékai just said he'd return the money soon.

In September, the twenty-fifth, twenty-fourth . . . that was when the terrible accident happened, the machete blow. Lorenzo had left on Saturday; he went to Sucúa with rice. I was with Lorenzo because I was going to accompany him there to go buy some eggs, and Lorenzo continued on.

Lorenzo returned on Sunday; the accident happened on Sunday, Sunday around 5 P.M. We had been moving the cattle that belonged to Gonzalo of Huambi. My son and I were leaving the house, and I realized it was late. I asked him what time it was. "4:45 P.M.," he told me.

But we ran into danger with these people. We didn't know what Luis was planning to do. So this is what happened, Son, to your brother Lorenzo.

Lorenzo was complaining to Luis, and Luis kept on talking; he said, "I'll show it to you."

Then Luis said to Lorenzo, "You had said, Nephew, that you were going to drag me by my balls, that you were going to tie Luis Kajékai's balls to a horse and drag him by his balls to turn him into the police."

"I hadn't said that to you, Uncle."

And the man said, "I don't believe you at all."

So, in this manner, Lorenzo said, "All right, you'll see; you'll pay, or you won't pay. But then I'll come for you." But we didn't have anything, not a single weapon.

So, at that time my sister Chavela [Luis's wife] was seated there, and she came out: "You don't have any blood; you have congealed blood, black blood!" she said to Lorenzo. "You aren't in tune! Who did you hit? Whose ribs did you break? You hit him and denied that you had done it. You are like this! You have no shame!"

And in that moment Luis struck. He hit Lorenzo with the machete, Luis Cornelio Kajékai did. In the very moment that she said that word, he said, "You're going to pull me with the horse" and struck him in the head.

Luis grabbed Lorenzo, because he was going to give Lorenzo another blow with the machete. Lorenzo took off running. "Where is Baudillo? Where is Baudillo?"

"Here I am."

He broke off a stick—he should have thrown a rock . . . he was going to throw a rock. But instead he grabbed a stick that I had cut down when we were moving the cattle.

He died in Shell, on the way to Quito. We took him to the hospital and then to Shell, where he died.

There is a word in English for a person whose parents have died; there is a word for a person whose spouse has died. I know of no word for a person who has lost a child. And I never thought to ask Alejandro if there was such a word in Shuar.

For years I dreamed of going back to Utunkus, of sleeping once more in Maria's house, of joking around with her and her children. . . . But I will never be able to go back to the site of my first fieldwork. Some time after Lorenzo's murder, Alejandro went to Macas to consult with lawyers . . .

. . . and when I came back, Esteban was dismantling the house. He said, "Dad, we're going to move the house to the plaza." He ordered the others to take down the house—but without orders from me! So, I got very angry with him.

I said to him, "Who told you to take down the house? Why did you take down the house? The work of your mother, my work . . . because I was the one who built the house, and with my money. This house was for the little ones; they have to live here, the little children. You—you're a man, you should work to get what you need. I can give you land, but not the house!"

Then I said, "Why are you doing this?"

He said, "Because Mercedes, mom's sister, said that 'It's no good

Lorenzo Tsakimp holding his son, Jamil

that I suffer each time I come here; I'm sad because I see that house where my sister lived. For this reason, take it down, change it, get rid of it,' she told us."

I almost killed Maria's sister, my sister-in-law!

Esteban had made a deal with his brothers. He gave Nantu a chainsaw as payment for his share of the house. They used parts of the house to build on the parcels of land that belong to Rudolfo and Efren, so that they could have their own houses. They did this together and lied to me. . . .

Fifty years after Andrés first settled in Utunkus, his grandchildren are still confronting colonialism head-on. Maria's children, now adults, took apart the house in which they grew up to make homes for themselves around the plaza of the *centro*. Efren and Nantu are working for *colonos*, trying to earn enough money to buy cattle. And although Esteban still maintains his property in Nayumpim, he has built a traditional Shuar house on the site of Maria's old house and has returned to make Utunkus his primary residence.

This confrontation with colonialism, however, inevitably leads to conflicts among Shuar. And for Alejandro, this conflict with his children was an ending of sorts. With his first wife and one son dead, and the house he had shared with them gone forever, he left Utunkus. It is too soon to tell whether this is a retreat or, as was the case when his father fled after the death of Tséremp, a tactical withdrawal. He has moved with Marta and their children to the other side of the Cutucú, to Macuma, where she has family and land, and where, they hope, they have some sort of future.

14

Informant

The deaths of Maria and Lorenzo provide an ending, of sorts, for me as well. I can go back to the Federation, to Utunkus, even to Alejandro; but I will be going back to see how things have changed, not to learn more of the same. In a way, I see my notes and recorded interviews as similar to the boards and nails of Maria's house. In them I tried to reduce the lives of my informants into manageable fragments, which I now reassemble in the form of a book. This is the vocation I have chosen for myself.

In chapter 1 I expressed my hope that in writing this book I would come to a better understanding of Alejandro and his relationship with his culture. In retrospect, this was a naive expectation. Despite my motivations and intentions, reviewing transcripts of our interview was often an exercise in nostalgia. And while editing and framing his stories, I was generally more concerned with pleasing my editors and attracting the interest of future readers of this book. As a writer, I alternated between extremes of attachment and detachment that left little room for me to encounter Alejandro in a new light.

Yet writing accomplishes a strange form of magic. As a writer, I had to detach myself from Alejandro; while writing I sought to express myself, and my words seemed to be a part of me. After I write, however, these same words appear to me as something new and even sometimes strange. They take on an existence independent of me and invite me to read them as if they were someone else's words. Maurice Blanchot argued that this strangeness is precisely what makes texts valuable and powerful: "The reader has no use for a work written for him, what he wants is precisely an alien work in which he can discover something unknown, a different reality" (1981: 27). Now that my words are detached from me, they beckon me to reapproach and reconsider these stories. In order to rediscover the man behind them, I must become a reader.

When I lived with Alejandro I was often irritated by the way he would alternate between expressing his commitment to help others, both as a healer and leader in his community, and baldly revealing his desire for money and power. I thought that these two traits were morally incompatible, and I wondered which reflected the real Alejandro and which was the guise. Is he a genuine healer, compromised by the poverty and social dislocations imposed on his people by colonialism? Or is he a selfish and self-aggrandizing opportunist, hiding behind the mystique of Shuar shamanism? In the end, I tried to ignore his various sermons and harangues as I tried to collect information on shamanic beliefs and practices and Federation politics.

Reading Alejandro's stories, however, forces me to take these features of his personality seriously. One of the things that emerges most starkly from these stories is how intimately—and consistently—intertwined his commitments and his desires are. For Alejandro, wanting to help others while helping himself is not a contradiction. Moreover, his vocation as a healer is not particularly Shuar (he was inspired in part by Dr. Ferguson and studied with non-Shuar shamans), and his desire for wealth and power is not entirely a product of Western influence. Indeed, the oppositions between selfless and selfish men, and genuine and spurious Indians, were discourses I had brought with me to the field. But Alejandro's narration of himself overwhelms these simplistic oppositions. In these stories, his personality is not an incidental distraction from or obstacle to my work; it is an expression of his engagement with the conditions of his life, a reflection of his situation.

Alejandro's narrative, then, is about far more than himself. For one thing, his story is the story of his father and his sons; it is the history of the Tsakimps. Andrés's influence, not only as a father but as a healer and a leader as well, on Alejandro is enormous; for Alejandro, the struggle to better his own situation is identical to the struggle to help his family. But the respective murders of Andrés and Lorenzo, and Alejandro's disputes with Esteban, are not merely family tragedy. In the context of the changing relationship between Shuar kinship and the colonial economy, they are political events, with control over *centro* Utunkus at stake.

The Tsakimps—the descendants of Andrés (whose Shuar name was Tsakimp)—appear to be what anthropologists call a patrilineage: a group constituted through demonstrated descent from a common ancestor, traced exclusively through the male line. Yet early ethnographers of the Shuar make no mention of patrilineages;[1] rather, they define the household as the primary unit of Shuar social organization (Harner 1984: 41, 78; Karsten 1935: 183). This is consistent with the general picture of Amazonian societies. In a brief review of the ethnographic literature, Robert Murphy concluded that "there are very few true lineage systems in lowland South America. Rather, what is usually found are clusters of co-resident kin who are not bound by careful reckoning of common descent nor unified by a unilineal ideology. If a rule exists, it is one of residence, and the resultant groups are ad hoc in nature rather than jural" (Murphy 1979: 218–19). Drawing on ethnography from other parts of the world (e.g., Worsley 1956; Meggitt 1965), Murphy argued that lineages are important when they organize control over a scarce resource such as land. Since most Amazonian societies combine shifting cultivation with hunting, control over land is not an issue.

Indeed, Harner pointed out that among Shuar the limiting factor on production was labor, not land; since women provided most of, and the most important, productive labor among Shuar, control over labor was a matter of control over women (1975: 127). The control was located in the household, organized by rules regarding marriage (rather than descent). Polygyny, for example, organized a man's control over his wives' labor. Matrilocality secured a man's control over his daughter's labor. One of the consequences of these marriage rules is to promote the importance of affinity over consanguinity. That is, the ties between brothers-in-law would supersede ties among brothers, and the ties between a father-in-law and a son-in-law would supersede ties between fathers and sons. As Maurice Bloch has noted, by forging links among people who live in different places, ties of affinity can render households more mobile (Bloch 1975: 215–16).

Colonialism, however, has radically transformed Shuar space (see Rubenstein 2001). What was for the Ecuadorian and Peruvian states a conflict over their boundary in the Upper Amazon was for the Shuar the institution of an absolute limit to their mobility, codified through law and enforced by the military. The territorially bounded character of the modern state is mirrored at the local level through the formation of *centros* and at the personal level through institution of private ownership of land.[2] This legal fiction immediately renders land a scarce resource, and the influx of Euro-Ecuadorian colonists from the highlands has intensified this scarcity. The state supports Shuar ownership of land, but only if they make it economically productive. It expects Shuar to invest in their land, preferably in the form of intensive cattle production, and (according to the Agrarian Reform Law of 1973) people must maintain at least 40 percent of their land as pasture in order to keep title to land. Moreover, according to Ecuadorian law, property rights do not dissolve upon the owner's death, but rather devolve to his or her children. Thus, although title to land is mobile, one of its effects has been to encourage the people who live on the land to become sedentary.

These circumstances provide the conditions for the development of lineages. Whereas kinship relations once served primarily to organize control of labor, they now organize control over land. When Andrés first settled along the Utunkus River, he did so precisely to establish a legal claim to land. Although his children were following Shuar custom when they took his Shuar name as a surname, they were also signifying their new status as heirs. Thus, his sons' children departed from Shuar custom and have kept his name as their surname, rather than their father's name. Imelda's children are Tsenkushes, and Teresa's children are Tunkis; but Valentín's and Alejandro's children are Tsakimps. These names are Shuar, but their use to identify families is a colonial practice.

One might predict that as patrilineality becomes institutionalized among Shuar, they will abandon matrilocality.[3] Today postmarital residence patterns among Shuar are in flux, in part because under Ecuadorian law both men and women have a right to own and inherit land, and in part because Shuar still rely on affinal ties for mobility. Sedentarization, which has coincided with conflicts over increasingly scarce land, along with the intensification of conflict that occurs with rising population density, has ironically promoted the relocation of people fleeing conflict. Alejandro, for example, is bilocal. When he married Josefina, she moved to Utunkus but maintained her household in Waríns, where she had inherited land from her first husband. Marriage has give Alejandro access not only to her labor but to her land as well. Alejandro has also turned to Marta's kin to help him acquire land in the Cutucú. He relied on his wives and affines when he fled Utunkus, in the wake of first his father's death and then his first wife's death.

Where matrilocality persists, it has taken on new functions. Whereas marriage once gave a father-in-law greater access to his sons-in-law's labor, it now gives sons-in-law access to their father-in-law's land. Thus, Calisto Tsenkush and Pedro Tunki moved to Utunkus when they married Andrés's daughters. Their claims to Andrés's land have brought them—and their wives—into tragic conflict with Andrés's son Alejandro. Alejandro has declared that he was never opposed to Calisto moving into Utunkus, only to Calisto's claim to more than what Alejandro thinks is a fair share of Andrés's estate. Of course, according to Alejandro (and Ecuadorian law) each of his children has a right to a fair share of the inheritance as well. Alejandro's eldest son, Lorenzo, married a woman who had no land, and when he lost his job working on a *colono*'s ranch, Alejandro insisted that Lorenzo be given land in Utunkus. And shortly after Lorenzo was murdered, Alejandro's second son, Esteban, left his property in Nayumpim (where his father-in-law had sold him land) and returned to Utunkus, to assert the Tsakimp claim. Matrilocality and patrilineality bring Andrés's sons-in-law and grandchildren into conflict.[4]

Just as patrilineages give corporate form to Shuar families, and *centros* give corporate form to Shuar communities, the Federation itself gives corporate form to the Shuar people. Indeed, I believe that it is the history of the Federation that has made possible the very notion of a Shuar people. As Harner noted, in their own language the word *shuar* simply means "man," "men," or "people" and is used "to refer to any Indian or group of Indians . . . without regard to cultural or linguistic affiliation" (1984: 14). I have even heard Shuar refer to me as an "*inkis-shuar*," a foreign person. Before the formation of the Federation there was no formal or practical basis for Shuar unity. Thus, Stirling insisted that "the Shuar" were not a tribe, nor were they divided into tribes: "The Jívaro-speaking peoples are divided into scores of so-called tribes. These tribal divisions, however, are merely artificial denominations given by whites to groups more or less isolated in certain geographical units such as rivers or divides. Tribes in this sense have no existence in the minds of the Indians themselves" (1938: 38). Just as private ownership of land provides a material basis for the formation of lineages, the institution of the Shuar reserve, originally under the control of the Salesian missionaries but now under the control of the Federation, provides a material basis for the formation of the tribe. Today, the Federation constitutes an internally differentiated, hierarchically organized, and territorially bounded material and practical basis not merely for members to act as one, but even for them to think of themselves as one. The word *shuar* is Shuar, but its use to refer to a tribe, people, or nation is a colonial practice.

Like patrilineages, the Federation is a Shuar response to colonialism that provides an institutional basis for collective Shuar identity and action. Unlike patrilineages, the Federation is chartered by the state, mimics the form of the state, and is at times an instrument of state policies.[5] By representing the Ecuadorian state in its hinterland (through surveying and registering land and adjudicating local disputes), the Federation also serves to promote private property and a complex division of labor. Thus, while Shuar are converted into Ecuadorian citizens, they are also converted into farmers, wage earners, and salaried workers. Although the Federation represents "Shuar," it is also promoting the division of Shuar into economic classes. And as Alejandro's ambivalent feelings suggest, leaders of the Federation seem to benefit from this process disproportionately.

These contradictions are epitomized in the disaster of 1986, when then-president Bartolome Juep and the Federation representative in Quito, Enrique Nurínkias, were expelled from the Federation and left to form the rival Shuar Organization of Ecuador. First, they claimed that they were promoting Shuar unity and autonomy by renouncing the Federation's ties with the Salesian missionaries, yet they precipitated the most traumatic fission in the history of the Federation. Second, they claimed to be serving the Shuar people, yet Alejandro (and every other partisan of the Federation with whom I spoke) believes that they were interested only in enriching themselves. This is an extreme case, and many still argue passionately over who was right. Yet almost every leader of the Shuar Federation has been subject to charges of sectarianism and corruption. Many *colonos* have pointed this out to me as evidence that Indians are incapable of honest and effective governance (despite the fact that the last several governments of Ecuador have been weakened by, or have even fallen because of, far greater scandals). I, however, take this pattern not as a sign of some failure of Shuar leadership but rather as a sign of the difficulties of negotiating between Shuar autonomy and their dependence on outside organizations for political and economic support and of the impossibility of improving the lives of all Shuar equally by incorporating them into an economic system based on inequality.

What appear to be family squabbles in *centros* or political struggles within the Federation reflect a fundamental contradiction in Shuar life created by colonialism. Gerald Sider has referred to this contradiction as the antagonism between work and production. By this he means that the work people must actually do in order to maintain their way of life is in conflict with the very conditions and means provided by society to do that work (Sider 1993: 11–12). Shuar must have land and capital to live, but what they must do in order to get and keep land and capital is determined by a legal and political framework that leads many of them to fight, and some to lose. And so the ironic fact that Alejandro depicts leaders of the Shuar Federation in precisely the same way that I have depicted him—as someone who cannot serve his people without promoting himself—is a sign not of his hypocrisy but rather of the situation that he and those whom he criticizes share.

The complexity of this situation owes not only to the fact that the antagonism between work and production is unresolvable, but to the fact that this antagonism is far more than a feature of the economic lives of Shuar. It defines the very terms of their existence, for the legal and political frameworks that organize work and production are not extrinsic—they are the lineages, *centros*, and Federation that make Alejandro a Tsakimp and a Shuar. Anthony Giddens argued that agency is possible only within or against a given structure, and social structures perdure only through human agency. I would take his suggestion that agency and structure are not opposed, but rather are linked, one step further. Individually held collective identities such as "Tsakimp" and "Shuar" reveal that agency and structure are not two different things but two ways of talking about the same thing. Consequently, one cannot help the collective unless one has power, and an individual has no power except through one's position in a collective.

It is thus often impossible to distinguish between helping others and helping one's self, and the tangle between these two orientations often gets people into trouble. This principle is one of the cornerstones of shamanism, at least in the Upper Amazon. One cannot help others unless one works within the same framework that hurts others. The power to kill and to cure is the same because it is embodied in the same instrument: *tsentsak*. Whenever a shaman diagnoses witchcraft and attempts a cure, he or she is calling attention to the work of distant shamans—both the *yajauch uwíshin* who is presumably the cause of the illness and some other *penker uwíshins* with whom the shaman trained and from whom the shaman acquired his or her own *tsentsak*. Every act of healing presupposes and constitutes a connection between the good and bad aspects of shamanism and confronts the shaman with his or her own capacity to do evil (see Brown 1988). Every shaman, then, is in a precarious position: when the veteran shaman Tséremp would not (or could not) heal Chúmpi's son, Chúmpi concluded that the shaman was a killer. And so when Tsamaraint asked the novice shaman Alejandro to cure his son, Alejandro could not refuse; although he was terrified of failing, he was more scared of saying no. In his role as shaman, Alejandro performs the dialectic of agency and structure that makes any form of power a double-edged sword.

In this understanding, such identities as shaman, Tsakimp, and "Shuar," are not primordial things; they are responses to the colonial encounter in the Ecuadorian Amazon, responses that provide the conditions for both colonial expansion and domination, and local resistance.[6] Accordingly, they are loci of deeply ambivalent sentiments and actions. Alejandro consistently expresses pride in being a shaman, a Tsakimp, and a Shuar. His vocation, family, and people are the most important things in his life, for they are the terms through which he defines himself and expects others to define him. And yet, he knows that shamanism exposes him to danger, and he began his training and practice with serious doubts. Similarly, throughout his life he has been embroiled in conflicts with members of his family and the Federation. His tales blaspheme the sacred status of these institutions and deflate any myths about his culture.

That Alejandro's narrative often undermines his own authority and that of his culture does not mean that either he or his culture is inauthentic. I have asserted that his various identities are responses to colonialism, but this does not mean, as writers like Malinowski and Perkins might suggest, that he is somehow not himself. His narrative should not lead us to alter our view of Alejandro or the Shuar; rather, it challenges us to change the way we think about "culture," to abandon the Western opposition between culture and history. Alejandro's ambivalence toward shamanism, the family, and the Federation does not owe to their being influenced by, or even products of, recent history. Rather, it owes to the fact that it is through these terms that he embodies and expresses his engagement with a profoundly ambiguous situation. This is the very character of authenticity, which, as Sartre defined it, "consists in having a true and lucid consciousness of the situation, in assuming the responsibilities and risks that it involves, in accepting it in pride or humiliation, sometimes in horror and hate (1948: 90). If Alejandro's consciousness of his situation has not always appeared lucid to me, the fault lies not in him but in the ways my own culture has taught me to read the lives of indigenous people. For reading is neither a passive nor an innocent activity.

As I first was writing this book, I saw Alejandro as my protagonist, at times comic, at times tragic. But as I take on the role of reader, I begin to see him as the writer—and realize that he is neither comic nor tragic but is rather telling me about a world that is both. And what I had once seen as a weird and sometimes disturbing mixture of selflessness and selfishness in his character I now see as a quixotic determination to live in that world, to reflect on it and thus, necessarily, to reflect it. In this reflection the space between history and culture, and the myths people—not just anthropologists but Shuar and *colonos* and even Alejandro himself—hold about culture unravel. And in this unraveling, Alejandro is just a *shuar*, just a person, living the best he can.

This reading of Alejandro's stories is motivated by the fact that I lived with him for several years, and I wanted to understand the man better. I was desperate to reconcile my appreciation for all he has given to and done for me with my irritation (verging on disgust) for his almost incessant requests for money, without resorting to some crude calculation. When I first moved in with him and his family, I offered to pay a regular rent, but he refused; he never denied that both of us were benefiting from our living and working together, but a *quid pro quo* exchange was incompatible with his understanding of our relationship. In turn, I wanted to find a way to give an account of his life without becoming an accountant, trying to balance the good and bad aspects of his character.

In order to reach an understanding, I have used his stories to portray a situation and to depict his struggle within and against that situation. But this struggle is necessarily with and against other people, and his stories are about them as well. These stories can be read in many different ways, and I am very anxious about whether my intentions in writing this book are justified when considering the possibly dangerous uses to which it could be put against Shuar. In chapter 1 I suggested that the kind of deconstruction Alejandro performs through his life is far more dangerous, and meaningful, than my deconstruction of texts in

Alejandro Tsakimp

the safety of my office. This suggestion, however, is nothing but a last-ditch effort to deny my responsibilities by invoking the opposition between home and the field.[7] The writing of scholarly texts has only the appearance of safety, for words can be as dangerous as *tsentsak*.

For one thing, any book about Shuar should be available to Shuar. Although Alejandro knew that I was going to write a book, and this book draws only on what he allowed me to tape-record, I will share some responsibility for how Alejandro's neighbors react to his stories about them when they are published in Spanish. More immediately, I worry about how its publication in English will affect the Shuar community. As a matter of fact, before I left for Ecuador one colleague discouraged me from working with the Shuar. She had considered fieldwork among them but decided that her research would likely embarrass or compromise the Federation. Her concerns were legitimate—Alejandro was hardly the only Shuar willing to tell me about problems within the Federation. And Alejandro was certainly an excellent informant, providing me with not only passion but details as well.[8] In his stories, every collective effort—whether in the form of the patrilineage, the *centro*, cooperatives, or the Federation itself—collapses under the weight of the contradictions of the colonial situation. Although I have tried to use these stories to learn something about the man and his situation, I worry that others will use them against the Federation.

Of course, this is exactly how Alejandro used them. After all, the meaning of these stories depends not only on the situation of the storyteller but on his or her relation to the audience as well—and during the course of the interview, I was the audience. When I first met him, he defined his relationship to me in opposition to the Federation. "I am a Shuar," he told me, "The Federation has no right to tell me what to do. I am a man, and do what I please. If the Federation won't give you permission, you can still work with me." And so another way to read these stories is as an extended explanation as to why I should work with Alejandro, rather than with leaders of the Federation.

This explanation involves not only a critique of the Federation but a celebration of the relationship between fathers and sons. After all, although it is an accident that my name in English and the Spanish name of Alejandro's second son (born the same year as I) are equivalent, my having been incorporated into Alejandro's family was an accomplishment. Alejandro's stories stress the importance of his lineage not just because it is important to him; he wants it to be important to me.

I do think of Alejandro as a second father. But although this sounds nicer than thinking of him as an informant, I am not just his *inkis-uchiru*. I am an anthropologist who has worked within the Shuar Federation, with the authorization of the Federation and the unfailing support of its leadership. My obligations to them are of a different sort than my obligations to Alejandro and the Tsakimps, but they are just as important. How can I help them, when the stories I have presented here are so threatening? Is there any other way that I can read these stories? How can they be of use to the Federation?

Ultimately, this is a misleading question. It is not for me to say how leaders of the Federation can or should use these stories. It is up to them, if they choose to use these stories at all. And what effect this book has on my relationship with the Shuar community is up to them as well. More importantly, although I do hope that leaders of the Federation will one day read this book, they do not constitute its primary intended audience. The pressing question is, how will college students—and perhaps other Euro-Americans interested in the struggles of indigenous peoples—use these stories? That is, the issue now is my relationship to my own people.

I believe that the best way I can help people like Alejandro Tsakimp and Miguel Puwáinchir is to write a book that can somehow be used against my own community. Indeed, I *want* my words to be dangerous to Euro-Americans, to those who benefit, however indirectly, from the colonization of the Amazon and its inhabitants. Half or more of Ecuador's foreign income comes from the sale of oil extracted from the Amazon, and much of this oil goes to the United States and other industrialized countries. There was a time when Europeans and Euro-Americans justified their colonization of places like the Amazon by arguing that its inhabitants were savages who needed to be civilized. Ironically, today many justify the continued exploitation of such places by arguing that its inhabitants have "lost their culture" and no longer have legitimate corporate rights to the territories they occupy. And others promote sustainable development and eco-tourism as ways to help Indians maintain their "traditional" culture, while strengthening their ties to the world capitalist economy.

I have tried to argue, however, that the issue is not whether indigenous people are entirely outside of or within the state. The opposition between savagery and civilization, between traditional and acculturated (or assimilated) Indians, is a language game that Indians lose no matter how they play. The issue is precisely how this Western discourse that separates culture from history is a discourse of colonialism. People like Alejandro, who struggle within and against the material practices of colonialism, necessarily struggle within and against this discourse as well.

The Federation and its leaders also struggle within and against colonial practices and discourses. Like marginalized people around the world, the Shuar Federation depends on the economic support of international organizations, and Shuar count on political and economic pressure to support indigenous rights that the international community puts on the Ecuadorian government. Yet much of this support and pressure is based on romantic notions of Indian life that leaves no room for the complexity of their struggle—a struggle that necessarily requires compromises and failures (see Conklin and Graham 1995). However much I have tried to write against the romanticization of the Shuar, and for their right to be human and flawed, I know the power of the oppositions I have tried to deconstruct. The history of colonialism is one of hypocrisy, in which its ills are blamed on its victims, who somehow are held to a higher standard than others.

So Alejandro is not the only one who gets into trouble as he tries to help others while helping himself. Peace Corps volunteers and Dutch development workers, U.S. consumers of gasoline and Rain Forest Crunch ice cream, and, of course, anthropologists do, too. And so it has taken me a long time to write this book. But I have argued that the problems of the Shuar are not just their problems but ours as well, and I have learned from Alejandro that one must face the responsibilities of one's situation rather than seek to escape them. I never promised Miguel Puwáinchir, Alejandro Tsakimp, or the people of the *centros* in which I worked that I would buy them a chainsaw. I did, however, promise that I would write a book about their lives. There is no one way to read Alejandro's stories, and how people will use them depends on their own situation. I have written this book in the hope that in reading it, Euro-Americans will see that their own situation, at the core of the world economy, is only distant—but not separate—from that of people, such as Alejandro, who live in its margins.

15

Friend

Alejandro retreated from the colonial frontier to find some peace and security for his family; I retreated from the frontier in order to write a book. But every retreat contains the hope of return, and I went back to Ecuador in June 1998. I was anxious: I had not been very good about maintaining contact with people—an occasional letter or postcard—and I felt guilty. The only people who knew I was coming were a few friends in Quito; I wondered if the others remembered me, and if they even cared.

On the airplane to Macas, I thought back to my very first flight to Morona Santiago. I had sat next to a nun. When we broke through the clouds and could see the forest below, a river shone in the sunlight like a silver snake. She asked me if that was the Upano, and I replied that I didn't know. Now I looked down, trying to identify the farms of people I knew.

I had brought a student with me. I didn't want to have to worry about loading all our gear, and the presents I had brought for people, on a bus, so we took a taxi to Sucúa. I thought I would be excited to share the vistas with the student, but instead I felt as if I were in a dream. I remembered half of everything—and I was not sure which things had changed and which things I had merely forgotten.

I was also preoccupied with settling in. I knew an archaeologist at the City University of New York who was conducting research in Sucúa. He told me about a new hotel in town (with hot water and cable television!) at which we could stay our first night. He was renting an apartment and would be coming down later in the summer, but he said we could stay there if we could get the key from the landlady, a Mrs. Yanez. Once we were settled in, I would have to meet the new president of the Federation. And finally, I needed to track down Alejandro—Elke had told me that he had left Utunkus and was now living with Marta on the other side of the Cutucú, in Macuma. I had only two months to continue my research in the Upano valley and didn't look forward to spending a week or two looking for Alejandro on the other side of the Federation. But I knew that the student would enjoy a trip away from the colonization frontier. More importantly, I could not return to Ecuador without seeing him.

We registered at the hotel and carried our bags up to the room, and I asked the owner of the hotel if she knew where Mrs. Yanez lived. She didn't know but told me that the sister and brother-in-law owned an ice-cream shop down the road, just past the Federation headquarters.

It was late, but the shop was still open, and a young girl was tending the counter. I told her who I was, and she went to get her mother. Then I heard a voice from the street call out to the girl, "*Desculpa, señora,*" [excuse me, ma'am]. I turned around.

His face was more worn than I remembered, and he had lost about as many pounds over the past six years as I had gained, but his hair was still jet black and his eyes twinkled. "Nanki!" he said.

"Alejandro!"

We walked toward each other and embraced, and—for just a moment—my regrets about the past, and my anxieties about the future, lifted.

I would like to think that—for just a moment—they lifted for my friend as well.

Steven Rubenstein and Alejandro Tsakimp

Series Editors' Afterword

Since the 1960s, anthropology's engagement with history has taken several turns. Some of these have been responses to changes going on in anthropology's conventional fieldwork milieu (Stocking 1992; Vincent 1990); others have been responses to changes in the intellectual climate in which ethnography is read and written (Clifford and Marcus 1986). These two issues are not, historically speaking, distinct. Indeed, it is increasingly clear that the latter—the change in the way that anthropology is written and read, or better put, produced and reproduced "here"—is directly related to the same global forces that have reorganized production and social reproduction "out there" (Roseberry 1996).[1] Yet the effort to historicize ethnography itself—by placing people "without history," be they ethnographic subjects or ethnographers themselves, into specific historical contexts—is not nearly the political panacea it was once hoped it might be (see Sider 1993: xxiii). Using history to deconstruct conventional ethnographic practice and conventional ethnographic subjects carries with it a host of political consequences that seem no less threatening to those involved (and perhaps even more threatening) than the history-less and largely idyllic ethnographic naivete that historical anthropology sought to replace.

These consequences make plain that anthropologists have, even recently, used history rather simply and in a rather self-centered way: primarily to place our ethnographic focus in the context of a coherent historical narrative, despite warnings from feminists that the coherence and linearity of narrative actively misrepresents the lives of the powerless (see Scott 1988; Walkowitz 1992). Simply placing our ethnographies in a history of a place or region—one narrative, at the expense of multiple and often conflicting ones—gives us apparent depth at the cost of further erasing, further simplifying, all the tensions, ruptures, and gaps that separate yesterday from today, today from a sense of impending tomorrows.[2] Such spaces between yesterday, today, and tomorrow are continually made and remade, often in small and insignificant ways, and occasionally in larger and more significant ways. These spaces are necessarily filled by people living, or trying to live, their lives. The always exceptional, always diverse ways that people deal with rupture and discontinuities are an important part of the way time becomes history, and thus an ethnography of one life is, at its best, an anthropology of history.

When we realize, however, that the people we study both "have" a history yet may also have an antagonistic relationship to their own sense of history, historical anthropology becomes a difficult and more complex matter. Several anthropologists have made this point, chief among them John and Jean Comaroff (1991) and Johannes Fabian (1983). We are, however, putting much more firmly in quotes the notions that people "have" their own sense of history. For, just like history itself, people's sense of their own history is not just out there waiting to be told. It is, instead, a precarious and potentially significant presence in a continually negotiated social world, one that potentially sets Alejandro against as well as within Shuar society.

Thus, as Steven Rubenstein points out, life history is precariously situated in this process. As a story of an individual through time—or more precisely, as the story of an individual's engagements with processes of historical change—it speaks to the concerns of both historical deconstruction and ethnography. Beyond this, however, by talking about the engagement of Alejandro Tsakimp with the unfolding of Ecuadorian statehood in the Western Amazon, this life history points to the fact that there is no easy separation between the "us" and "them" of standard colonial-historical-ethnographic discourse. Rubenstein writes in chapter 2:

> Alejandro's story of what happened thus overwhelms any easy distinction between Shuar and settler vices and virtues. He was equally afraid of the police and Tséremp's family. Some Shuar cooperated with the police in the relocation of Andrés's family, while others helped hide the refugees; some settlers took advantage of the situation, while others offered aid. This is not a story about leaving Shuar culture to enter the space of the state. It is a story that simultaneously embraces and rejects different images of both Shuar and settlers. The geographical distance between Sucúa and Utunkus is clear, but the cultural boundary between them is not.

The ability of life history to do, in perhaps more intimate and detailed fashion, the deconstructive work of historical anthropology reveals its potency—its ability to call to the foreground the conflicted engagement of native people(s) with the societies that seek to absorb them. For in the life history form, the engagement between the teller-author and the listener-author—an engagement that usually shapes both partners—allows us to deconstruct (literally, to take apart) the usual perspective of historical anthropology.

Anthropologists have talked about "deconstructing" each other's and their informants' texts as if it were a kind of game, with little at stake besides academic reputations. We must, however, situate our current practice of pulling "texts" apart within our recognition of actual practices aimed at pulling apart people's families and social lives (Shkilnyk 1985). Indeed, lives are at stake in the contingencies of understanding that underlie what are called, rather innocently, "the constructedness of society." One need only think of the power of U.S. corporations, post-NAFTA, to radically enter and withdraw from even the most remote margins of Mexico—a power they have had in areas like the Philippines for much longer—to be confronted with the stakes involved in such "social construction." Under these circumstances, historical deconstruction—even by best-intentioned anthropologists—can seem much more significant to actual human lives, and much more dangerous, than would appear possible for what is ostensibly a recent intellectual trend in cross-cultural understanding. As Ward Churchill (citing the Mexican theorist of indigenismo Guillermo Bonfil Batalla) implies, some things must be held steady over place and time in order for distinctive, alternative politics to emerge (Churchill 1996a). In such cases, historical deconstruction can seem as much a threat as a boon to radical organizing.[3]

Because life history sits precariously atop this dilemma—a dilemma as much political and moral as it is intellectual—it remains a critical form of inquiry and engagement even while other staples of ethnographic work (like "the field"—see Gupta and Ferguson 1997) have given way. For while life histories such as this one offer stories that inevitably deconstruct ethnographic "webs of meaning," they simultaneously attest to people's attempts to "grasp," to hold on to, to hold their place in a turning world. Thus, while life histories point out the impossibility of our finding anything approaching conventional ethnographic notions of culture—the functionally integrated, institutionally reproduced Malinowskian *weltanschauung*—they simultaneously attest to the near constant efforts of people to "culture" their world, not in the sense of reading it according to a set of categories, rules, or textual relations, but in the sense of struggling—with and against those around them—to make a world worth living in, a world that can be lived in, a world in which one's own emerging intuitions about the way things might and ought to be are given at least a reasonable chance of success. Lives such as that of Alejandro Tsakimp remind us that a person's *weltanschauung*, if and when such a thing exists, must be made and remade on a continual basis, amid the efforts and contingencies of others, differently positioned and differently self-directed, who may seek to do the same.

A historical presentation of Alejandro Tsakimp's life—his struggles with and against his siblings, Imelda and Valentín; his suspicions of the Shuar Federation amid Federation leaders' struggles to mediate the egalitarian feelings of Shuar and the creeping hegemony of the Ecuadorian state—points to historical contingency and agency as pragmatic accomplishments created between people(s), with results that, though often short-lived, nevertheless provide critical points from which people seek to hold or change their place in time. For indigenous peoples, such efforts are perhaps more heavily burdened with the weight of ongoing survival than are the efforts of others in the margins.

Rubenstein shows (and as innumerable others have pointed to as well), for native peoples like the Shuar, holdings one's place in time and thus in the larger society often means more than simply holding back some things from the wash of historical deconstruction. It means both doing this—and in so doing, marking and describing the solidarity produced, its value and its virtue, as something "out of time" or "without history"—while simultaneously arguing against most of the assumed negative consequences of doing this in the eyes of the surrounding society.

To remain indigenous is, as power sees it, to be outside of "civilization." One of the central fantasies of power is that civilization is based on law, and thus to be seen outside civilization is, by extension, to be utterly without intrinsic legal rights—without any rights other than those that power chooses to "give." The task of being—of remaining—indigenous is thus, necessarily, collectively dangerous. The task of being an indigenous individual is even more difficult and doubly dangerous. In the specific case of the Shuar, the Federation is thus left with the clearly disjunctive job of arguing to the Shuar that they, the Shuar, remain significantly different from the surrounding society, while simultaneously arguing to the state that these differences ought not matter in so far as the recognition of rights of people and the obligations of the state are concerned. Such strategies necessarily embrace contradictions rather than avoid them, and throw open to question the efforts of those who pursue them, both in the eyes of the surrounding society and in the eyes of their own constituencies. Alejandro's suspicion of the Federation can be understood as an example of this. The Federation looks to ordinary Shuar like an agent of the state when it replicates state projects of settlement, democratization, corporatization, and centralization in order to secure for them the sorts of social organizational recognition received by other clients of the state. To the surrounding Ecuadorian society, the Federation looks like an organization aimed at promoting the sorts of difference that require its own mediation and whose main function is to suspend the normal operation of the state in favor of some people (and not others).

The clearest case in which the dilemmas of this strategy play out is that of land. When native peoples in general hold out egalitarianism and communalism as both the basis and benefit of specifically native sorts of solidarity—solidarity that is a virtue in its own right, but one that is also necessitated by the ongoing efforts of the surrounding societies to obtain native land and labor—this often means that solidarity is fashioned at a cost of acknowledging the overlap between those in the group and those beyond. There are both pragmatic and rhetorical troubles created by this strategy (see, e.g., Churchill 1996b). As Rubenstein notes, the discourse of communal solidarity and egalitarianism and the discourses of individualism—endorsed by capitalism and underlying the nation-state—contain many similarities, and Alejandro's marked distrust of those who claim to represent him to the outside makes differentiating communal egalitarianism from state-sponsored individualism, in even the most pragmatic projects, almost impossible. A similar dilemma confronts the Federation as well. For the Federation, differentiating native from non-native, Shuar from colono—again, in the interest of creating the sorts of solidarity capable of resisting the immense power of an encroaching state—often means submerging not just the overlaps between Shuar senses of property and person and those of the settlers; it also means simultaneously arguing that the differences identified ought not to matter in the eyes of the state—that is, that Shuar claims to property and individual rights ought to be afforded the same state protections as those rights of all citizens.

Because life history seems particularly capable of identifying and revealing the tensions between the individual and the collective in any society—a topic that Rubenstein shows to be very old in anthropology, but that has nonetheless been little remarked upon for a long time—it seems a particularly critical media for capturing the specific tensions faced by native peoples in this process. For, as we have argued (separately) elsewhere, native people(s) bear a far more contentious relationship with the sources and signs of their own cultures than do others in the margins (Dombrowski 2001; Sider 1993). Forced at once to define themselves as native—and thus to root their solidarity in a fixed "cultural" form—in order to combat encroachment, native people(s) become bound to the sources and dynamics of this identity. This means that the relationship between native people(s) and the institutional and ideological bases of their cultures take on a far more conservative hue than does the relationship between other people(s) pushed to the margins. The latter are thus often granted a sort of cultural flexibility that is denied indigenous people(s), and in that way they retain the ability to make and remake the institutional and ideological bases of their own solidarity, freedom that native people(s) are not given.

This same point is raised in the two previous works in this series. In Bruce Miller's *The Problem of Justice* (2001), the tensions created through the efforts of Salish communities to form and make workable their own "native courts"—either traditional-style courts with roots in an older social organization, on the one hand, or courts modeled on the surrounding society but run by and for native people(s), on the other—mark these same fault lines (Miller 2001). There, arguably, the most successful native courts were the ones whose structures were imposed from the outside. These courts were free to adjudicate local solidarity where other, more ostensibly "indigenous," courts were more bound to represent a fixed and intractably partial (in both senses: incomplete and interested) solidarity. In Dombrowski's *Against Culture* (2001), corporate co-optation of native identity symbols caused some village residents to separate issues of local solidarity from the signs and institutions of native culture. In the process, new kinds of solidarities are sought and created, some of which feature much more prominently issues of class and access to wealth and resources; and some of which feature new, intense religious communities. Such strategies are clearly contentious, because they pit one kind of solidarity against another. In all such cases, each resulting party or side can point to the historical contingency of the other—the development-based corporate sponsors of native dance groups versus the history of missionization that lay behind the "anti-cultural" church groups; the imposed structure of federally constituted native courts versus the freezing of some versions of custom (and not others) into customary law—and, in so doing, call into question the ability of their opponents to hold their place in time or within the larger, surrounding society.

Struggles like these allow us to lose sight of the fact that what is at stake is not a clearer picture of historical authenticity or inauthenticity. What is at stake, on both sides, is the continuing struggle for solidarity amid forces whose aims are at best unclear and, more often, intensely destructive. As Sider (1993) points out, and Steven Rubenstein echoes here, under such conditions, no strategy can possibly achieve what, minimally, it must, and as such every strategy will be the source of intense struggle, hope, disappointment, and renewal.

All of the complexities in indigenous life—individual versus society, conflicting solidarities, known vulnerabilities versus novel organizing strategies—all can be summed up in the realization of the limits of hope. These limits do not, however, free anthropology from the demands of struggle and the necessity of partisanship. Nor does it permit us to wash our hands in or of the complexities of social life. It is, rather, a call to use the case studies presented here and in the other books in the series to construct a more rooted partisanship, one that cannot simply and innocently take one "side" or another, any more than it could sit back and watch individual and social lives be torn apart.

Kirk Dombrowski   Gerald Sider

NOTES

1. The scare quotes around "here" and "out there" are meant to indicate that it is precisely the concrete connection between the events "out there" and intellectual climates "here" that call into question the utility of notions like "out there" and "here." Another way of putting this is to note that

anthropology as a practice takes place in the same social field as the social practices it seeks to understand. This is the failure of the "scholastic point of view," as Pierre Bourdieu puts it (1990).

2. As William Roseberry pointed out, there is a critical difference between history and histories, ethnography and ethnographies (1989).

3. Linda Tuhiwai Smith notes that some Maori organizations are reluctant to allow even Maori researchers to begin work "until they have developed a sufficiently strong base" (1999: 172).

REFERENCES

Bourdieu, Pierre. 1990. "The Scholastic Point of View." *Cultural Anthropology* 5(4): 380–91.

Churchill, Ward. 1996a. "I am Indigenist: Notes on the Ideology of the Fourth World." *From a Native Son: Selected Essays on Indigenism, 1985–1995.* Pp. 509–48. Boston: South End Press.

————. 1996b. "False Promises: An Indigenist Perspective on Marxist Theory and Practice." *From a Native Son: Selected Essays on Indigenism, 1985–1995.* Pp. 461–82. Boston: South End Press.

Clifford, James, and George E. Marcus. 1986. *Writing Culture: The Poetics and Politics of Ethnography.* Berkeley: University of California Press.

Comaroff, John, and Jean Comaroff. 1991. *Of Revelation and Revolution: Christianity, Colonialism and Consciousness in South Africa.* Vol. 1. Chicago: University of Chicago Press.

Dombrowski, Kirk. 2001. *Against Culture: Development, Politics and Religion in Indian Alaska.* Lincoln: University of Nebraska Press.

Fabian, Johannes. 1983. *Time and the Other: How Anthropology Makes Its Object.* New York: Columbia University Press.

Gupta, Akhil, and James Ferguson. 1997. "Discipline and Practice: 'The Field' as Site, Method, and Location in Anthropology." In *Anthropological Locations: Boundaries and Grounds of a Field Science.* A. Gupta and J. Ferguson, eds. Pp. 1–46. Berkeley: University of California Press.

Miller, Bruce. 2001. *The Problem of Justice: Tradition and Law in the Coast Salish World.* Lincoln: University of Nebraska Press.

Roseberry, William. 1989. *Anthropologies and Histories: Essays in Culture, History, and Political Economy.* New Brunswick: Rutgers University Press.

————. 1996. "The Unbearable Lightness of Anthropology." *Radical History Review* 65:5–25.

Scott, Joan Wallach. 1988. *Gender and the Politics of History.* New York: Columbia University Press.

Shkilnyk, Anastasia M. 1985. *A Poison Stronger than Love: The Destruction of an Ojibwa Community*. New Haven: Yale University Press.

Sider, Gerald M. 1993. *Lumbee Indian Histories*. New York: Cambridge University Press.

Smith, Linda Tuhiwai. 1999. *Decolonizing Methodologies: Research and Indigenous Peoples*. New York: Zed Books.

Stocking, George. 1992. "Postscriptive Prospective Reflections." *The Ethnographer's Magic and Other Essays in the History of Anthropology*. Pp 362–74. Madison: University of Wisconsin Press.

Vincent, Joan. 1990. *Anthropology and Politics: Visions, Traditions and Trends*. Tucson: University of Arizona Press.

Walkowitz, Judith. 1992. *City of Dreadful Delight: Narratives of Sexual Danger in Late-Victorian London*. Chicago: University of Chicago Press.

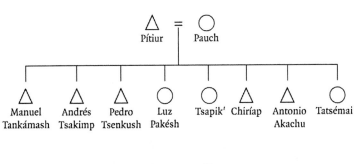

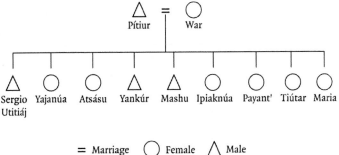

= Marriage ○ Female △ Male

Chart 1. Pítiur's Wives and Children

263

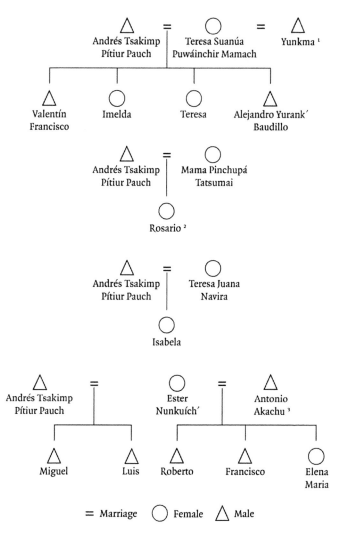

= Marriage   ◯ Female   △ Male

1. Teresa was first married to Yunkma; they had two children who live in the northern part of the country. After Yunkma died, Teresa married Andrés.
2. Rosario was adopted from Mama's classificatory sister.
3. Ester was first married to Antonio Akachu. After Antonio died, Ester married his brother Andrés, and Andrés reared Antonio's three children (Roberto, Francisco, and Elena Maria), who were his classificatory children.

Chart 2. Andrés Tsakimp Pítiur Pauch's Wives and Children

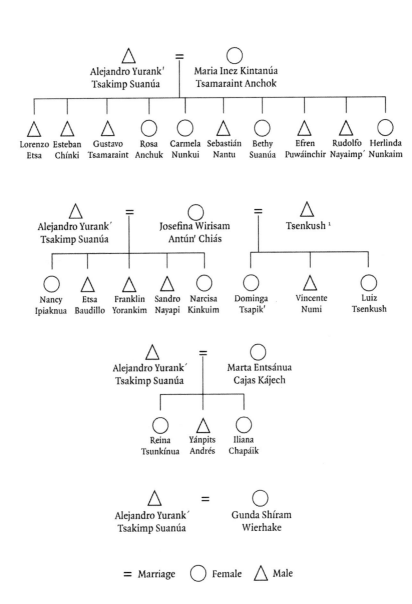

Alejandro Yurank'
Tsakimp Suanúa

Maria Inez Kintanúa
Tsamaraint Anchok

Lorenzo Etsa | Esteban Chínki | Gustavo Tsamaraint | Rosa Anchuk | Carmela Nunkui | Sebastián Nantu | Bethy Suanúa | Efren Puwáinchir | Rudolfo Nayaimp' | Herlinda Nunkaim

Alejandro Yurank'
Tsakimp Suanúa

Josefina Wirisam
Antún' Chiás

Tsenkush [1]

Nancy Ipiaknua | Etsa Baudillo | Franklin Yorankim | Sandro Nayapi | Narcisa Kinkuim | Dominga Tsapik' | Vincente Numi | Luiz Tsenkush

Alejandro Yurank'
Tsakimp Suanúa

Marta Entsánua
Cajas Kájech

Reina Tsunkínua | Yánpits Andrés | Iliana Chapáik

Alejandro Yurank'
Tsakimp Suanúa

Gunda Shíram
Wierhake

= Marriage   ◯ Female   △ Male

1. Josefina was first married to Tsenkush. After Tsenkush died, Josefina married Alejandro, who adopted her three children (Dominga Tsapik', Vicente Numi, and Luiz Tsenkush).

Chart 3. Alejandro Tsakimp's Wives and Children

265

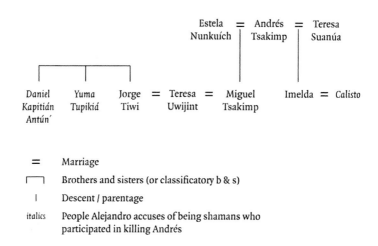

=	Marriage
⌐¬	Brothers and sisters (or classificatory b & s)
I	Descent / parentage
italics	People Alejandro accuses of being shamans who participated in killing Andrés

Chart 4. Accused Shamans and Their Relationship to Andrés Tsakimp

Cast of Characters

Note: Because of the common use of first names in the text, names are listed alphabetically by first letter of first name.

Achayat' first friend of Andrés Tsakimp

Aíjiu shuar name of Alfredo Germani

Alberto Mejéant classificatory brother of Alejandro, who lives in Sintuch and is an acquaintance of Pichík'

Albino Gomezcuello itinerant Salesian missionary who advised the Shuar from 1948 to 1960 and who organized the first Shuar *centros*

Alfredo Germani salesian missionary who, with Juan Shutka, helped found the Association of Sucúa

Ampush in-law of Andrés

Andrés alejandro's father; first *síndico* of Utunkus

Angel Sharup'Uwijint husband of Elena Akachu, father of Natividad

Angel Tsamaraint former president of the Federation

Antonio Akachu son of Pítiur and Pauch; brother of Andrés; father of Elena Akachu

Antonio Tankámash son of Manuel Tankámash; classificatory brother of Alejandro

Antonio Nekta uncle of Maria

Antún' uncle of Alejandro

Atsásu daughter of Pítiur and War; sister of Andrés

Augustín son of Chúmpi

Augusto Abad first provincial director of CREA; deputy of the province when I conducted my first fieldwork in Morona Santiago

Bartolome Juep former president of the Federation; founder of the Shuar Organization of Ecuador

Bartolome Máshumar former president of the Federation

Benigno Abarca *Colono*

Benjamín Chiríap son of Pítiur and Pauch; brother of Andrés

Bethy Suanúa Tsakimp seventh child of Alejandro and Maria (born 1977)

Bosco Chiríap son of José Chiríap; former *síndico* of the Utunkus

Bosco Chuínt former *vice-síndico* of Saip; served on the founding committee of the Association of Sucúa

Calisto Tsenkush fourth husband of Imelda Tsakimp

Carlos Kunamp President-of the Association of Sucúa before Alejandro

Carlos Olvera *Teniente político* of Sucúa when Alejandro was a boy

Carmela Nunkui Tsakimp fifth child of Alejandro and Maria (born 1971)

Carmelina Antúnish daughter of Teresa Mamach and Pedro Tunki; wife of Rafael Antúnish

Chavela Isabela Tsakimp, daughter of Andrés and his third wife, Teresa Navira; wife of Luis Kajékai

Chínki *Teniente político* in Yaup'

Chinkiásu aunt of Maria

Chúmpi classificatory brother of Teresa Suanúa

Cristina secretary for Father Juan Shutka

Cristobal confidant of Alejandro

Daniel Kapitián Antún' classificatory brother of Jorge Tiwi

Dionicio Atamaint President of the Association of Sucúa during the time of my first fieldwork

Domingo Antún' former president of the Federation

Domingo Kúkush' brother of Juan José; nephew of Andrés Tsakimp

Eduardo Tunki former *síndico* of Utunkus

Efren Puwáinchir Tsakimp eighth child of Alejandro and Maria (born 1981)

Ela Ficke North American Evangelical missionary; wife of Miguel Ficke

Elena Akachu daughter of Antonio Akachu; classificatory sister of Alejandro; wife of Angel Sharup'Ushap Uwijint; mother of Natividad

Elena Nekta daughter of Antonio Nekta; classificatory sister of Maria

Emilio son of Luz Pakésh; *saich* of Alejandro

Enrique Ferguson North American chiropractor who worked in Sucúa when Alejandro was a young man

Enrique Nurínkias former representative of the Federation in Quito

Ernesto Tséremp former *síndico* of Saip; served on the founding committee of the Association of Sucúa; son of Yankúr; *saich* of Alejandro

Esteban Chínki Tsakimp second child of Alejandro and Maria (born 1962)

Eugenio Samík former secretary of Asunción; served on the founding committee of the Association of Sucúa

Felipe Abarca third husband of Imelda Tsakimp

Filimon Lopez Colono with land adjacent to and in Utunkus

Francisco also Valentín; first son of Andrés and his first wife, Teresa Suanúa

Francisco Monticone Salesian acolyte from Italy

Germán Mancheno provincial director of CREA during the time of my first fieldwork; deputy-elect during the time of my second fieldwork

Gunda Wierhake fourth wife of Alejandro Tsakimp; German anthropologist and author of Cultura Material Shuar en la Historia; also called Shíram

Gustavo Molina Evangelical missionary who taught in Sucúa from 1948 to 1957

Gustavo Tsamaraint Tsakimp third child of Alejandro and Maria (born 1966)

Herlinda Nunkaim Tsakimp tenth child of Alejandro and Maria (born 1986)

Hilario Tunki former vice-síndico of Utunkus

Huayna-Capac Inca; son of Tupac-Yupanqui

Imelda Tsakimp second child of Andrés and his first wife, Teresa Suanúa

Janet Hendricks anthropologist; author of To Drink of Death

Jean Ferguson son of Dr Enrique Ferguson

Jiúkam classificatory brother of Teresa Suanúa; father of Pedro Tunki and Antonio Nekta

Jorge Lopez Colono in Macas; evangelical; operated a lumber mill; father of Judith

Jorge Kuja first vocal (representative) of Saip; served on the founding committee of the Association of Sucúa

Jorge Tiwi former husband of Teresa Uwijint

José Chau childhood friend of Alejandro

Cast of Characters

Josefina Josefina Wirisam Antún' Chies; second wife of Alejandro

José Maria Velasco Ibarra five-time president of Ecuador

José Nantip' classificatory son of Alejandro; of Natemtsa

Juan Achayat' shaman in Napo, with whom Maria Chúmpi studied

Juan Bosco Mashu Shuar teacher; my first Shuar friend and *compadre*

Juan Jorge Kajékai first treasurer of Utunkus

Juan Pinínkias Chiríap classificatory brother of Alejandro

Juan Shutka Salesian missionary who first organized the Shuar Federation

Julio Saant former *teniente político* of Sevilla don Bosco; served on the founding committee of the Shuar Federation; two-time president of the Federation

Julio Zuniga *Colono*; involved in a dispute with members of Utunkus

Kasent classificatory brother of Andrés

Katan' shaman in Chiguaza, with whom Maria Chúmpi studied

Lorenzo Etsa Tsakimp first child of Alejandro and Maria (born 1960)

Lorenzo Vargas shaman in Napo

Lucho son of Andrés and his fourth wife, Ester Nunkuich

Luis Carollo Salesian missionary

Luis Cornelio Kajékai secretary of Utunkus; accused of killing Lorenzo Tsakimp

Luis Mánkash shaman from Corazon de Jesus

Lupe Narvaiz wife of Pepe Narvaiz

Luz Pakésh daughter of Pítiur and Pauch; sister of Andrés

Maria Maria Ines Kintanúa Tsamaraint Anchok; Alejandro's first wife

Maria Chúmpi shaman; Alejandro's "political aunt" (her parents were classificatory brothers of his grandfather)

Maria Ornes Peace Corps volunteer during the time of my first fieldwork

Maria Troncatti nun

Mariana mother-in-law of Gustavo

Marta Marta Entsanua Kajas Kajéch; third wife of Alejandro

Mashiant husband of Maria Chúmpi

Mercedes elder sister of Maria

Miguel Ficke North American Evangelical missionary

Cast of Characters

Michael Harner North American anthropologist who conducted fieldwork among the Shuar in 1956–57

Miguel Minki Miguel Minki Tankámash; former *síndico* of Asunción; served on the founding committee of the Association of Sucúa; first president of the Association; first (and three-time) president of the Federation; classificatory brother of Alejandro (their mothers are classificatory sisters)

Miguel Pillco *Colono*

Miguel Puwáinchir President of the Federation during the time of my first fieldwork; mayor of Palora during my second fieldwork

Miguel Tankámash son of Pitior and Pauch; brother of Andrés

Miguel Tankámash Chiríap former *vice-síndico* of Utunkus; served on the founding committee of the Association of Sucúa; catechist; son of Benjamín Chiríap

Miguel Tiwi *Saich* of Alejandro

Miguel Tsakimp son of Andrés and his fourth wife, Ester Nunkuich; brother of Alejandro; husband of Teresa Uwijint

Nantu Sebastián Tsakimp sixth child of Alejandro and Maria (born 1975)

Natividad Uwijint daughter of Elena Akachu and Angel Sharup' Uwijint

Nohemi Chiríap daughter of Benjamín Chiríap; wife of Rafael Mashiant

Pedro Kayáp man in Nejempaim

Pedro Kunkúmas former president of the Federation

Pedro Tunki husband of Teresa Mamach; *saich* of Alejandro

Pepe Narvaiz *Colono*

Philip III crowned Hapsburg Emperor in September 1598

Pichík' best friend of Alejandro; Achuar from Wichim'

Piruch *Saich* of Andrés

Quirruba leader of the Shuar uprising of 1599

Rafael Kunkúmas son of Ernesto Kunkúmas; brother of Pedro Kunkúmas; former husband of Natividad

Rafael Mashiant former representative of the heads of households of Utunkus; served on the founding committee of the Association of Sucúa; later *vice-síndico* of Utunkus; husband of Nohemi Chiríap

Reina Tsunkínua first child of Alejandro and his third wife, Marta

Ricardo Rubio policeman in Sucúa when Alejandro was a boy; second husband of Imelda

Ricardo Tankámash brother of Miguel Minki

Roberto North American friend of Dr Ferguson who came to Sucúa to make a movie about the Shuar

Rosana also Tsunkínua; classificatory sister of Alejandro; reared by the Fickes

Rosa Anchuk Tsakimp fourth child of Alejandro and Maria (born 1970)

Rosario daughter of the classificatory sister of Andrés's second wife, Mama; adopted by Andrés and Mama

Rudolfo Nayemp Tsakimp ninth child of Alejandro and Maria (born 1982)

Segundo Tsakimp classificatory brother of Alejandro; studied shamanism with Alejandro; lives in Tsuntsuim

Segundo Yasakam' shaman in Puyo

Shimpiúkat son of Tsamaraint; first person treated by Alejandro; from Waríts

Shíram Gunda Wierhake; fourth wife of Alejandro

Sofia classificatory sister of Alejandro; daughter of the sister of Teresa Suanúa

Suanúa the wife of Tséremp

Tarcicio Kuja interim president of the Federation after the coup

Teresa Mamach third child of Andrés and his first wife, Teresa Suanúa

Teresa Suanúa first wife of Andrés; mother of Alejandro

Tiwi classificatory brother of Andrés

Tsachímp' son of Tséremp and Suanúa

Tsapik' Tukup' first wife of Valentín

Tséremp brother of Andrés's second wife, Mama

Tsunkínua Shuar name for Alejandro's classificatory sister Rosana and his daughter Reina

Tsunkuman Kishíjint classmate of Alejandro

Tupac-Yupanqui Inca

F. W. Up de Graff North American adventurer who traveled around Ecuador from 1894 to 1901

Utitiáj former *síndico* of Shimpis; served on the founding committee of the Association of Sucúa

Valentín also Francisco; first child of Andrés and his first wife, Teresa Suanúa
Vicente Jíntiach' former president of the Federation
Vicente Kuja uncle of Alejandro

Wampíu man who lived in Asunción; believed to have died from witchcraft
Wanít famous shaman; accused of witchcraft and shot dead
Wíakach' *Saich* of Pichík'
Wisúm mute man from Asunción

Yankúr classificatory brother of Teresa Suanúa; *saich* of Andrés; uncle of Alejandro
Yuma Tupiki classificatory brother of Jorge Tiwi

273

Glossary

abstraction A process that starts with particular, concrete events that occurred in different contexts; claims that the meaning of these events has little or nothing to do with the contexts in which they occurred, and that these events are really examples of particular kinds of events and patterns; and ends with generalizations.

agouti A large rodent. In Spanish, *guatuza*; in Shuar, *yunkitz*.

ají (Spanish) Chili pepper; along with salt, it is the basic condiment for both Shuar and Euro-Ecuadorians.

ajija (Shuar) Ginger.

aishman (Shuar) Man.

alama (Spanish) Pejorative term for Quichua.

anakma (Shuar) An object that a shaman has cursed; anyone who touches it becomes sick.

apache (Shuar) A non-Shuar, non-indigenous Ecuadorian.

arútam (Shuar) Vision.

arútam wakaní (Shuar) The Salesian missionaries use this word to mean soul, but Shuar translate it as a kind of power one may possess.

awankim (Shuar) Cloth.

ayahuasca (Quichua) An infusion made from a vine; also called *yagé*, in Shuar, *natém*; the botanical name of the vine is *Banisteriopsis caapi*. It contains the alkaloid harmine.

ayampaco (Quichua?) A stuffed leaf that is roasted and then eaten.

bifurcate merging A kinship terminology; also called Iroquois or Dravidian kinship terminology. In the parental generation, siblings of the same sex are merged. Thus, people call their mother's sisters "mothers" and their father's brothers "fathers." In one's own generation, there is a sharp distinction between consanguineal and affinal kin. Parallel cousins are treated as brothers and sisters, and cross cousins are treated as spouses or in-laws. When necessary, Shuar can identify their classificatory fathers, mothers, and siblings with the word *kana*.

They also use the word *kana* to identify people related solely through marriage.

brujo (Spanish) Witch; in Shuar, *uwíshin*.

caracha (Spanish) A bottom-feeding fish; in Shuar, *nayump'*.

centro (Spanish) Center. Among Shuar it refers to a central plaza that is used for soccer games and community assemblies. The plaza is generally surrounded by a schoolhouse, a chapel, a meeting hall, and houses. More generally, *centro* refers to all the people who have concentrated around this plaza, and the land to which they collectively or as individuals hold title; a nucleated settlement.

chicha (Quichua) Fermented manioc beverage; in Shuar, *nijiamanch'*.

chucchu (Shuar) A medicinal hallucinogenic plant, also *pirípiri*.

chuntak (Shuar) A rubbery phlegm involved in shamanism.

colono (Spanish) Settler. Any non-Shuar Ecuadorian who has settled in or near Shuar territory.

CREA Acronym for the Economic Reconversion Center for the Austro (southern Ecuador), also known as the Economic Reconversion Center for Azuay, Cañar, and Morona Santiago; the state's development agency for the region.

cross cousin A child of one's mother's brother or father's sister. Shuar prefer to marry their cross cousins.

cumpachuma (Spanish) Pejorative term used by members of the Shuar Federation to refer to members of the rival organization, the Shuar Organization of Ecuador.

curandero (Spanish) Healer; in Shuar, *uwíshin*.

encomendero (Spanish) A person granted control over Indian labor by the Crown in return for converting them to Christianity.

ethnographic present The exclusive use of the present tense to describe events, beliefs, and practices.

ethnography A book describing and analyzing a particular society, based on particiapnt-observation fieldwork.

fiscal (Spanish) A school run by the state.

fiscomisional (Spanish) A school run by missionaries on behalf of and with the support of the state.

FODERUMA Acronym for the Fund for the Development of Marginal Rural Areas; an instrument of the state.

guayusa (Shuar) A plant from which Shuar and *colonos* make an herbal tea. *Colonos* mix it with sugar and claim that once people drink *guayusa*, they will always yearn to stay in the Amazon. Shuar used to drink huge quantities in the early morning as an emetic.

IEOS Acronym for the Institute Ecuatoriano de Obras Sanitarias; the Ecuadorian Institute for Sanitary Works.

IERAC Acronym for the Ecuadorian Institute for Agrarian Reform and Colonization; the state agency in charge of land title.

inchinkian (Shuar) A clay pot.

inkis (Shuar) A non-Ecuadorian.

itíp' Cloth worn by men as a skirt.

iwianch (Shuar) The Salesian missionaries use the Shuar word *Iwianch* to mean Satan or the Devil, whereas the Shuar use the term *iwianch* to refer to a demon or goblin.

jefe político (Spanish) Political chief. Appointed by the governor, this person represents the executive arm of the state at the level of the county and functions as a magistrate.

Jívaro (Spanish) Pejorative term for Shuar.

kakáram (Shuar) Warrior.

kaonak (Shuar) Dried plantain leaf.

kana saich (Shuar) A person related by marriage only; someone who was not considered to be an affine (or relative) prior to marriage.

kare (Quichua) Strong.

maikiúa (Shuar) An infusion made from a plant; in Spanish, *floripondia;* of the genus *Brugmansia*. This is related to the genus *Datura* in North America and the Old World; in English, the plant is called thorn apple. The *maikiúa* used for punishment is *B. sanguinea*. The plant contains tropane alkaloids.

minga (Spanish) Laborers contracted for community service.

mikiut (Shuar) *Maikiúa* for use by shamans.

mingas (Shuar) Work parties consisting of adults from the community.

muisak (Shuar) The spirit of a dead person.

nampi (Shuar) A nut.

namur (Shuar) A talisman.

Nanki (Shuar) Spear; my Shuar name. The diminutive form is *Nankichi*.

nanku (Shuar) A papaya stick.

ñaña (Quichua) Sister.

ñaño (Quichua) Brother; the diminutive form is ñañito.

napi (Shuar) A snake.

natém (Shuar) An infusion made from a vine; in Quichua, *ayahuasca* or *yagé*; the botanical name of the vine is *Banasteriopsis caapi*. It contains the alkaloid harmine.

nayump' (Shuar) A bottom-feeding fish; in Spanish, *caracha*.

nijiamanch' (Shuar) Fermented manioc beverage; in Quichua, *chicha*.

oriente (Spanish) The east; the Amazon.

panki (Shuar) Anaconda.

parallel cousin A child of one's mother's sister or father's brother. Shuar consider parallel cousins to be their brothers and sisters. When necessary, Shuar use the word *kana* to indicate that a brother or sister is not the child of their own birth mother or birth father.

pasuk (Shuar) A shaman's familiar. It is animate, often takes the form of an animal, and lives outside the shaman's body, but it is under the control of the shaman, who often uses it for errands.

patrilineage A group constituted through demonstrated descent from a common ancestor, traced exclusively through the male line.

peccary A piglike animal indigenous to the New World; Shuar use the term *sajino* or *paki*.

pinink' (Shuar) A cup.

pirípiri (Quichua?) A medicinal plant that shamans use to gain power; also *chucchu*.

polygyny The practice of one man having more than one wife.

real (Spanish) A unit of Ecuadorian currency equal to ten *centavos*.

reification The process by which generalizations are given names and then treated as if they were particular, concrete things.

Runa (Quichua) Quichua.

saich (Shuar) Alejandro's pronunciation of the Shuar word for affine (a person who is, or can be, related by marriage); for Shuar men this would include a sister's husband or a male cross cousin); the Shuar Federation uses the term *sai*; Harner (1984) and Hendricks (1993) transcribe the term as *sái*. Shuar translate this word as *cunado* (Spanish), brother-in-law.

serbish Acronym for the Sistema de Educación Radiofónica Bicultural Shuar; the Shuar Radiophonic Bicultural Educational System; the educational branch of the Shuar Federation.

shinshínk (Shuar) A sheaf or handful of palm leaves that shamans rustle rhythmically during their treatments.

shushui (Shuar) Armadillo.

sierra (Spanish) The highlands.

síndico (Spanish) Trustee. The elected chief of a *centro*. This person has no coercive power but may be called on to resolve disputes within the *centro*, to represent the *centro* to outsiders, and to elect the president and directorate of the Federation.

snv Acronym for the Nederlandse Ontwikkelingsorganisatie; (Spanish) Servicio Holandes de Cooperación al Desarollo; the Netherlands Development Organization.

sucre (Spanish) The Ecuadorian unit of currency; named after a military hero.

supai (Quichua) The spirit of a dead person; Achuar shamans use the term to refer to *pasuk* or *tsentsak*.

tankámash (Shuar) The male side of the house.

tarabita (Spanish) A gondola or basket that is attached to a pulley suspended from a cable and used to cross over a river in a deep gorge.

teniente político (Spanish) Political lieutenant. Appointed by the *jefe político*, this person represents the executive arm of the state at the level of the parish; functions as a sheriff or justice of the peace.

tsaniri (Shuar) Girlfriend.

tsantsa (Shuar) Shrunken head.

tsentsak (Shuar) A weapon that only shamans can see and control, but that can cause illness or death. Shuar translate this word as "little arrow."

Tsunki Refers to a class, or member of a class, of mythic beings with supernatural powers; it can also refer to a specific man in Shuar myth. Tsunkinua is the term for any female Tsunki; it can also refer to the daughter of the man called Tsunki in Shuar myth.

tumank (Shuar) A jew's harp, made from a hard reed and a string.

uchiru (Shuar) Alejandro's pronunciation of the word for "son"; the Shuar Federation uses the term *uchirí*; Harner (1984) and Hendricks (1993) transcribe the term as *uchi*.

umpum (Shuar) Food that a shaman has blown on, generally so that when anyone eats it, that person becomes sick, although *umpum* may also be used for good purposes.

uxorilocal A married couple that lives with or near the wife's parents.

uwíshin (Shuar) A part-time specialist in killing and curing through the use of *natém* and *tsentsak*. Shuar translate *uwíshin* as "witch" or "healer." Shamans that heal are called *penker uwíshin* or *tsuakratin*; shamans that do not heal or who harm are called *yajauch uwíshin* or *weawekratin*.

vocal (Spanish) A councilor.

wánip' (Shuar) A pythonlike red snake that lives in trees.

washim (Shuar) A wooden grill or a trap for catching fish made out of reeds.

yagé (Quichua) An infusion made from a vine; also called *ayahuasca* or, in Shuar, *natém*; *Brugmansia caapi*. It contains the alkaloid harmine.

yápu A large bird of prey.

yatsuru (Shuar) Alejandro's pronunciation of the word for "brother"; the Shuar Federation uses the term *yatsu*; Harner (1984) and Hendricks (1993) transcribe the term as *yachi*.

Notes

1. MEETING ALEJANDRO

1. Maurizio Gnerre has argued convincingly that the term *Jívaro* evolved from the sixteenth-century Spanish spelling of *shuar*, in which the *x* (which was later replaced by the *j*) was used to represent the *sh* sound, and the *v* was used to represent the *u* sound (as there was no letter *u* in the Roman alphabet). Whatever the derivation of the word *Jívaro*, though, today it is used to mean something other than *Shuar*.

Anthropologists have used the term *Jivaroan* to refer to a number of groups speaking mutually intelligible or otherwise closely related languages and characterized (or formerly characterized) by similar subsistence and settlement patterns and similar social and political organization, such as the Shuar, Achuar (see Descola 1994, 1996; Gippelhauser and Mader 1990; Taylor 1981), Aguaruna (see Brown 1985), and Shiwiar (see Seymour-Smith 1988). Euro-Ecuadorians use the word *Jívaro* pejoratively, as if the word were not the name of a specific people but rather a synonym for "savage."

I therefore prefer not to use the word *Jivaroan* for two reasons. First, Shuar consider the term an insult. As Michael Harner (1984) proposed, "academic taxonomic ideals must take second place when they interfere with the rightful aspirations of oppressed peoples." Second, each group has a different experience of colonialism and consequently a different understanding of their own identity. After over a century of colonialism, it no longer makes sense to collapse these groups into one "academic taxonomic ideal."

The works of Brown, Descola, Gippelhauser and Mader, Seymour-Smith, and Taylor continue to provide important comparative material and analysis relevant to the study of the Ecuadorian Shuar. Nevertheless, research among one group is not necessarily generalizable to another. My research was conducted within the Shuar Federation and in the Upano valley in Ecuador; my analysis is limited to this population.

2. The literature on colonialism (see Fanon 1963 and Memmi 1965) and postcolonialism (see Bhabha 1994, Guha 1982–89, Said 1978, Spivak 1988) is too extensive to engage in any depth here. Most of these works grapple

with the legacy of French and British colonialism in the nineteenth and twentieth centuries, a time of capitalist expansion. Part of this legacy is the difficulty and danger in developing a national identity in the periphery of the world system.

Ecuador, however, was colonized by Spain in the sixteenth century, a time of merchant-capitalist expansion, and achieved independence from Spain in 1822. Consequently, the postcolonial challenges of nation building in Ecuador have taken a different form from those in Africa, the Middle East, and India. Moreover, one important component of Ecuadorian postcolonial politics has been the continuation of the conquest and colonization of indigenous peoples. In other words, what is the postcolonial epoch for Euro-Ecuadorians is still a colonial epoch for people like the Shuar.

Nevertheless, this book takes seriously some of the larger questions raised by postcolonial theory, specifically, how (and by whom) is knowledge about subordinate people produced, and how (and by whom) is it used?

3. As I hope to make clear in the following chapter, Shuar have good reason to be suspicious of anthropologists. Nevertheless, I never heard a Shuar criticize or complain about a specific anthropologist. Their complaint was with the asymmetrical relationship between them and Europeans and Euro-Americans, in general. In their experience, foreigners too often took their material or cultural resources without providing adequate, if any, compensation. The most common complaint was that visitors took photographs of them and never offered them copies (thus, when I returned, I brought with me a Polaroid camera and plenty of film). Unfortunately, I eventually discovered, many of these visitors were tourists who identified themselves to Shuar as anthropologists.

4. In 1969 the American Anthropological Association resolved that "members . . . shall not engage in any secret or classified research," and that "fieldworkers shall not divulge any information orally or in writing, solicited by government officials, foundations or corporation representatives about the people they study that compromises and/or endangers their well-being and cultural integrity." The current code of ethics states that: "Anthropological researchers have primary ethical obligations to the people, species, and materials they study and to the people with whom they work. These obligations can supersede the goal of seeking new knowledge, and can lead to decisions not to undertake or to discontinue a research project when the primary obligation conflicts with other responsibilities, such as those owed to sponsors or clients."

5. I spent almost half of my time in Utunkus and more time in Sucúa, where I interviewed Federation officials and settlers, and which I used as a base to visit, or host, shamans from other communities.

6. *Deconstruction*, despite appearances, is not the opposite of *construction*; it means both something less and something more than "take apart." Of course, there is a long tradition in academe of reducing something to its components in order to better understand its origin, function, and meaning—in short, "analysis" or "critique." Deconstruction, however, is applied to a narrower range of phenomena. It is based on the observation that many practices (especially discursive ones) rely on particular oppositions, and that such oppositions are often asymmetrical: one term of the opposition is considered superior or prior to the other. Furthermore, deconstruction goes far beyond taking such oppositions apart in order to understand them. It is a political strategy for dealing with such practices. Strictly speaking, it relies first on reversing the opposition and then on displacing it, usually by redefining one of the terms of the opposition. The intention behind these two movements is to challenge the power that operates through hierarchical oppositions—without denying their power or attempting to replace them. By "relying on distinctions that it puts in question, exploiting oppositions whose philosophical implications it seeks to evade" (Culler 1982: 151), deconstruction seeks to destabilize claims to absolute truth or knowledge (see Derrida 1973, 1976, and 1981). It is this intention that motivates my use of the term.

7. Of course, this is not always or necessarily true. But although many books have been banned or burned, and many authors imprisoned or killed, I know that the worst thing that can happen to me is my words being left unread.

2. HISTORY AND CULTURE

1. My point is not that many, let alone most, anthropologists are directly responsible for genocide or ethnocide. For one thing, these are extreme cases that, however horrible, distract us from the everyday abuses of colonialism and imperialism. Shuar, for example, have not been victims of genocide and ethnocide—but they have been subject to a set of practices that promote the exploitation of their land and labor. Precisely because these practices are more common and less abhorrent, they are more insidious.

Furthermore, these extreme situations distract us from scrutinizing ethnographic practices that are ethical and legal and perhaps even good science, yet still problematic. Most anthropologists working among the

Shuar, for example, have in fact been critics of colonialism. And although some missionaries and government officials in Ecuador have read ethnographies of the Shuar, they developed their policies and practices on their own. Nevertheless, there are significant similarities among the ways Western scientists, artists, administrators, merchants, soldiers, and clergy categorize and represent the world, and these patterns reflect a history of domination and attempted domination of the world. My point is that even the most rigorous anthropologist working with the best of intentions cannot completely escape his or her own culture.

2. Strictly speaking, the word *critique* refers to the traditional philosophical exercise of making explicit and scrutinizing those assumptions implicit in our forms of thought. Today, *critical theory* is sometimes used very narrowly to describe the project of a group of scholars known as the Frankfurt School, but many people, including members of the Frankfurt School itself, use the term more broadly. According to a member of that school, the philosopher Jurgen Habermas, the rise of positivism (which he also called empirical-analytic science), hermeneutics, and critical theory reflects the dissolution of traditional philosophy in the modern epoch. Traditionally, philosophy sought to guide human action through knowledge that is free from human interests. The distribution of philosophical activity into positivism, hermeneutics, and critical theory, however, reveals that knowledge is always constituted by human interests, and that different interests constitute different kinds of knowledge. Thus, *positivism* (see note 4 below) is motivated by a desire for technical control over the world; *hermeneutics* is motivated by a desire to understand the meaning of human actions; and *critical theory* is motivated by a desire to emancipate one's self from illusory notions of reality. Since such notions are socially produced, critique and emancipation necessarily occur in the context of a social struggle. That is, it is not enough to emancipate just one's self; one must also emancipate social arrangements from illusions (Habermas 1971; Horkheimer 1972).

The first two of these domains seem to map out onto the structure of the modern university rather easily: positivism corresponds to the natural and social sciences, and hermeneutics corresponds to the humanities. Nevertheless, some sort of critical theory has been of increasing importance in the social sciences and humanities—although in different ways. On the one hand, many disciplines use the word *criticism* differently from Habermas. In the social sciences the word signifies a desire to fight social injustice (see Gouldner 1970; Mills 1959) or a commitment to identity politics; in the humanities it signifies a way of seeing (or reading) and talking about art (see Frye 1957). On the other hand, some people in the social sciences and humanities have appealed to the Frankfurt School's understanding of critical theory, either as an alternative or as a supplement, to positivism and hermeneutics. Consequently, the words *critical theory* have taken on a variety of meanings and have been put to a variety of uses (see Agger 1998; Bronner 1994; Calhoun 1995, Fay 1987; Foster 1983; Hall 1992; Held 1980; Hunter 1992; Kellner 1989).

Unlike positivism, both hermeneutic and critical approaches problematize the possibility of cross-cultural communication and objective or universally valid (or meaningful) knowledge—but in very different ways.

3. Although I did not study *critical theory* until I returned from Ecuador, it was this approach, more than any other, that drew me to the academic life. It is true that universities often reproduce popular (and all too often limited and dangerous) discourses about ourselves, others, and the world we share. But they are also among the few, and safest, places where one may question these discourses.

4. Of course, many people have argued over what might constitute a scientific method in cultural anthropology. Ethnographic research occurs under uncontrolled circumstances rather than in a laboratory, and the first anthropologists claimed that theirs was a natural, rather than experimental, science (in other words, more like geology or astronomy than chemistry). Like other scientists, however, their program was *positivist*, meaning, immediately, the attempt to provide a general description of a phenomenon based on systematic and objective observation and, ultimately, the attempt to derive from such descriptions "laws" that could equally explain past, and predict future, phenomena.

5. There is a growing body of literature on surrounding indigenous groups, such as the Achuar in Ecuador (see Descola 1994, 1996; Taylor 1981) and the Achuar (Gippelhauser and Mader: 1990), Aguaruna (Brown 1985), and Shiwiar (Seymour-Smith 1988) in Peru. A recent book by Mader (1999) provides a comparative analysis of Shuar and Achuar cosmology (and draws on research in San José Utunkus). Individually, these books illustrate the range of interests and styles in contemporary ethnography; collectively they provide a rich portrait of the region.

6. In English and Spanish, words such as *brother* and *brother-in-law* have fairly specific meanings: a brother is the son of one's own parents, and a

brother-in-law may be the husband of one's sister or the brother of one's wife. This is the case among Shuar as well. Nevertheless, Shuar use words such as *brother* and *brother-in-law* to include many more people than do the English and Spanish words. Shuar use Iroquois kinship terminology (see note 16 in this chapter) to classify a large number of people as either kin (brother or sister, mother or father, son or daughter) or affine (people who are, or can be, related by marriage). Therefore, it is better to think of words such as *brother* and *brother-in-law* as designating a general class of relatives, rather than a specific relationship.

7. See Gunter Gebauer and Christoph Wulf's analysis of forms of political representation during the epoch of absolutist monarchies in Europe: "The king is an ideal actor, for, in the history of his time, he is the only actor on earth. What he produces becomes history. He is the producer of historical time, a singular time created by a singular individual to which the times of all other individuals are linked" (1992: 122).

8. From the point of view of European-Ecuadorian relations, this account comes from a colonial period that ended in 1822 when Ecuador achieved independence from Spain and became part of Gran Colombia. From the point of view of Euro-Ecuadorian and Shuar relations, of course, this account is of an early episode in an ongoing colonial process.

9. I borrow this phrase from Lévi-Strauss (1966: 233). Lévi-Strauss recognized that "all societies are in history and change" (234) but that different societies respond differently to this situation. He argued that "people without history" seek to deny change by representing their world through transcendental categories. Unfortunately, he paid rather less attention to how anthropologists have represented such peoples and their representations. See my discussion of Lévi-Strauss and myth below.

10. I use the terms *history* and *myth* in their colloquial senses, the former being an account of change, the latter an account of the social or moral order. I do so, however, in order to make the point that this opposition reveals something about Western culture. Much recent research in South America has demonstrated that many non-Western peoples have a variety of ways of talking about events and the social order, and that the forms and functions of these accounts cannot be reduced to two opposed genres (see Hill 1988).

11. This is a partial description of "conventional history." As Stirling's work also illustrates, moreover, historians have generally limited themselves to written records as evidence and have focused on the history of

states. Although these features still define much academic and popular history, many historians have challenged the dominant model.

In the 1960s, "social historians" began studying subordinate groups within states, such as peasants and workers (see Thompson 1963; Hobsbawm and Rude 1968), African American slaves (see Genovese 1974), and women (see Lerner 1986, 1993). Other historians turned their attention to non-Europeans (see Cohen 1985; Feierman 1993). These shifts required new methods, including innovative uses of written documents as well as oral history (see Dunaway and Baum 1996).

More recently, some have turned attention to the political uses of history and have explored the political conditions under which certain kinds of history become possible while others are dismissed (see Wallace 1996). From this perspective, "objectivity" is no longer a stance to which historians should aspire, but a political claim that needs to be questioned. In this vein, others have questioned the epistemological and discursive bases of history. Specifically, some have questioned the very possibility of identifying an "object" of study, or a "subject" of history, and have explored what is at stake in identifying groups or classes of people as objects or subjects of history (see Ranciere 1994; Joan Scott 1996a). Others have explored the varied uses of different narrative styles and have questioned how "objectivity" is achieved rhetorically (see White 1973).

12. Given these assertions, many were shocked by the publication in 1967 of Malinowski's diary, in which he wrote of his boredom in the field and general dislike of "the natives." Although many have concluded that Malinowski was a racist, and that his pretensions to a humanistic science was hypocritical, I am instead impressed by his determination to bracket his personal feelings in his professional writings.

The fundamental problem with his ethnographies, I argue in this chapter, is not that they either reveal or hide his racism, but that they serve, however unconsciously, the colonialist project, through their separation of culture and history. (See Clifford 1988 for further reflections on Malinowski's influence on ethnographic discourse.)

13. Based on my own experience, these figures seem exaggerated. Nevertheless, I must stress that high levels of chicha consumption are not tantamount to alcoholism. Chicha that has been fermented for four days is extremely intoxicating and is served only at parties. Fermentation for one day merely transforms a bland starch into a refreshing drink.

14. Men prefer, but are not required, to have more than one wife.

15. Shuar distinguish between cross and parallel cousins. Cross cousins are the children of one's mother's brother or one's father's sister. Parallel cousins are the children of one's mother's sister or one's father's brother. Shuar consider their parallel cousins to be brothers and sisters and forbid marriage between them. They do, however, prefer (but do not require) marriage between cross cousins.

16. Bifurcate-merging kinship terminology is also called Iroquois or Dravidian kinship terminology. In the parental generation, siblings of the same sex are merged. Thus, people call their mother's sisters "mothers" and their father's brothers "fathers." In one's own generation, there is a sharp distinction between consanguineal kin (related by blood) and affinal kin (related by marriage). Parallel cousins are treated as blood relatives, and cross cousins are treated as spouses or in-laws.

17. Alejandro once described them to me as microbes, because under normal circumstances they are invisible.

18. These people purchase and learn how to control *tsentsak* by apprenticing themselves to more experienced shamans. Shamans often apprentice themselves to many such shamans over the years (see Alejandro's story in chapter 9). Conversely, there are a few very experienced and powerful shamans who have many apprentices; these shamans are called *bancos*. This is a Spanish term that Whitten translated as "seat" (1976: 149) and Harner translates as "repository" (1984: 119), but in this volume I gloss it as "mage."

19. This is not an effect solely of the "ethnographic present." Even had I used the past tense, there would still be no account of how these beliefs and practices developed—and, consequently, an implication that they existed for ages, unchanged until only recently.

20. Not all anthropologists were optimistic; although Boas agreed that the search for general laws of culture is the ultimate task of anthropology, he argued that the diversity of cultural forms and the difficulties in understanding their development render the task practically impossible, and any attempt to formulate such laws almost perpetually premature.

21. For an instructive example of this dilemma, see Derrida's 1976 critique of Lévi-Strauss's *Tristes Tropiques* (1973). Lévi-Strauss believed that anthropology could provide people with an objective vantage point from which one could understand human nature and thus judge all cultures. Among other things, Derrida points out that this construction of human nature ultimately reflects a Western view and is not objective.

22. Although Perkins does not identify himself here with the "New Age" (the back cover identifies it as a book on "Ecology/Native Spirituality"), his attitude and approach correspond with many points made by members of the New Age movement. See Heelas 1996 for an overview. For a critique of the Native Spirituality movement written by a leader of the American Indian Movement, see Churchill 1994a and 1994b. For a critique of the articulation between Native Spirituality and ecology, see Churchill 1994c.

23. Perkins's romanticization of humankind's past probably reflects a nostalgia for his own childhood. His book is replete with fond memories of his childhood and suggestions that Indians today remember what Euro-Americans once knew as children but have forgotten as adults. He does not confront the implication that adults living in the Amazon are somehow childlike. This implication, however, is basic to the Western discourse of the savage (see Derrida 1973).

24. This is slightly different from a *stereotype*, which is a perceived probabalistic description of a group (see McCauley, Jussim, and Lee 1995). Stereotypes may be essentialist, but even people who use stereotypes in the crudest, most demeaning ways might admit that a member of a group can act against type. An essence *defines* a type, however; if an individual acts against type, then he or she is no longer "really" a member of that group.

25. Michaels's larger point is that any notion of identity, if it is to be effective, must be essentialist; for critiques see Boyarin and Boyarin 1993; Gordon and Newfield 1994.

26. In this approach I am following Wolf's response to essentialism. He argued that "by understanding these names [of nations, societies, and cultures] as bundles of relationships [rather than as things], and by placing them back into the field from which they were abstracted, [we can] hope to avoid misleading inferences and increase our share of understanding" (1982: 3).

27. When Perkins asks his shaman friend how a former teacher at a Catholic mission school could believe in shamanism, the Shuar replies that there are many commonalities between *ayahuasca* shamanism and Christianity. "You see . . . the Shuar and Christians—true Christians—believe the same thing. We are all connected, all brothers and sisters in the deepest possible sense, because we are the same, hatched from a common egg" (1994: 65).

This man's remarks echo those made by a Cocama shaman to a missionary early in this century: "Well, you priests, when you baptize people, don't you blow, spit, pour over salt and oil, and do lots of other stupid things? Well, we do the same" (Espinosa 1935: 146). Peter Gow comments that "this Cocama shaman's statement was not, I suspect, a piece of cultural relativism, but a revelation of the inner logic of *ayahuasca* shamanic practice" (1994: 108). Similarly, I would suggest that we might learn more from this Shuar shaman's claim that Christianity and *ayahuasca* shamanism hatch from the same egg if we understand him rather more literally than metaphorically. His observation is not an assertion of relativism but of a historical connection.

28. This argument is speculative but accounts for a variety of facts concerning *ayahuasca* shamanism: it is found primarily in the Western Amazon, that is, at the frontier of the highland colonial economy; it is a regional, not a local, practice; it is pervasive among urban *mestizos* (claiming descent from both indigenous and European peoples); its lexicon is heavily Quichua—the *lingua franca* of the colonial Catholic missions; many shamans explain their beliefs and practices in terms of Catholic beliefs and practices; and it is today found among all Amazonian peoples who were linked to the colonial rubber economy and is not found among those peoples in the Western Amazon who were not (such peoples use *ayahuasca*, but not for shamanic purposes).

29. Both the Ecuadorian and Peruvian governments, believing that there was petroleum under the forest floor, claimed the same region of the Upper Amazon. In 1920 the Leonard Exploration Company of Delaware, a front for Standard Oil of New Jersey, began oil exploration in the Ecuadorian Amazon. In 1931 the government granted the company a concession of 2.5 million hectares. The contract allowed for a twenty-year study period, a six-year exploration period, and forty years of tax-exempt exploitation.

In 1937 the government, citing six years of exploration without results and an unpaid debt, canceled the contract with the North American company. It then granted an expanded concession of 10 million hectares to the Anglo Saxon Petroleum Company, Ltd.—a front for Royal Dutch Petroleum. At that time Standard Oil also had a front in Peru, the International Petroleum Company. IPC received from the Peruvian government the concession to explore and exploit the Amazon, and in 1941 the company gave Peru financial and political support in a war against Ecuador.

Preoccupied with World War II and anxious to support U.S. capital, the U.S. government met with representatives of both countries in Brazil and negotiated a cease-fire in 1942. According to the Rio de Janiero Protocol, signed 29 January 1942, Ecuador ceded 200,000 square kilometers of territory (more than half of its claimed national territory) to Peru. The new border ran exactly along the limits of the concession that Ecuador had granted the Anglo-Dutch company, and Peru immediately granted IPC the concession for its newly acquired territory. Later Ecuadorian governments have repudiated this settlement but have never been able to recover their ceded claim (NACLA 1975: 30–31). Nevertheless, at the time of my research all Ecuadorian maps (published by the Instituto Geográfico Militar, or Military Geographical Institute) use pre-1942 boundaries. These maps include the 1942 border as a dotted line (and marked "unenforceable") "to remind citizens of the 'forgotten' fact of the country's dismemberment" (Radcliffe and Westwood 1996: 63). The dispute over the border between Peru and Ecuador was not fully resolved until 1998.

30. Every two years the members of each *centro*—all men and women over the age of sixteen—elect a *síndico* (trustee), who chairs community meetings, represents the *centro* to nonmembers, and mediates local disputes, but who has no coercive power); a *vice-síndico*; a secretary; and a treasurer. The *síndicos* assemble every two years to elect the president of their association, and the president, vice president, and directors of the Federation.

31. The uses of writing affect its style. Gebauer and Wulf argued that "historians who report on historical time likewise produce it in their texts; they keep their own persons with their own time out of the historical text" (1992: 122). That is, when "history" is the history of the state—when the king is "author" of all that happens—then the authority of historians (meaning, those who literally write histories) is based on the evacuation of their own voices from their texts. Ironically, the "objective" voice is the disguised voice of the king's subjects. Consequently, the "subjective" voice can speak only to matters that are private; it literally lacks authority. In other words, the king's history effects a stunning reversal: in grammar, the subject is that which acts, and the object is that which is acted upon; in politics, however, the subject is that which is acted upon, and authority is "objective."

Writing that attacks the authority of the state necessarily attacks more general notions of authority and authorship. Thus, I believe that if one is to mobilize the fairy tale against the state, one must rely on a more personal form of writing too. When subjectivity is harnessed to political ends, political power is also revealed to be subjective.

3. LIFE HISTORY

1. Years later Vincent Crapanzano echoed these doubts: "We must ask whether or not the life history is in fact the best or even a possible strategy

for illuminating an individual's options. Indeed, given its retrospective nature, are we analyzing 'real' options—the options at the time—or selected options that justify choices already made? We have to ask, too, whether or not the life history is suited to the formulation of dynamic models of social change. I believe a case can be made for formulating such models from the dynamics of the interview in which the life story is, so to speak, invented, but not from the life historical text. The text provides us with a conventionalized gloss on social reality that, from a strict epistemological point of view, we cannot know. We may be discussing the dynamics of narration rather than the dynamics of society" (1984: 959).

2. Cf. Cora Dubois's (with the collaboration of Abram Kardiner and Emil Oberholzer) The People of Alor (1944) for the opposite strategy, an attempt to synthesize anthropological and psychological approaches.

3. Cf. Leo Simmons's Sun Chief for a more mechanical, rather than dialectical, approach to the relationship between culture and the individual. He argued that individuals relate to their cultures in various roles: as creatures, creators, carriers, and manipulators (1942: 388). By treating the individual and culture as separate variables, however, he grants them unmerited a priori status.

In fact, all individuals are produced through and exist in social relations, and no society exists independent of individuals. Ruth Benedict suggested that we often think of individual and society as being opposed because of our experience with the law as subjects of modern states (1934: 252). Perhaps students of anthropology too often conceive of agents and structures as existing independently because of the conventions of ethnographic description. Nevertheless, just as Benedict argued that there is no opposition between an individual and culture, Anthony Giddens has argued that there is no opposition between agency and structure (1979). Agency is only possible within or against a given structure, and social structures perdure only through human agency.

4. Unfortunately, owing to limitations of space, this book lacks a full account of Alejandro's marriage to his German wife, Gunda Wierhake. Although I did meet with and interview her, she was not at the time living with Alejandro, and he and I never spoke extensively about their relationship.

5. Structuralism takes as its object of study (and promotes as an explanatory or interpretive device) relationships among the parts of a system, rather than the parts themselves. Although the term "structuralist" is commonly

taken to refer to theories influenced by the linguists Ferdinand de Saussure (1966) and Roman Jakobson (1990), I use the term more generally to include theories influenced by the philosopher Immanuel Kant (1990, 1996) or the sociologist Emil Durkheim (1965, 1984). I thus include A. R. Radcliff-Brown (1965) and his students, who were concerned with the relationships among social roles or institutions (i.e., social structure), as well as the most famous "structuralist," Claude Lévi-Strauss (1963, 1966), and his students, who see such structures as reflections of the structure of the mind. Following "poststructuralist" critics, I am especially concerned with how these approaches use the notion of "system" to hierarchize difference, subordinating differences within a system to differences between systems.

4. WORKING WITH ALEJANDRO

1. Before I left for Ecuador one of my advisers warned me that a tape recorder would distract interviewees. Although Alejandro asked me, on one occasion, to turn off the recorder, I never met a Shuar who expressed any discomfort or inhibition because of the presence of the recorder or microphone. One reason may be that the Federation maintains a radio station from which any Shuar in Sucúa may broadcast a message to his or her *centro*; thus, many Shuar already have experience communicating through microphones.

2. Boas warned that a story can change with each telling, in part because of lapses of memory and in part because of the changing circumstances of the telling. Over the months I often reintroduced a topic or event, to elicit a new telling. Sometimes Alejandro told the same story several times, in response to different questions. Although his chronology was often inconsistent, his various accounts of any particular event never contradicted one another. Many of the stories I present here are composites of his different tellings of the same event.

3. See Sartre (1948: 59–60) for a discussion of the situationality of the human condition.

5. FIRST OF ALL . . .

1. Nanki is my Shuar name and also Shuar for "spear." The diminutive is Nankichi.

2. Just like Stirling, Alejandro here seems to believe that history begins when Shuar enter the space of the state. I do not know whether this reflects what he has learned about "history" from his non-Shuar teachers, employers, and friends, or whether he believes he is responding to my own

interests. In any event, I do not take this as evidence of a Shuar notion of history. As I have suggested in chapter 2, and as Alejandro illustrates in chapter 6, many significant events occurred in his life before he moved to Sucúa.

3. There are four kinds of schools in Morona Santiago: *Fiscal* are state run; *Misional* are missionary run; *Fiscomisional* are missionary run on behalf and with the support of the state; and *Bicultural* are run by the Shuar Federation on behalf and with the support of the state.

4. The Huambisa are neighboring groups that speak dialects of the same language and have similar cultures. The Achuar and Shuar used to have hostile relations.

6. SON AND BROTHER

1. A plant from which Shuar and *colonos* make an herbal tea. *Colonos* mix it with sugar and claim that once people have drunk *guayusa*, they will always want to stay in the Amazon. Shuar used to drink huge quantities in the early morning as an emetic.

2. *Tankámash* refers to the male side of the house and things associated with men. The woman's side of the house is called *ekenta*.

3. According to his identity card, Alejandro was born 24 November 1944. Thus, in 1954 he would have been ten, not six. (Of course, the dates on identity cards are frequently made up.) I often asked Alejandro when something occurred, and I have not tried to reconcile contradictions between his age and the year of an event. I have tried to order these accounts chronologically, but this arrangement is necessarily imprecise.

4. Many Shuar are polygynous; Andrés had several wives, as has Alejandro. Alejandro called Teresa, his birth mother, "mother" and called his other mothers *madrastra*, or "stepmother." When Alejandro first told me about his stepmother Mama I was confused; *mama* is, in Spanish as in English, a word for mother. When I asked Alejandro what Mama's name was, he looked at me and said "Mama." I eventually figured out that this was her name; *mama* is also the Shuar word for manioc.

5. Shuar classify their mother's sisters as "mother," and their father's brothers as "father." They therefore classify the children of these other mothers and fathers (in anthropological lingo, "parallel cousins") as brothers and sisters. In Spanish they call them *primos hermanos* and *primas hermanas.*

Some Spanish speakers use the phrase *primo hermano* to mean cousin, but settlers in Morona Santiago use only the word *primo.* When Shuar refer to someone as the cousin of a non-Shuar, they too use the word *primo;* they never apply the word alone to their own relatives.

7. STUDENT AND WORKER

1. Shuar and settlers identify all non-Catholic Christian churches and sects as "Evangelical."

2. The *sucre* was the Ecuadorian unit of currency. Between 1950 and 1960 the official exchange rate was 15 sucres to the dollar; in 1961 it was 16.50 to the dollar; from 1962 to 1969 it was 18 to the dollar; from 1970 to 1979 it was 25 to the dollar. When I first arrived in Ecuador in 1987 the commercial exchange rate was around 200 to the dollar, and when I returned at the end of 1988 it had reached 500 to the dollar. In 2000 the government fixed the exchange rate at 25,000 to the dollar in anticipation of phasing out the national currency in favor of the exclusive use of dollars by the end of the year.

8. HUSBAND AND FATHER

1. A couple of months later, in another context, Alejandro further reflected on this experience. He told me, "When I was young, around seventeen, I thought of marrying a white woman. I thought I would be happier and proud of myself if I were the only one married to a white. I told Judith that she was the only one for me, but that I didn't know if her parents would allow me. We were a couple, but I was insecure. I thought, 'She is not my race, and when I am with my people I am happier.' If I had married her, she would have manipulated me, because I see how white women manage their husbands; some women are superwomen. Well, this is what I thought when I was young. But I thought about it and realized that if I left my father to be with other people, they would make us inferior, they would crush my father and manipulate us. So it is better that I stay with my father before going off to be with other people."

2. Maria was born June 14, 1940.

3. The capital of Napo, the province to the north of Pastaza.

4. The capital of Pastaza, the province to the north of Morona Santiago.

5. Shuar do not generally sleep in or otherwise use hammocks; they sleep on bamboo or wooden platforms.

6. Alejandro's declaration to Marta's stepfather and mother was meant to convey his commitment to Marta and her family. Although marriage is not considered as sacred to the Shuar as it is to some North Americans, it is a serious commitment.

7. After marrying, Chínki Esteban moved to the *centro* of his wife

and parents-in-law, Nayumpim, across the Cutucú, between Taisha and Macuma.

8. A Catholic mission and Shuar *centro* on the eastern slopes of the Cutucú.

9. SHAMAN

1. The name of both a *centro* and an association in the northern part of the province.

2. In Spanish, *flechita*. Alejandro is referring to *tsentsak*, the shaman's weapon, which Shuar translate as "little arrows."

3. Sangay is a prominent volcano in Morona Santiago and is among the world's most active volcanoes.

4. The east; what Ecuadorians call the Amazonian region of the country.

5. Presumably the talisman fell in a river. Alejandro always spoke of his talismans as if they were inanimate objects; I don't know whether the phrase "I drowned it" reflects a special relationship between the shaman and the object, or the peculiar charms of Shuar Spanish.

6. In Spanish, *tigre*. Shuar use this word to refer to jaguars.

10. THE SHUAR FEDERATION

1. That is, from the road from Sucúa, where it passes Huambinimi.

2. Pedro Kunkúmas, like Alejandro Tsakimp, is a shaman. Although I never heard either one of them accuse the other of witchcraft or malpractice, and neither of them seemed to object to my working with both of them, they nevertheless competed for clients.

3. Kimi is land owned by the Federation just to the south of Sucúa and is the site for courses, special programs, and the annual assembly.

11. FRIEND AND ENEMY

1. Literally, *mi costumbre*. In part thanks to anthropological theory, the English word *custom* now has a technical meaning that emphasizes conformity and that is commonly applied to indigenous peoples. Ironically, Carlos's and Alejandro's usage evokes the earlier sense of *habit* and emphasizes individuality. I translate *costumbre* as "custom" because I want English-speaking readers to see how (some) indigenous people use the word themselves.

2. During the time of my research, Peace Corps volunteers in Morona Santiago worked for CREA (the Economic Reconversion Center for the Austro). Owing to the history of hostility between CREA and the Federation, it did not assign any volunteers to work with the Shuar. A number of

volunteers, however, did work on their own time with individual Shuar. Maria Ornes befriended Alejandro and was instrumental in his acquiring funding, material, and expertise from the government to build a well and aqueduct to bring water to each household in 1989. This primarily benefited women and girls, who otherwise would have to walk to the river for water.

3. Lorenzo told me, "Calisto had this problem in Yaup' with his own brother. Calisto had gone to his brother and said, 'Give me cattle.' He took and he took, and finally the brother said, 'All right. How is it, Brother, that you are taking away all my cattle? These cattle belong to the bank.' So the people in Yaup' no longer wanted Calisto among them; they were fed up. So they said, 'All right, Mr. Calisto, you go, you're gone. You're making trouble here, so it's better that you take your things and go to where you want to live.' This was three or four, maybe five, years ago, I think, something like that. Chínki was the *teniente político* who sent him away. The brothers took possession of his land. So now he is making trouble here."

12. ORPHAN

1. Alejandro's Shuar name for Maria Ornes. Maria's primary job for CREA was to help *colonos* dig and stock fish ponds with carp and talapia. *Apup* is a freshwater dolphin.

2. Our interview was in Spanish, although Alejandro occasionally quoted a Shuar phrase. Sometimes he immediately translated the Shuar phrase into Spanish; other times he did not. I have translated his Spanish narrative into English and have left Shuar phrases in Shuar.

13. AT A LOSS

1. As Crapanzano might put it, I was experiencing something like counter-transference.

2. According to Freud, the original experience of the self through the intervention of another occurs when a boy (in the classic oedipal scenario) realizes that he has a rival for his mother's attentions. Strict Freudians believe that the growing boy then seeks substitutes for the mother. In other words, people attach themselves to "others" who are *other than the mother.* Following Lacan, however, Crapanzano argues that the various others to whom we attach are not substitutes for an original attachment. All such "others," including one's mother, "are surrogates for the empty space of desire," that "Other" that is simply "not me" (1980: 9–10).

3. Although I shall share whatever royalties I may earn from this book with Alejandro, I doubt that the sum will come close to the income I

have as an assistant professor, made possible by my having finished my dissertation, thanks in large part to what I learned from him.

14. INFORMANT

1. Harner does mention a "slight patrilineal tendency" among Shuar but does not identify specific patrilineages; indeed, he states that there is "an absence of unilineal kin groups" (1984: 78) and stresses the primacy of the personal bilateral kindred instead (97).

2. In 1975 the Federation and the government signed an accord establishing a "global" system of land ownership, in which individual families had title that could be bought, sold, and inherited only within the community; that is, members of the Federation could sell land only to other members of the Federation. This practice has limited the commoditization of land—in effect, the Federation owns the land, and members buy and sell use rights. Since most members of the Federation are subsistence farmers, prices for land are relatively low. Some Shuar have argued that the global system keeps Shuar poor, since they cannot sell the most valuable commodity they own for profit. Others argue that the global system ensures Shuar autonomy.

As with other *centros* formed before the Federation, Utunkus does not participate in the global system; Andrés held individual title to his land. But Utunkus is the exception that proves the rule: none of its members have ever raised the possibility of selling their land to a non-Shuar. For them, the real effect of individual title is how it has affected relations within the Shuar community. Similarly, even in communities with global title, patrilineages are forming, neighbors fight over boundaries, and children fight over their inheritance.

3. Cf. Murphy (1956) for the converse, a case where matrilocality developed over patrilineality.

4. Murphy acknowledged that matrilocality and patrilineality are an unstable combination, and he suggested that sustained matrilocality among Mundurucu could lead to a decline in patrilineality. Since Shuar women can own land, it is possible that matrilocality and patrilineality will coexist in Shuar culture, or that both will disappear in favor of bilocality or neolocality and the disintegration of descent groups.

5. The Federation is, in fact, a perfect example of what Morton Fried called a "secondary tribe": a polity precipitated through contact with, and actions by, a state (1975: 99–105). Fried suggested that tribe formation is a common feature of colonialism. Although he recognized that there are a variety of catalysts for this process, two of the most common are

attempts by states to rule indirectly the peoples on their frontiers (see Chanock 1985; Fried 1952) and attempts by peoples on the frontiers of states to organize resistance to state encroachment (see Evans Pritchard 1949; Wolf 1982: 347- 49). One may view the case of the Shuar Federation as an example of the coincidence and intermingling of these two causes. This perhaps paradoxical combination of causes (or effects) seems common in the Americas (see Chaumiel 1990; Jackson 1991; Sider 1993; Smith 1985).

6. Pace Wolf, these names refer to bundles of relationships within an historical field (1982: 3).

7. And, as Derrida would point out, between writing and speech.

8. Conventionally, the term *informant* conveys the fact that anthropologists learn *from* others through a personal relationship (unlike, for example, sociologists or psychologists, who typically learn *about* others through surveys or experiments). Recently, many anthropologists have expressed some discomfort with the term, because it is perilously close to *informer*. Indeed, Alejandro was often as much an informer as an informant. I believe that this reflects an unavoidable and necessary tension inherent in any vocation that involves asking people about their lives. In the ambiguous and conflict-ridden situation of fieldwork, there are no good labels, only ambivalent ones.

References

Abya-Yale. 1986. *Los Shuar y los Animales.* 3rd ed. Preface by Father Juan Bottasso. Quito: Abya-Yala.

Agger, Ben. 1998. *Critical Social Theories.* Boulder: Westview Press.

Asad, Talal, ed. 1973. *Anthropology and the Colonial Encounter.* London: Ithaca Press.

Benedict, Ruth. 1934. *Patterns of Culture.* Boston: Houghton Mifflin.

————. 1948. "Anthropology and the Humanities." *American Anthropologist* 50:585–93.

Benjamin, Walter. 1968. "The Storyteller." *Illuminations.* New York: Schocken Books.

Bhabha, Homi. 1994. *The Location of Culture.* London: Routledge.

Blanchot, Maurice. 1981. "Literature and the Right to Death." *The Gaze of Orpheus.* Barrytown NY: Station Hill.

Bloch, Maurice. 1975. "Property and the End of Affinity." *Marxist Analysis and Social Anthropology.* London: Malaby Press.

Boas, Franz. 1940. "The Methods of Ethnology." *Race, Language and Culture.* Chicago: University of Chicago Press.

————. 1943. "Recent Anthropology." *Science* 98(2545):311–18.

Boyarin, Daniel, and Jonathan Boyarin. 1993. "Diaspora: Generation and the Ground of Jewish Identity." *Critical Inquiry* 19:693–725.

Bronner, Stephen. 1994. *Of Critical Theory and Its Theorists.* Oxford: Blackwell.

Brown, Michael F. 1985. *Tsewa's Gift: Magic and Meaning in an Amazonian Society.* Washington DC: Smithsonian Institution Press.

————. 1988. "Shamanism and Its Discontents." *Medical Anthropology Quarterly* 2(2): 102–20.

Calhoun, Craig. 1995. *Critical Social Theory.* Oxford: Blackwell.

Chanock, Martin. 1985. *Law, Custom, and Social Order: The Colonial Experience in Malawi and Zambia.* New York: Cambridge University Press.

Chaumiel, Jean-Pierre. 1990. "Les Nouveaux Chefs: Pratiques Politiques et Organizations Indigenes en Amazonie Peruvienne." *Problemes d'Amerique Latine,* 87–107.

References

Churchill, Ward. 1994a. "Indians Are Us?" *Indians Are Us.* Monroe ME: Common Courage Press.

———. 1994b. "Do It Yourself 'Indianism.' " *Indians Are Us.* Monroe ME: Common Courage Press.

———. 1994c. "Another Dry White Season." *Indians Are Us.* Monroe ME: Common Courage Press.

Clifford, James. 1988. "On Ethnographic Authority." *The Predicament of Culture.* Cambridge: Harvard University Press.

Cohen, 1985. 1985. "Doing Social History from Pim's Doorway." In *Reliving the Past: The Worlds of Social History.* Olivier Zunz, ed. Chapel Hill: University of North Carolina Press.

Conklin, B., and L. Graham. 1995. "The Shifting Middle Ground: Amazonian Indians and Eco-Politics." *American Anthropologist* 97(4): 695–710.

Crapanzano, Vincent. 1980. *Tuhami: Portrait of a Moroccan.* Chicago: University of Chicago Press.

———. 1984. "Life Histories." *American Anthropologist* 86:953–60.

Culler, Jonathan. 1982. *On Deconstruction.* Ithaca: Cornell University Press.

Derrida, Jacques. 1973. *Speech and Phenomena.* Evanston IL: Northwestern University Press.

———. 1976. *Of Grammatology.* Gayatri Spivak, trans. Baltimore: Johns Hopkins University Press.

———. 1981. *Positions.* Chicago: University of Chicago Press.

Descola, Philippe. 1994. *In the Society of Nature.* N. Scott, trans. Cambridge: Cambridge University Press.

———. 1996. *The Spears of Twilight.* Janet Lloyd, trans. New York: New Press.

DuBois, Cora. 1944. *The People of Alor.* Minneapolis: University of Minnesota Press.

Dumont, Jean-Paul. 1978. *The Headman and I: Ambiguity and Ambivalence in the Fieldwork Experience.* Austin: University of Texas Press.

Dunaway, David K., and Willa K. Baum, eds. 1996. *Oral History: An Interdisciplinary Anthology.* 2nd ed. Walnut Creek CA: AltaMira Press.

Durkheim, Emile. 1965. *The Elementary Forms of Religious Life.* New York: Free Press.

———. 1984. *The Division of Labor in Society.* New York: Free Press.

Escobar, Arturo. 1995. *Encountering Development.* Princeton: Princeton University Press.

Espinosa, P. Lucas. 1935. *Los Yupi del Oriente Peruano: Estudio Linguistico y Etnografico*. Madrid.

Evans-Pritchard, E. E. 1949. *The Sanusi of Cyrenaica*. Oxford: Clarendon Press.

Fabian, Johannes. 1983. *Time and the Other: How Anthropology Makes Its Object*. New York: Columbia University Press.

Fanon, Frantz. 1963. *The Wretched of the Earth*. New York: Grove Press.

Fay, Brian. 1987. *Critical Social Science: Liberation and Its Limits*. Ithaca: Cornell University Press.

Feierman, Steven. 1993. "African Histories and the Dissolution of World History." In *Africa and the Disciplines*. Robert Bates, V. Y. Mudimbe, and Jean O'Barr, eds. Chicago: University of Chicago Press.

Ferguson, James. 1994. *The Anti-Politics Machine*. Minneapolis: University of Minnesota Press.

Ferguson, R. Brian, and Neil Whitehead, eds. 1992. *War in the Tribal Zone*. Santa Fe: School of American Research.

Fortes, Meyer, and E. E. Evans-Pritchard. 1940. Introduction. *African Political Systems*. London: Oxford University Press.

Foster, Hal, ed. 1983. *The Anti-Aesthetic*. Seattle: Bay Press.

Fried, Morton H. 1952. "Land Tenure, Geography and Ecology in the Contact of Cultures." *American Journal of Economics and Sociology* 11: 391–412.

————. 1975. *The Notion of Tribe*. Menlo Park CA: Cummings.

Friedlander, Judith. 1975. *Being Indian in Hueyapan*. New York: St. Martins Press.

Frye, Northrop. 1957. *Anatomy of Criticism*. Princeton: Princeton University Press.

Fuss, Diana. 1989. *Essentially Speaking: Feminism, Nature, and Difference*. New York: Routledge.

Gebauer, Gunter, and Christoph Wulf. 1992. *Mimesis: Culture—Art—Society*. Don Renean, trans. Berkeley: University of California Press.

Geertz, Clifford. 1973. *The Interpretation of Cultures*. New York: Basic Books.

Genovese, Eugene. D. 1974. *Roll, Jordan, Roll: The World the Slaves Made*. New York: Pantheon Books.

Giddens, Anthony. 1979. *Central Problems in Social Theory*. Berkeley: University of California Press.

Gippelhauser, Richard, and Elke Mader. 1990. *Die Achuara-Jívaro: Wirtschaftliche und Soziale Organisationsformen am Peruanischen Amazonas*. Wien: Verlag der osterreichischen Akademie der Wissenschaften.

References

Gnerre, Maurizio. 1973. "Sources of Spanish Jívaro." *Romance Philology* 27(2): 203–4. Berkeley: University of California Press.

Gordon, Avery, and Christopher Newfield. 1994. "White Philosophy." *Critical Inquiry* 20:737–69.

Gordon, Robert J. 1992. *The Bushman Myth*. Boulder CO: Westview Press.

Gouldner, Alvin W. 1970. *The Coming Crisis in Western Sociology*. New York: Basic Books.

Gow, Peter. 1994. "River People: Shamanism and History in Western Amazonia." In *Shamanism, History, and the State*. N. Thomas and C. Humphrey, eds. Ann Arbor: University of Michigan Press.

Graham, J. D. 1976. "Indirect Rule: The Establishment of 'Chiefs' and 'Tribes' in Camaron's Tanganyika." *Tanzania Notes and Records* 87:1–9.

Graves, Adrian. 1983. "Truck and Gifts: Melanesian Immigrants and the Trade Box System in Colonial Queensland." *Past and Present* 101:87–124.

Guha, Ranajit, ed. 1982–89. *Subaltern Studies*, vols. 1–6. Delhi: Oxford University Press.

Habermas, Jurgen. 1971. *Knowledge and Human Interests*. Boston: Beacon Press.

Hall, Stuart. 1992. "Cultural Studies and Its Theoretical Legacies." In *Cultural Studies*. Lawrence Grossberg, Cary Nelson, and Paula Treichler, eds. New York: Routledge.

Harner, Michael. 1975. "Scarcity, the Factors of Production, and Social Evolution." In *Population, Ecology, and Social Evolution*. Steven Polgar, ed. The Hague: Mouton.

———. 1984. *Jívaro: People of the Sacred Waterfalls*. Rev. ed. Berkeley: University of California Press.

Heelas, Paul. 1996. *The New Age Movement*. Cambridge: Blackwell.

Held, David. 1980. *An Introduction to Critical Theory*. Berkeley: University of California Press.

Hendricks, Janet. 1993. *To Drink of Death*. Tucson: University of Arizona Press.

Hill, Jonathan D. 1988. *Rethinking History and Myth*. Urbana: University of Illinois Press.

Hobsbawm, Eric, and George Rude. 1968. *Captain Swing: A Social History of the Great English Agricultural Uprising of 1830*. New York: W. W. Norton.

Horkheimer, Max. 1972. *Critical Theory: Selected Essays*. New York: Continuum.

Hunter, Ian. 1992. "Aesthetics and Cultural Studies." In *Cultural Studies*.

Lawrence Grossberg, Cary Nelson, and Paula Treichler, eds. New York: Routledge.

Hymes, Del, ed. 1969. *Reinventing Anthropology*. New York: Random House.

Jackson, Jean. 1991. "Being and Becoming an Indian in the Vaupes." In *Nation States and Indians in Latin America*. Greg Urban and Joel Sherzer, eds. Austin: University of Texas Press.

Jakobson, Roman. 1990. *On Language*. Linda Waugh and Monique Monville-Burston, eds. Cambridge: Harvard University Press.

Kant, Immanuel. 1990. *Critique of Pure Reason*. J. M. Meiklejohn, trans. Amherst: Prometheus Books.

———. 1996. *Critique of Practical Reason*. T. K. Abbott, trans. Amherst: Prometheus Books.

Karsten, Rafael. 1935. *The Headhunters of Western Amazonas: The Life and Culture of the Jibaro Indians of Eastern Ecuador and Peru*. Helsinki: Societas Scientiarum Fennica, Commentationes Humanarum Littararum, vol. 7(I).

Kellner, Douglas. 1989. *Critical Theory: Marxism and Modernity*. Cambridge: Polity Press.

Kuhn, Thomas S. 1962. *The Structure of Scientific Revolutions*. Chicago: University of Chicago Press.

Lerner, Gerda. 1986. *The Creation of Patriarchy*. New York: Oxford University Press.

———. 1993. *The Creation of Feminist Consciousness: From the Middle Ages to Eighteen-Seventy*. New York: Oxford University Press.

Lévi-Strauss, Claude. 1963. *Structural Anthropology*. Claire Jacobson and Brooke Grundfest Schoepf, trans. New York: Basic Books.

———. 1966. *The Savage Mind*. George Weidenfeld, trans. Chicago: University of Chicago Press.

———. 1973. *Tristes Tropiques*. John and Doreen Weightman, trans. New York: Penguin Books.

Lewis, Oscar. 1961. *The Children of Sanchez*. New York: Vintage Books.

———. 1964. *Pedro Martinez*. New York: Random House.

Mader, Elke. 1999. *Metamorfosis del Poder: Persona, Mito, y Vision en la Sociedad Shuar y Achuar*. Quito: Ediciónes Abya-Yala.

Malinowski, Bronislaw. 1922. *Argonauts of the Western Pacific*. Prospect Heights IL: Waveland Press.

———. 1929. "Practical Anthropology." *Africa* 2:22–38.

Maybury-Lewis, David. 1965. *The Savage and the Innocent*. Boston: Beacon Press.

McCauley, Clark, Lee J. Jussim , and Yueh-Ting Lee. 1995. "Stereotype Accuracy: Toward Appreciating Group Differences." In *Stereotype Accuracy: Toward an Appreciation of Group Differences*. Yueh-Ting Lee, Lee J. Jussim, and Clark R. McCauley, eds. Washington DC: APA Books.

Meggit, Mervyn J. 1965. *The Lineage System of the Mae-Enga of New Guinea*. Edinburgh: Oliver & Boyd.

Memmi, Albert. 1965. *The Colonizer and the Colonized*. Boston: Beacon Press.

Michaels, Walter Benn. 1992. "Race into Culture: A Critical Genealogy of Cultural Identity." *Critical Inquiry* 18:655–85.

Mills, C. Wright. 1959. *The Sociological Imagination*. New York: Oxford University Press.

Mintz, Sidney. 1960. *Worker in the Cane: A Puerto Rican Life History*. Yale Caribbean Series, vol. 2. New Haven: Yale University Press.

Mundo Shuar. 1977. *Plantas*. Preface by Father Juan Bottasso. Sucúa: Mundo Shuar.

Muratorio, Blanca. 1991. *The Life and Times of Grandfather Alonso*. New Brunswick: Rutgers University Press.

Murphy, Robert F. 1956."Matrilocality and Patrilineality in Mundurucu Society." *American Anthropologist* 58:414–34.

———. 1979. "Lineage and Lineality in Lowland South America." In *Brazil: Anthropological Perspectives*. Maxine Margolis and William Carter, eds.. New York: Columbia University Press.

North American Congress on Latin America (NACLA). 1975. "Ecuador: Oil Up for Grabs." *Latin America and Empire Report* 9(8):2–38.

Pels, Peter, and Oscar Salemink. 1994. "Introduction: Five Theses on Ethnography as Colonial Practice." *History and Anthropology* 8(1–4):1–34.

Perkins, John. 1994. *The World Is as You Dream It*. Rochester VT: Destiny Books.

Popper, Karl. 1959 *The Logic of Scientific Discovery*. New York: Harper & Row.

Powdermaker, Hortense. 1966. *Stranger and Friend*. New York: W. W. Norton.

Rabinow, Paul. 1977. *Reflections on Fieldwork in Morocco*. Berkeley: University of California Press.

Radcliffe, Sarah, and Sallie Westwood. 1996. *Remaking the Nation*. New York: Routledge.

Radcliffe-Brown, A. R. 1965. *Structure and Function in Primitive Society*. New York: Free Press.

Radin, Paul. 1913. "Personal Reminiscences of a Winnebago Indian."
Journal of American Folklore 26:293–318.

——. 1963. *The Autobiography of a Winnebago Indian*. New York: Dover.

Ranciere, Jacques. 1994. *The Names of History: On the Poetics of Knowledge*.
Hassan Melehy, trans. Minneapolis: University of Minnesota Press.

Ranger, Terence. 1983. "The Invention of Tradition in Colonial Africa."
The Invention of Tradition. E. Hobsbawm and T. Ranger, eds. Cambridge:
Cambridge University Press.

Ricoeur, Paul. 1974. *The Conflict of Interpretations*. Don Ihde, ed. Evanston IL:
Northwestern University Press.

Rosaldo, Renato. 1976. "The Story of Tukbaw: 'They Listen as He Orates.' "
In *The Biographical Process: Studies in the History and Psychology of Religion*. F.
Reynolds and D. Capps, eds. The Hague: Mouton.

Rubenstein, Steven. 1995. "Death in a Distant Place: The Politics of Shuar
Shamanism." Ph.D. dissertation, Columbia University, New York.

——. 2001. "Colonialism, the Shuar Federation, and the Ecuadorian
State." *Environment and Planning D: Society and Space* 19(3): 263–93.

Sahlins, Marshall. 1981. *Historical Metaphors and Mythical Realities: Structure in
the Early History of the Sandwich Islands Kingdom*. Ann Arbor: University of
Michigan Press.

Said, Edward. 1978. *Orientalism*. New York: Random House.

Salazar, Ernesto. 1981. "The Federación Shuar and the Colonization
Frontier." In *Cultural Transformations and Ethnicity in Modern Ecuador*.
Norman E. Whitten Jr., ed. Urbana: University of Illinois Press.

Sapir, Edward. 1922. "Sayach'apis, a Nootka Trader." In *American Indian
Life*. Elsie Clews Parsons, ed. New York: B. W. Huebesh.

——. 1938. Foreword. *Left Handed, Son of Old Man Hat*, by Walter Dyk.
Lincoln: University of Nebraska Press.

Sartre, Jean-Paul. 1948. *Anti-Semite and Jew*. New York: Schocken Books.

Saussure, Ferdinand de. 1966. *Course in General Linguistics*. New York:
McGraw-Hill.

Scott, James C. 1998. *Seeing Like a State*. New Haven: Yale University Press.

Scott, Joan. 1996a. "After History?" *Common Knowledge* 5(3): 9–26.

——. 1996b. *Only Paradoxes to Offer*. Cambridge: Harvard University
Press.

SERBISH (Sistema de Educación Radiofónica Bicultural Shuar), in
collaboration with FONCULTURA BEDE. 1988a. *Nuestro Atlas*. Intro. by
Miguel Puwáinchir. Sucúa: Editorial SERBISH.

————. 1988b. *Chicham Nekatai: Apach Chicham-Shuar Chicham*. Preface by José Miguel Jembékat; intro. by Emanuele Amodio. Sucúa: Editorial SERBISH.

Seymour-Smith, Charlotte. 1988. *Shiwiar: Identidad Etnica y Cambio en el Rio Corrientes*. Quito-Lima: Abya Yala-CAAP.

Shostak, Marjorie. 1981. *Nisa*. New York: Vintage Books.

Sider, Gerald. 1993. *Lumbee Indian Histories*. Cambridge: Cambridge University Press.

Simmons, Leo, ed. 1942. *Sun Chief: The Autobiography of a Hopi Indian*. New Haven: Yale University Press.

Smith, Richard Chase. 1985. "A Search for Unity within Diversity: Peasant Unions, Ethnic Federations, and Indianist Movements in the Andean Republics." In *Native Peoples and Economic Development: Six Case Studies from Latin America*. Theodore MacDonald Jr., ed. Occasional paper no. 16. Cambridge MA: Cultural Survival.

Spivak, Gayatri. 1988. "Can the Subaltern Speak?" In *Marxism and the Interpretation of Culture*. Cary Nelson and Lawrence Grossberg, eds. Urbana: University of Illinois Press.

Stirling, M. W. 1938. *Historical and Ethnological Material on the Jívaro Indians*. Bureau of American Ethnology Bulletin no. 117. Washington DC: U.S. Printing Office.

Stocking, George W., ed. 1991. *Colonial Situations*. Madison: University of Wisconsin Press.

Sumner, William Graham. 1906. *Folkways*. Boston: Gin.

Taussig, Michael. 1987. *Shamanism, Colonialism, and the Wild Man*. Chicago: University of Chicago Press.

————. 1992. *The Nervous System*. New York: Routledge.

Taylor, Anne-Christian. 1981. "God-Wealth: The Achuar and the Missions." In *Cultural Transformations and Ethnicity in Modern Ecuador*. Norman E. Whitten Jr., ed. Urbana: University of Illinois Press.

Thompson, E. P. 1963. *The Making of the English Working Class*. New York: Vintage Books.

Todorov, Tzvetan. 1984. *The Conquest of America*. New York: Harper & Row.

Torgovnick, Marianna. 1990. *Gone Primitive*. Chicago: University of Chicago Press.

Trouillot, M. 1991. "Anthropology and the Savage Slot: The Poetics and Politics of Otherness." In *Recapturing Anthropology*. R. G. Fox, ed. Santa Fe: School of American Research Press.

References

Up de Graff, F. W. 1923. *Head Hunters of the Amazon: Seven Years of Exploration and Adventure*. Garden City NY: Garden City Publishing.

Visweswaran, Kamala. 1994. *Fictions of Feminist Ethnography*. Minneapolis: University of Minnesota Press.

Wallace, Michael. 1996. *Mickey Mouse History and Other Essays on American History*. Philadelphia: Temple University Press.

Warren, Kay B. 1998. *Indigenous Movements and Their Critics*. Princeton: Princeton University Press.

White, Hayden. 1973. *Metahistory: The Historical Imagination in Nineteenth-Century Europe*. Baltimore: Johns Hopkins University Press.

Whitten, Norman E., Jr. 1976. *Sacha Runa: Ethnicity and Adaptation of Ecuadorian Jungle Quichua*. Urbana: University of Illinois Press.

Wilmsen, Edwin. 1989. *Land Filled with Flies*. Chicago: University of Chicago Press.

Wolf, Eric. 1982. *Europe and the People without History*. Berkeley: University of California Press.

Worsley, Peter M. 1956. "The Kinship System of the Tallensi: A Revaluation." *Journal of the Royal Anthropological Institute* 86:37–75.

Index

Abad, Augusto, 181–82
Abarca, Benigno, 56
Abarca, Felipe, 200–201
abstraction technique, 33
Achuar tribe, war between Shuar and, 197
Against Culture (Dombrowski), 258
agency-structure dialectic, 60–61, 243, 244
Agrarian Reform Law (1973), 177, 178, 240
agriculture: of Ecuadorian colonization (twentieth century), 52–53; family gardens used for, 129; Shuar cultivation rights and, 34–35, 53; slash and burn technique used in, 34. *See also* land
Añiu, Father (Alfredo Germani), 169, 170, 183, 185
Akachu, Antonio, 198
Albino, Father, 167
Aldrete, Juan, 25
Alejandro's stories. *See* Tsakimp, Alejandro (life history interviews)
Amazon discourses, 52
American Athropological Association, 13, 282 n.4
anthropologists: abstraction/reification approach used by, 41–42; as both subversive and conservative, 12–13, 248; culture shock experienced by, 217–18; current code of ethics for, 282 n.4; as informant, 299 n.8; participant observation dilemma of, 218; relationship to the state struggle by, 13; relative isolation of, 228; responding to requests of participants, 228–29, 231; respon-

sibility for genocide/ethnocide by, 283 n.1; Shuar interactions with, 282 n.3; Western biases of, 64–65
anthropology: authenticity notion and, 42; changes in intellectual climate of, 253; debate over scientific method in, 285 n.4; ethnocentrism vs. relativism approach of, 31; life history tradition in, 60; separation of home and field in, 14–15; striving for universal understanding of culture, 44–45; subversive/conservative paradox and history of, 12–13. *See also* ethnography; Malinowskian ethnography
apaches (non-Shuar): Shuar abused by, 170; Shuar Federation as protection against, 172; See also *colonos*
apartheid logic, 229
Argonauts of the Western Pacific (Malinowski), 31–32
arútam practice, 39, 40
arútam wakaní, 39
Atamaint, Dionicio, 189
authenticity, 42, 244–45
ayahuasca. See *natém* (hallucinogenic plant/infusion)

Barzallo, Alfonso, 176
behavior: and cultural expectations of male Shuar, 44; notion of culture to understand, 49–50
Benedict, Ruth, 62, 292 n.3
Benjamin, Walter, 57, 58, 67
best friend story, 111–14
Boas, Franz, 13, 61, 62, 63, 64, 288 n.20, 293 n.2
brujo. See shamanism

fifteenth-century attempts to conquer, 24; inheritance issues facing modern, 81; interactions between anthropologists and, 282 n.3; land conflicts between *apaches* and, 170; relations between *colonos* and, 52–54; relations between Spanish and, 25–31; Spanish failure to conquer, 51–52; two class divisions of modern, 69; war between Achuar and, 197; Westernized vs. "noble" savage members of, 47

Shuar religion, 104–5

Shuar violence myth: civilization-nature opposition discourse and, 27–31; "the Jívaro Revolt" (sixteenth century) as origins of, 25–27; narrations supporting, 28–30. *See also* myth

Shunta, Umberto, 130

Shutka, Father Juan, 87, 134, 135, 167, 168, 169, 170, 171–72, 175, 185

Sider, Gerald, 65, 67, 242, 259

Simmel, Georg, 226

Simmons, Leo, 64, 292 n.3

SNV (Netherlands Development Organization), 231–32

social structure: creation of solidarities within, 258–59; ethnography focus on, 60–61; link between individual agency and, 243, 244; present tense/normative effects of using, 61; Shuar household defined as primary, 238–39. *See also* power structure

society: "hot" and "cold," 30; insiders and outsiders of, 63, 73; relationship between individual and, 60; relative isolation/cultural differences of Amazonian, 4; social structure of, 60–61

solidarities, 258–59

Spanish: conquest of Inca by, 24, 25; failed efforts to conquer Shuar by, 51–52; "the Jívaro Revolt" (sixteenth century) against, 25–27; relations between Shuar and, 25–31; reports on Shuar people by, 28–30

state: clash between indigenous people and, 46; relationship of anthropologists to struggle by, 13; study of subordinate groups within, 286 n.11; subjective nature of history of the, 291 n.31. *See also* Ecuadorian state

stealing story, 99–100

stereotypes, 289 n.24

Stirling, M. W., 19, 24, 25, 27, 28, 29–30, 31, 46, 47, 56, 57, 241, 286 n.11

stories: Alejandro's personality revealed through, 238; cultural boundaries images revealed in, 254; Euro-American reading of, 23–24; on events after Tséremp's death, 54–57; hermeneutical issues of understanding, 17–20, 244–45, 248–49; historical vs. ethnographic reading of, 23–24; impact on Shuar community by Alejandro's, 246–47; judgment passed through, 31; lying/lies theme throughout, 78, 79; question/answer prior to, 85–88; into realm of fairy tale, 57–58; on Tséremp and Chúmpi, 20–23, 31, 40–41, 44, 52, 54. *See also* life history; Tsakimp, Alejandro

stories (on being friend/enemy): on comparing friends and relatives, 193–94; on disputes over land, 198–202; on envy, 196–97; on hopes/dreams/customs of people, 191–92; on the unforgiven, 201–2

stories (on being husband/father): on extramarital relationships, 134–38; on first *colono* girlfriend, 119–20; on first house/growing family, 122–25; on first sexual experience, 117–18; on future of country, 139–40; on happiness, 115–16; on his sons, 129–34; on lies told by Lorenzo, 129–33; on making money, 138–